POLITICAL RUMORS

PRINCETON STUDIES IN
Political Behavior
Tali Mendelberg, Series Editor

Political Rumors

Why We Accept Misinformation and How to Fight It

Adam J. Berinsky

PRINCETON UNIVERSITY PRESS
PRINCETON AND OXFORD

Published by Princeton University Press
41 William Street, Princeton, New Jersey 08540
99 Banbury Road, Oxford OX2 6JX

press.princeton.edu

Library of Congress Cataloging-in-Publication Data

Names: Berinsky, Adam J., 1970– author.
Title: Political rumors : why we accept misinformation and how to fight it / Adam J. Berinsky.
Description: Princeton, New Jersey : Princeton University Press, 2023. |
    Series: Princeton studies in political behavior | Includes bibliographical references and index.
Identifiers: LCCN 2022059384 (print) | LCCN 2022059385 (ebook) |
    ISBN 9780691158389 (hardback) | ISBN 9780691247571 (ebook)
Subjects: LCSH: Political culture—United States. | Misinformation—United States. |
    Truthfulness and falsehood—Political aspects—United States. | United States—
    Politics and government—Public opinion. | BISAC: POLITICAL SCIENCE /
    Political Process / General | POLITICAL SCIENCE / American Government / General
Classification: LCC JK1726 .B474 2023 (print) | LCC JK1726 (ebook) |
    DDC 306.20973—dc23/eng/20230109
LC record available at https://lccn.loc.gov/2022059384
LC ebook record available at https://lccn.loc.gov/2022059385

British Library Cataloging-in-Publication Data is available

Editorial: Bridget Flannery-McCoy and Alena Chekanov
Production Editorial: Nathan Carr
Jacket/Cover Design: Chris Ferrante
Production: Erin Suydam
Publicity: Kate Hensley and Kathryn Stevens
Copyeditor: Molan Goldstein

This book has been composed in Adobe Text and Gotham

Printed on acid-free paper. ∞

Printed in the United States of America

10 9 8 7 6 5 4 3 2 1

To my family: Deirdre, Ben and Lila

CONTENTS

LIST OF FIGURES AND TABLES

Figures

Tables

ACKNOWLEDGMENTS

I have been working on this book for a long time. A very long time. But after more than a decade, here I am at the end. With such a long journey, there are many institutions and people I want to think. Almost certainly, I am going to forget some valuable contributions, suggestions, and support I received along the way. If I had delivered this book when I said I would—June 2014, according the terms of my contract with Princeton University Press—perhaps my memory would serve me better. So it is entirely my fault, and I sincerely apologize for my omissions.

This book began during a sabbatical I took at the Center for Advanced Study in the Behavioral Sciences during the 2009–2010 academic year. At that time, I had recently gotten tenure, just finished a book on public opinion and war, and was trying to figure out what I wanted to do next. I knew that I wanted to do something on the topics of political behavior and democratic dysfunction but I wasn't sure what. Over the course of the year, I was able to recharge, think, and—most importantly—engage in a series of discussions with a group of social psychologists that inspired me to think about my work in new and creative ways. Lunches, coffees, and seminar discussions with Nick Epley, Sander Koole, Daphna Oyserman, Norbert Schwarz, and the late Nalini Ambady were incredibly rewarding, introducing me to ideas that pushed my work in new directions. My cohort was strong not just in social psychology, but in all subfields of psychology: having Edith Chen, Margie Lachman, and Greg Miller there as well made the ride even more fun (both personally and professionally). By the end of the year, inspired by the concurrent rise of the birther and death panel rumors on the political scene and invigorated by my intellectual experience at the center, I was off and running. I am grateful to the center for providing this opportunity.

Despite what is printed on the title page, no book is written by a single individual. The one saving grace of having spent so long working on this book is that I have had the good fortune to work with many people in the field as students, collaborators, and co-authors. This list begins with Briony

Swire-Thompson, Ullrich Ecker, and Stephen Lewandowsky, who collaborated on the work presented in chapter 6 and were kind enough to allow me to reprint that material here. Our research partnership began in the fall of 2015, when Briony came to MIT on a Fulbright because she was interested in the phenomenon of Donald Trump. At the time, I told her that we would have to collect data quickly because I was sure that Trump would be gone from the scene by early March. I was wrong about Trump, but working with Briony, Uli, and Steve over the next few years was a pleasure. In addition, I had a tremendous team of research assistants working on this project—many of whom have since gone on to become professors themselves. I thank Sarah Beech, Justin de Benedictis-Kessner, Laurel Bliss, Paige Bollen, Zachary Burdette, Daniel de Kadt, Seth Dickinson, Natasha Dumas, Esteban Fernandez, Alejandro Frydman, Meg Goldberg, Daniel Guenther, Krista Loose, Michele Margolis, Zachary Markovich, Tom O'Grady, Robert Pressel, Hari Ramesh, Blair Reed, Tesalia Rizzo, Leah Rosenzweig, Mike Sances, Kathryn Treder, D. Camilla Valerio, Anna Weissman, Nicole Wilson, Chloe Wittenberg, and Lukas Wolters for supporting my work. I could not have done any of this without them.

I also received great feedback from many friends and colleagues when presenting my work at a variety of professional venues. I thank seminar participants at Brigham Young University, California Institute of Technology, East Carolina University, Florida State University, MIT, Princeton University, the University of Michigan, University of California–Berkeley, UCLA, University of Chicago, University of Georgia, University of Houston, University of Illinois, University of Virginia, the West Coast Experiments Conference, and Vanderbilt University. In addition, I am deeply indebted to Jamie Druckman, Gabe Lenz, Neil Malhotra, Tali Mendelberg, Brendan Nyhan, Michael Tesler, and Nick Valentino for especially detailed comments and counsel over the last decade. Special thanks to John Sides for invaluable eleventh-hour input on the introduction and conclusion, and Matthew E. Dardet, Addie New-Schmidt, and Dominic Valentino for a detailed and thoughtful read of the manuscript before I sent the final draft to Princeton University Press. I also thank the (multiple) editors at the Press who were far more patient and encouraging than I deserved as I worked through this project: Chuck Myers, Eric Crahan, and Bridget Flannery-McCoy.

This book is dedicated to my family—the Blogan clan. When I began this project, Ben had just turned five and was in the midst of his first year of kindergarten. Lila was one and a half and had just started walking. Now, they are both in high school, with Ben soon off to college. I thank them and, as always, Deirdre for being by my side on the long road to completing this book.

POLITICAL RUMORS

1

Introduction

Did you know that Joe Biden and the Democrats stole the 2020 US presidential election? Maybe you heard how an intricate web of domestic and foreign agents thwarted the election's real victor, Donald Trump, by using computer servers in Italy and Germany to replace his true vote totals? Perhaps you read about the absentee ballots cast for Trump that somehow ended up in a river in Wisconsin . . . or was that a ditch? This is to say nothing of the mail carriers in West Virginia who sold ballots in the weeks before the election.

If you were listening to some of the political rhetoric surrounding the 2020 election, you probably encountered at least one of these claims. But none of these allegations are true. Absentee ballots were never found in any river or ditch. And there was no foreign hacking of vote counts. The evidence against claims that the 2020 election was stolen is overwhelming and clear. For example, on November 12, 2020, in the immediate wake of the election, a national coalition of election security officials announced that "there is no evidence that any voting system deleted or lost votes, changed votes, or was in any way compromised."[1] In June 2021, an official Michigan State Senate Committee of three Republicans and one Democrat published a report that systematically debunked voter fraud claims in that state. No information has emerged since to challenge the conclusions of the fact-finding committees and the intelligence community in any serious—or even semi-serious—way.[2]

But the rumors and intimations have only continued. For example, more than eight months after the election, at the July 2021 meeting of the

Conservative Political Action Conference (CPAC), Donald Trump still publicly declared that the 2020 election was "rigged"—a claim that many other CPAC speakers and participants repeated. And into the fall and winter of 2021, Trump continued to issue statements seeking to rally citizens and politicians to his cause of overturning the results of the 2020 election. On October 13, 2021, Trump released a statement claiming, "If we don't solve the Presidential Election Fraud of 2020 (which we have thoroughly and conclusively documented), Republicans will not be voting in '22 or '24. It is the single most important thing for Republicans to do."[3]

And as the 2022 midterm elections approached, it was not just Trump who was touting claims of voting fraud. Doug Mastriano, the Republican candidate for governor in Pennsylvania—who as a state legislator led his state's "Stop the Steal" campaign and had previously helped commission an off-the-books audit of voting machines in a rural Pennsylvania county— continued his election-denying rhetoric throughout his campaign.[4] In Arizona, Kari Lake won the Republican gubernatorial nomination after declaring in a June debate that she would not have certified Biden's victory in Arizona had she been governor, citing unfounded claims that 34,000 ballots "were counted two, three, and four times" in Arizona and that 200,000 ballots were trafficked by mules.[5] These candidates reflected a larger trend in the 2022 electoral landscape: a report by the States United Democracy Center concluded that election deniers were on the ballot in half of the races for governor, as well as more than one-third of races for secretary of state and attorney general.[6]

The persistence of false information like this is troubling for the prospects of our political system. If lies continue to crowd out the truth, how can Americans—citizens and politicians alike—maintain a meaningful dialogue about the pressing political issues of our time? If citizens believe that their leaders are capable of terrible actions—even going so far as to allow catastrophes to occur on American soil, an actual claim made by the "truthers" from across the ideological spectrum who believe that the destruction of the World Trade Center in New York and the attack on the Pentagon on September 11, 2001, were the result of an inside government job—how can they trust their government with any authority? Rumors consisting of lies, false narratives, and "alternative facts" can undermine the factual foundations of good public policies, taint faith in the political system, and even motivate violent political action. A democracy where falsehoods run rampant can only result in dysfunction.

This book takes up a critical question on the mass politics side of the equation: why do political rumors and misperceptions persist in the public consciousness, even when media organizations, political leaders, and experts across the ideological spectrum discredit those stories? We do need not go far to find examples of such rumors in the modern day. The hubbub surrounding the 2020 election is simply the tip of the iceberg on the political right. Consider these other dubious stories on the political stage: the innuendo that officials are planning government-run panels to decide whether or not individuals should be given access to life-saving health care; the notion that former president Barack Obama held office illegitimately because he was born in Kenya and not Hawaii; and even the disturbing fantasies of QAnon followers who claim that the world is run by a group of Satan-worshipping pedophiles, comprising top Democratic politicians, among others. Moreover, such rumors are not limited to the Right. For instance, though Russian efforts in spreading misinformation may have played a role in shaping the conversation about and opinions on the 2016 election, some on the political Left have gone even further by claiming that Russia directly tampered with vote tallies to get Donald Trump elected as president.

Of course, political rumors are nothing new. Over fifty years ago, John F. Kennedy's assassination in Dallas sparked an industry of conspiracy theories about his death—and the subsequent report by the Warren Commission, which found that Lee Harvey Oswald was the lone shooter involved in JFK's murder on November 22, 1963. In the wake of the US entry into World War II after the attack on Pearl Harbor, stories circulated that Franklin Delano Roosevelt had goaded the Japanese military into offensive action, even going so far as allowing the attack to proceed when he knew it was imminent.[7] And as far back as the American Revolution in the eighteenth century, false stories of British-instigated brutalities by Native Americans against the colonial population were spread to incite support for the revolutionary cause.[8] In short, fringe beliefs and people who believe them have always existed, not just in the United States but around the world.

But just because rumors are a longstanding political phenomenon does not mean that they do not pose a danger to the current political system. Patterns of rumors and other political misinformation can have broad-ranging consequences for the way in which ordinary citizens of all stripes interact with the political world. That is the subject of this book.

Rumors and Misinformation

What is a rumor? Questions of definition will be explored more thoroughly in the next chapter but, briefly, the term "political rumor" will be used in this book as follows. A political rumor is a type of unsupported claim, often with a conspiratorial edge. It is not simply the misstatement of fact or an incorrect answer to a factual question about politics. Rather a rumor is something more insidious, similar to what Weeks and Garrett refer to as "unverified stories or information statements."[9]

Here my terminology departs somewhat from the current academic conversation about unverified and unsupported political assertions. In the vast literature on misinformation and false beliefs that has emerged in the last few years, some scholars have used terms like "misperception" to represent belief in many of the same kinds of false or unsupported claims analyzed here and "misinformation" to describe the claims themselves. I recognize that the phenomenon I examine in this book largely fits these definitions, but I will use the term "rumor" throughout this book to refer to the fanciful stories at the heart of my analyses because I believe that this term more precisely describes the weaponized mistruths that circulate through the information ecosystem. That said, the lessons from this book fit well with the broader misinformation literature. Indeed, I look at the intersection of rumor and misinformation more directly in chapter 5.

Understanding Political Rumors

What does it mean when a sizable portion of the mass public endorses fanciful claims such as the contention that, despite evidence of a birth certificate proving Obama was born on August 4, 1961, in Honolulu, Hawaii, he is not a natural-born citizen and therefore ineligible to serve as president under the Constitution? Or that another group believes that political leaders instigated a crisis on September 11, 2001, that ultimately drew the United States into a war in Afghanistan? Is the widespread belief in rumors like these a reflection of a lack of knowledge or engagement by the public? Or is mass belief in these rumors a symptom of some deeper problem with how citizens relate to the political world?

In the years following the election of Obama in 2008, when rumors and misinformation began to capture the media consciousness, several commentators downplayed the societal consequences of such false information.[10] Take, for example, the various claims surrounding Obama's citizenship. Much of the discussion of these rumors focused on their implausibility and made analogy to other seemingly preposterous beliefs that many Americans cling to, such as the existence of witches and ghosts.[11] In a similar vein, other commentators, such as conservative columnist Jonah Goldberg, minimized the severity of this information crisis, arguing that conspiratorial worldviews exist across the ideological spectrum, noting that roughly equal proportions of Americans endorse the position of the "birthers"—who question Obama's citizenship—and that of the "truthers," who see sinister US government involvement in the events of 9/11.[12]

All told, arguments like Goldberg's imply that political misperceptions based on rumors are little more than random phenomena arising from widespread ignorance among the American public. In essence, these commentators suggest that one-fifth of the American public will believe just about anything, no matter how unsubstantiated and no matter its political valence.[13] While interest in rumors has increased in the second decade of the twenty-first century—especially alongside the rise of Donald Trump to prominence on the political stage after 2015—there was little systematic political evidence to turn to when the birther rumor—and other more general rumors about Barack Obama—first gained steam in 2008 and 2009.

I first became interested in learning more about the scope of the problem of political rumors during this period. Accordingly, I started collecting public opinion data in 2010 about the patterns of belief in specific rumors in the United States. That July, I conducted the first of many surveys designed to investigate the prevalence of rumor beliefs among the American mass public—starting with a set of seven rumors, six political and one nonpolitical. For each of the seven items, I asked respondents if they believed the rumor, rejected the rumor, or were not sure about its veracity.[14] These questions, listed below in table 1.1, were drawn from a combination of public opinion polls conducted by other individuals and questions about contemporary rumors that I wrote myself. Four of the six questions addressed rumors that cast liberal politicians and policies in a negative light, while two questions frame conservative politics through a negative lens.[15] For the rest of the book, I refer to the former as "Democratic-targeted rumors" and the latter as "Republican-targeted rumors" (though, strictly speaking, these questions do not explicitly refer to Republican politicians). The first category of questions can also be thought of as rumors about the political Left, while the second group can be thought of as rumors about the Right. The seventh question asked about a well-known incident of a supposed unidentified flying object (UFO) landing in Roswell, New Mexico, in 1947. This final question was designed to be explicitly nonpartisan; accepting the Roswell rumor entails endorsing the notion that the US government engaged in a cover-up that has lasted over sixty years but does not implicate either party directly. For present purposes, this rumor serves as a useful baseline for the other explicitly political and partisan rumors on the survey.

TABLE 1.1. Responses to Rumor Questions, July 2010

Question	Rumor Target	Endorse Rumor (%)	Reject Rumor (%)	Not Sure (%)
Do you believe that Barack Obama was born in the United States of America?	Democrat	27	55	19
Do you think the changes to the health care system that have been enacted by Congress and the Obama administration creates "death panels" which have the authority to determine whether or not a gravely ill or injured person should receive health care based on their "level of productivity in society"?	Democrat	33	46	22
Do you think that Senator John Kerry lied about his actions during the Vietnam War in order to receive medals from the US Army?	Democrat	35	34	31
Do you think the changes to the health care system that have been enacted by Congress and the Obama administration require elderly patients to meet with government officials to discuss "end of life" options including euthanasia?	Democrat	26	46	28
Do you think the FBI and the CIA make sure that there is a steady supply of guns and drugs in the inner city?	Republican	15	63	22
Do you think that people in the federal government either assisted in the 9/11 attacks or took no action to stop the attacks because they wanted the United States to go to war in the Middle East?	Republican	18	64	18
Do you believe that a spacecraft from another planet crashed in Roswell, New Mexico, in 1947?	Neutral	22	45	33

Note: Percentages are rounded. For all items except for the Obama citizenship question (which was reverse-scored), "Yes" responses are coded as rumor endorsement, and "No" responses are coded as rumor rejection.

Source: YouGov, July 2010.

Readers will probably have noticed that in my 2010 survey I asked about more rumors arising on the right than I did about rumors arising on the left. This imbalance reflects the political reality of the information ecosystem in the present day—there are simply more rumors in circulation on the right than there are on the left. For example, Allcott and Gentzkow found pro-Trump fake stories were shared 30 million times on Facebook during the 2016 election, compared with 7.6 million shares for pro-Clinton stories.[16] In a 2019 study, Garrett and Bond examined the most viral fake political news stories every two weeks for six months and found that 46 percent of the high-engagement stories benefited the political Right, while only 23 percent benefited the political Left.[17] While rumors originate and spread on both sides of the partisan divide, in the present day, they are far more prevalent on the conservative side.

What do the answers to these questions collectively say about the state of the public acceptance of political rumors? On the one hand, some of the news is good: a plurality of the public rejects six of the seven rumors. But, on the other hand, these findings unearth a troubling pattern. There are only two rumors that a majority of the respondents conclusively reject. Large swaths of the public either accept rumors as true or, by giving a "don't know" response, refuse to refute these rumors outright. In the chapters to follow, I will demonstrate that these "don't know" responses are especially consequential because, for some individuals, such responses indicate a skepticism of political facts that can, on occasion, be overcome with the provision of new information. For now, what is important is that acceptance of rumors—or at least the failure to reject them—was widespread in 2010. Numerous surveys I have conducted since then have yielded similar results (as a fuller accounting of the data in chapter 3 will show).

Moreover, the failure to reject rumors is not simply concentrated in a small, fixed portion of the citizenry. Instead, most people exhibit at least *some* belief in prevailing rumors. As figure 1.1 demonstrates, on average respondents endorsed about two rumors out of the seven and said they were "not sure" about another two. However, only 5 percent of respondents endorsed more than four rumors. These results underscore wide variation among individuals in their willingness to believe rumors. Moreover, while at least 15 percent of the respondents expressed support for each of the individual rumor statements, over 70 percent of respondents expressed support for at least one of the statements. Thus, it is not just that *some* people believe *a lot* of fanciful things. Rather, *a lot* of people believe *some* fanciful things.[18]

FIGURE 1.1. Distribution of Beliefs on Rumor Questions, July 2010

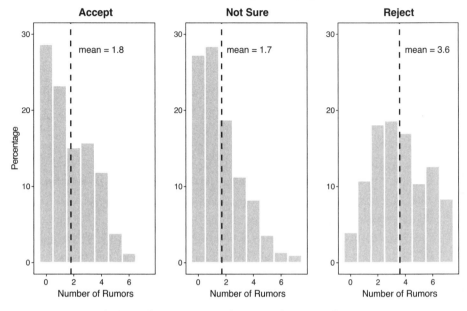

Note: The graph shows the distribution of rumor endorsement (acceptance, uncertainty, and rejection) across the seven rumor items (refer to table 1.1). The mean number of rumors accepted is equal to 1.8, uncertain is 1.7, and rejected is 3.6. *Source*: YouGov, July 2010.

Why Do Some People Accept Rumors?

Just because many Americans believe many different political rumors does not mean there is no rhyme or reason to their beliefs. There is, in fact, a structure to individuals' willingness to accept or reject the rumors in circulation in the political world. First, as psychologists have long known and political scientists have recently observed, individuals systematically vary in their willingness to embrace the kind of conspiratorial thinking at the heart of political rumors. Consider, for example, the kinds of people who are unwilling to lend credibility to conspiracy theories of any kind. These people lie at one end of a continuum. At the other end of this continuum are those individuals who embrace conspiracy theories of all sorts no matter how ridiculous they sound—the kinds of people you may try to avoid at family events because they always have a new outlandish story to share. And of course many individuals lie at points in between. Such tendencies do not necessarily reflect pathologies of reasoning. After all, at times, authoritative voices in government have not been truthful to the American public. Moreover, certain groups in society have been subject to more damaging misinformation than others—as the experience of Black citizens during the Tuskegee Syphilis Study in the 1930s and 1940s demonstrates. Thus, it might make sense for some people not to accept all official information unconditionally. But such tendencies are adaptive only to a point. There is a line between the scrutiny of government that is critical for active engagement by citizens and a problematic move to instead substitute claims based on flimsy standards of evidence for official voices. A healthy democracy requires a citizenry that, while appropriately skeptical of authority, does not cross this line.

Social scientists have measured individuals' placement along this continuum of conspiracism in various ways, ranging from a search for general factors that lead individuals to accept political rumors—such as a sense of alienation from a group or society—to the measurement of degrees of endorsement of specific conspiracy theories. But at the core, all these scholars are working toward capturing variation in some general tendency to accept conspiracies and rumors as truth—the tendency to embrace misinformation.

In this book, I focus on politically grounded rumors and misinformation. I use measures of individuals' general propensity to believe in conspiracies and rumors of all types, because some people are more susceptible than others to conspiratorial thinking, regardless of the topic area. I also use measures of belief in specific rumors because these rumors have distinctive *political* roots, especially related to people's partisan attachments. When it comes to belief in the veracity of political rumors that target a particular party or leader, where you stand depends in large part upon where you sit. The problem is widespread, and it affects citizens who sit on both the political Left and the political Right.

Jointly these factors—the tendency toward conspiratorial thinking on the one hand and partisan attachments on the other—shape patterns of rumor belief. The interaction of conspiratorial dispositions and partisan motivation predict who accepts rumors, who rejects them, and who is uncertain. Political partisans who are prone to conspiratorial thinking are also the least likely to question the veracity of rumors impugning their political adversaries. The refusal to reject political rumors therefore arises from the combination of political beliefs and conspiratorial orientation.

Rumors in a Democratic Society

Simply because unsubstantiated beliefs are widespread and structured in meaningful ways does not mean such beliefs are politically consequential. Perhaps rumors are akin to celebrity gossip—something to keep people entertained but of little import to politics and governance. When I began writing this book, many media commenters could and did make such a case. For instance, Matthew Yglesias in 2010 likened the belief that Obama was a Muslim to other fringe beliefs, including the belief in the existence of extrasensory perception.[19] In the resulting decade, it has become much harder to dismiss political rumors as frivolous entertainment.

On the contrary, rumors can have serious political consequences and carry tangible costs for society. Granted, rumors have been a persistent part of American politics, even stretching back to the early days of the republic. But just because rumors have always been with us does not mean that we should simply shrug our shoulders and accept them as facts of political life. Misinformation and rumors are dangerous for the functioning of democracy because they can pervade the political environment, shaping the beliefs not only of the hard-core believers but also of the more casual observers of politics.

Most concerningly, rumors might motivate some people to engage in political violence. As Cass Sunstein has observed, "Even if only a small fraction of adherents to a particular conspiracy theory act on the basis of their beliefs, that small fraction may be enough to cause serious harm."[20] The wider a rumor spreads, perhaps the greater the chance that harm will result. And such events are no longer mere hypotheticals. In December 2016, Edgar Maddison Welch came armed with a rifle to the Comet Ping Pong restaurant in Washington, DC, to investigate for himself the "Pizzagate" rumors that linked the restaurant to a nonexistent child sex trafficking ring allegedly run by Hillary Clinton and her political associates.[21] The insurrection on January 6, 2021—when hundreds of protesters stormed the US Capitol in a violent attempt to stop the counting of the electoral vote—demonstrated how belief in rumors might spiral into large-scale violence for some individuals.

All this being said, establishing a causal connection between political rumors and political action—or establishing a direct relation between misinformation and harm, more generally—constitutes an extremely difficult task. We know that rumors and real-world outcomes are almost certainly associated, but few scholars have established a direct causal link between the two.[22] But even if we cannot easily quantify the direct harms of misinformation by putting a monetary cost on its effects or by directly tying the existence of particular forms of misinformation to real-world outcomes, rumors can be important and powerful.

Especially troubling is the damage that political rumors can do to the shape of the larger information environment. Much political research has documented citizens' ignorance of basic political knowledge and facts,

a problem that plagues even highly educated citizens of both conservative and liberal persuasions. However, Kuklinski and his colleagues note
that the more serious problem for democracy is the prevalence of beliefs
in *misinformation*—factually incorrect information.[23] In other words, a
*mis*informed public may be even worse than an *un*informed one when it
comes to democratic outcomes. Political science research has effectively
demonstrated that such misperceptions are widespread among citizens in
the United States. For example, Americans overestimate the size of welfare
payments, the percentage of the budget that goes to foreign aid, and the
details of the provisions of the 2010 Affordable Care Act.[24] Unsubstantiated political rumors are an insidious form of misinformation that can be
particularly damaging for the functioning of democracy in several ways.

One of these ways is how the kinds of extreme beliefs encapsulated in false
rumors—such as the belief that the government is creating "death panels," or
that millions of illegal immigrants have voted in presidential elections—can
weaken trust in government. For instance, McKay and Tenove argue that,
by promoting false claims, online disinformation campaigns purposefully
offer opposing information that competes with established facts, encouraging debates over the "truth" in a context rife with conflicting claims.[25]
Echoing these concerns, Rosenblum and Muirhead warn of the dangers of
subscribing to a worldview embodying "new conspiracism" that codifies
conspiracy without the theory. Such a belief system seeks to delegitimize
all authority.[26] As they argue, "The new conspiracists seek not to correct
those they accuse, but to deny their standing in the political world to argue,
explain, persuade, and decide. And from attacking malevolent individuals,
conspiracists move on to assaulting institutions. Conspiracism corrodes
the foundations of democracy."[27] Such a strategy is especially pernicious
because it does not require individuals to actually accept political rumors;
the mere questioning of political reality can have serious downstream consequences because sowing doubt about political policies and claims is much
easier than resolving such doubt. In this view, purveyors of misinformation
do not need the public to accept one view of political reality; they just need
ordinary citizens to doubt and mistrust authoritative voices in the government—to say they are "not sure" if rumors are true or not. As I will demonstrate in the chapters that follow, such expression of uncertainty among
the less engaged portion of the public can be dangerous for the functioning
of democracy. An unwillingness to unconditionally accept facts as truth
fosters an environment of mistrust around the politicians and policies that
those facts implicate.

Finally, rumors may directly affect policy. If people rely on faulty information, they might oppose policies they would otherwise support or support policies they would otherwise oppose. As Hochschild and Einstein argue, "Developing public policies in response to pressures linked to misinformation risks making bad decisions and implementing them poorly."[28] One such example occurred in the summer of 2009 when a myth circulated that Obama's health care reform plan included "death panels" that would decide whether individual citizens should receive health care, based on a calculation of their level of productivity in society. In actuality, the plan included provisions to pay doctors to counsel patients about end-of-life options. This rumor started with statements made by the former lieutenant governor of New York, Betsy McCaughey, a Republican, and quickly spread across conservative media. A number of prominent Republican politicians added to the chorus, including Sarah Palin and Senator Charles Grassley, the ranking Republican member of the Senate Finance Committee.[29]

This rumor was patently false and had been widely discredited by media organizations from across the ideological spectrum. All the same, it took root among the American mass public. An August Pew Center poll found that 30 percent of the public thought the death panel rumor was true, and another 20 percent were unsure of the veracity of the statement. Even after the passage of the Affordable Care Act (ACA), the rumor persisted. In the July 2010 survey I described earlier, 33 percent of the public thought the death panel rumor was true, and 22 percent were unsure. This rumor also had important political implications. In early 2011, the Obama administration announced that it would revise Medicare fee policies to remove those provisions that provided funding for end-of-life counseling. The persistence of the death panel rumor hung heavily over this decision.

What Can Be Done?

To this point, I have painted a fairly grim, if realistic, picture of the modern political landscape. But that was not my goal. I began this project during the early days of the first Obama administration with the hope that by understanding how and why seemingly unbelievable stories about political figures and policies grab hold of the public mind, I could then offer strategies to effectively counter rumors. Demonstrating which types of people believe rumors to be true is important, but the more pressing task involves establishing a method to correct false information.

This is easier said than done. As we will see in the chapters that follow, I—and other scholars in the fields of political science, psychology, and communication—have made far more progress on identifying which types of people believe rumors than on convincing them that those rumors are false. That said, in the second half of the book, I explore ways to correct the rampant falsehoods afloat in society. A word of warning, though: rather than offering a "silver bullet" solution to fixing the problem of misinformation, I largely discuss the bounds on the effectiveness of such strategies and the limits of the various types of people that can be convinced to unconditionally reject political rumors.

THE STICKINESS OF MISINFORMATION

In 2000, Kuklinski and his colleagues called upon scholars to focus the field of political behavior on the implications of widespread misinformation, in addition to the well-established findings of the dearth of information among the public. Despite this admonition, academic interest in the dynamics of political misinformation was limited. What work was done suggested that correcting misinformation is, if anything, a more intractable problem than Kuklinski and his colleagues thought it to be. Nyhan and Reifler ran experiments where they attempted to correct false statements about the Iraq War and rumors about Obama's religion, both with little success.[30] In addition to these studies, my own work on opinions concerning war and that of Hopkins, Sides, and Citrin on immigration attitudes found that presenting citizens with political facts does not change their opinions on important political matters.[31]

In recent years, though, there has been an increased focus on misinformation, leading to a flood of work on the topic across the social sciences. The findings are too numerous to list here (though for a review of the literature circa 2019, see Wittenberg and Berinsky).[32] In some ways, this work has been promising. For example, Wood and Porter find that, across a variety of issues, it is possible to reduce misperceptions by providing citizens with factual information.[33] But even this explosion of scholarship has shown that there is still a long way to go. While there are some promising results, the search for a *solution* to the problem of misinformation remains elusive.

This is not surprising. Rumors are very hard to correct from a psychological standpoint. Political misinformation is especially pernicious because once misinformation takes seed, its effects extend even after it has been discredited—a phenomenon called belief perseverance.[34] For example, in her study of the evaluation of hypothetical political candidates, Thorson found that misinformation can generate "belief echoes"—persistent effects on attitudes even after false information has been corrected and the truth has been internalized.[35] Perhaps scholars of misinformation have not found workable solutions because such solutions are impossible.

THINKING ABOUT CORRECTIONS:
WHOM TO TARGET AND HOW

But we need not throw up our hands in defeat. First, while there may not be a single magic solution that can eliminate the scourge of misinformation, there are some corrective strategies that can help reduce misinformation's grip on the collective public mind. In chapter 4 I show that *who* debunks a rumor is just as important as *how* it is debunked. People who speak out against their apparent political interests—for example, Republican politicians countering the death panel rumors—can be even more effective than seemingly neutral "authoritative" sources. But my solution is just one approach. That strategy may not work, or even represent the best course of action, in every case. We need to focus on an inclusive toolkit—a collection of solutions.

A number of scholars have advanced a variety of solutions, and the scope of this work will surely only grow. These proposed solutions seek to tackle misinformation at all points in the process—through both ex ante interventions (advocated by other scholars) that preemptively inoculate against misinformation before individuals first encounter it and ex post interventions like mine that are deployed after exposure to try to correct misinformation. No one solution need take priority over another. Instead we should use *all* available solutions that are each imperfect in one way or another, yet offer a greater probability of success when combined. To combat the spread of COVID-19, some virologists advocate a "Swiss cheese model" of pandemic defense. This model entails the use of multiple layers of protections, such as masks, social distancing, ventilation, and testing and tracing. Individually each method is a slice of "cheese" with holes in it. But by stacking each of these layers, each with a different set of "holes," we can create a more effective barrier to the spread of the virus. The same is true for combatting misinformation. By combining different strategies, we may be able to create a collective response that works—a "Swiss cheese model" of information defense.

In addition to expanding the scope of solutions and interventions to consider, we can also change the kinds of people we target with those strategies. When I began my work, I focused on correcting the beliefs of individuals who fully embraced political rumors—a group I refer to as the "believers" of rumors. Over time, it has become clear just how hard it is to change their beliefs. In focusing solely on the believers, we may be overlooking people we can actually help. While some people, like the believers, are engaged with the political world, for the vast majority of Americans, politics is a secondary concern. Most of the public, most of the time, does not care about politics. People certainly do not care enough to deeply consider a particular issue, much less to go down a rabbit hole of misinformation. But all citizens live in a system of social interactions, both online and offline, and their casual attention can be weaponized.

We therefore also need to pay attention to the power of rumors to grip citizens beyond the core believers. Recall the distribution of responses to the rumor questions from my surveys I presented in figure 1.1. For every rumor question, there exists a substantial set of individuals who actively endorse that rumor. But there are also people who, though they do not fully embrace rumors, do not fully reject them either. Like the "believers," this group of "uncertain" citizens is both a symptom and a cause of the dangers of misinformation. Because rumors thrive in ambiguous environments, the presence of these uncertain citizens can aid the spread of rumors and undermine the legitimacy of the democratic system. Any position short of outright rejecting a rumor—even a "don't know" or "not sure" response—may enhance a rumor's credibility by suggesting cause for ambivalence or uncertainty. As I discuss in the chapters that follow, these people are important for understanding and ultimately defusing the power of rumors. The "uncertain" often represents a significant portion of the public, and these individuals come from all walks of life. But, more importantly, I find that it is sometimes possible to induce these uncertain individuals to reject political rumors.

I therefore believe that we need to expand our efforts to combat rumors and misinformation from a focus on the believers to a focus on the "uncertain" as well. This is not to say that we can never convert believers to disbelievers. Yet we must recognize that believers' minds are extremely hard to change. Thus, I argue for putting greater energy into moving the "uncertain." By focusing on this group, the social transmission of those rumors could be short-circuited, thereby reducing the spread of misinformation.

THE IMPORTANCE OF LEADERSHIP

Fighting political misinformation must also involve a change in the way political leaders talk to ordinary citizens. As I and many others have argued, the blame for the failings of the collective public to refute misinformation and rumors does not lie solely in their hands.[36] We must also address misinformation at its source—the elites and opinion leaders who strategically disseminate misinformation through the information ecosystem.

Over the past several decades, American politics has been rife with rumors. As I will discuss, the rise of Donald Trump and his public embrace of misinformation and innuendo has certainly affected the information ecosystem in a sizable and enduring way. But Trump is neither the cause nor the only instantiation of the rise of rumors. Over the long term, we need to think about the shape and nature of the larger information environment and what incentives can be deployed to convince leaders to forgo tactics of misinformation and rumor.

Once again, this is easier said than done. And this task is especially difficult because political leaders benefit from spreading rumors. The problem is further compounded because, as I will show in chapter 5, politicians may not necessarily pay a cost for their lies—especially in the United States. Even when misinformation is corrected—and people accept those corrections—their overall evaluations of the politicians who spread misinformation is largely unchanged. That said, there are some hopeful findings in other countries. In Australia, for instance, correcting misinformation *does* reduce citizens' evaluations of leaders who promote mistruths. Perhaps with a more targeted strategy, politicians in the United States could be held accountable as well.

Plan of the Book

Throughout the remainder of this book, I critically examine the challenge of political rumors through a metaphor of a pebble in a pond. When a pebble is tossed into a pond, waves ripple outward, diminishing in strength as they move away from the initial point of impact. When it comes to rumors, a similar pattern arises: after creators plant the first seeds of a rumor—in essence, dropping the pebble into the pond—its effects emanate outward into the mass public, with the strength of individuals' belief in the rumor diminishing as it moves from a core circle of believers to more uncertain individuals to active disbelievers. I use this theoretic framework to explore political rumors through a series of empirical studies of mass and elite political behavior.

In the first two empirical sections of the book, I focus on the mass public, with the dual goals of understanding why citizens come to believe some political rumors but not others, and identifying effective strategies for debunking rumors after they first take hold. In the final part of the book, I turn my attention to the elite actors who create and exploit rumors for their own political benefit. As part of this process, I investigate whether, and under what conditions, leaders may be held accountable by the public for spreading misinformation and document distinct patterns of elite rumor discourse across party lines. In doing so, I bring to light key opportunities and challenges for combating political rumors, conspiracy theories, and misinformation and offer guidance to scholars, practitioners, and other stakeholders about how best to tackle this growing threat. Note that an appendix to the book containing tables and figures not included in the text can be found at this book's website: https://press.princeton.edu/books/hardcover/9780691158389/political-rumors

I begin in the next chapter by providing a historical overview and describe the anatomy of rumors and misinformation. I then discuss how such rumors can spread through the public, including the role played by social media.

In chapter 3, I turn to the empirical study of rumor belief, exploring ten original surveys I collected from 2010 to the waning days of the Trump presidency. This broad span of data allows me to observe what has changed and what has stayed the same as American politics has unfolded, rather than focusing on just rumors and misinformation in the current environment. I then use a series of original experiments to demonstrate that the people who say that they believe that Obama is a Muslim or that George W. Bush allowed the 9/11 attack to occur are not simply venting anger or frustration at the president; they sincerely think these things are true. Finally, I move beyond a focus on the believers to explore the full distribution of belief in rumors—from the believers to the uncertain to the disbelievers. Although there are core believers who are likely to accept a rumor no matter its content, partisanship fundamentally shapes belief in political rumors. Republicans are more likely to reject rumors that implicate Republicans in wrongdoing, and similarly, Democrats are more likely to reject rumors about Democratic malfeasance. The failure to reject rumors therefore arises from a combination of generalized belief and specific interest. At the same time, I find a degree of partisan asymmetry in my data. The interaction of conspiratorial inclination and partisan attachments predict the degree of support for rumors among both Democrats and Republicans, but the importance of conspiratorial dispositions and partisan identity tends to be greater for rumors targeting Democrats. I return to this question of partisan asymmetry in the nature of rumor belief in later chapters. But putting this asymmetry aside for the moment, it is clear that rumors can gain traction among individuals of varied political stripes.

Showing which types of people believe certain rumors to be true is only half the story. A democracy in which lies and falsehoods run rampant cannot function properly. When citizens do not trust their leaders, disharmony and chaos are the result. Dispelling the rumors that plague today's political system is critical. As scholars have learned, and as the American public has repeatedly demonstrated over the past decade, this is a daunting task. We can see these processes in the experiences of two recent presidents—one who sought to combat rumors and another who tried to spread them. Take first the presidency of Barack Obama. The Obama administration repeatedly tried to dispel the rumors that plagued his term of office. During the 2008 presidential contest, Obama released a computer printout of his birth certificate on a campaign website, but this did little to quell the "birther" controversy. In April 2011, he released his long-form birth certificate. For a time, it appeared that this strategy was effective. In the week after he released the document, the public's rejection of the birther rumor increased greatly. The proportion of the public who said that Obama was born in the United States rose from just over half to two-thirds of the public. But the effect of Obama's action on public perceptions was short lived. Most of the increase in the percentage of respondents who say that Obama was born in the United States dissipated in a matter of months.

Obama also addressed the rumors surrounding the health care bill, directly refuting the death panel rumor at town hall meetings in New Hampshire in the summer of 2009. However, the administration's strategy similarly failed to stem the tide. Polls administered throughout 2010 showed that a large portion of the American public continued to believe that the government was prepared to enact death panels—a contention that still plagues discussions of health care reform to this day. The failure of the Obama administration to correct widespread mistruths and the difficulty involved in correcting these rumors demonstrate just how sticky rumors can be. However, in the second half of the book I show that by paying close attention to the types of factors that give rumors their power, we might be able to learn how to combat these rumors in a more effective manner.

In a rational society, expertise should carry weight in the public sphere in its own right. But this is not always the case. Because facts are not self-correcting, establishing facts and truth is only half the battle. In addition to the message, we need to pay attention to the messenger. Here we can potentially turn the power of partisanship on its head. In chapter 4, I use the ACA death panel rumor as a case study of one strategy that could be effective—namely using messengers who speak against their apparent interest.

But this strategy can only go so far. Targeting individual rumors and misinformation might work in the short term, but it is akin to playing Whac-A-Mole, batting down rumors as they pop up on the political landscape, only to have a new set appear. In chapter 5, I discuss this Whac-A-Mole strategy of political fact-checking in the context of the Trump presidency. One important point that underscores the lessons of chapter 4 is that the impact of corrections is short-lived. If this approach is similar to playing Whac-A-Mole, its effectiveness is like playing with a weak mallet.

Finally, I turn to the role played by politicians in forming misinformation. I lay much of the blame at the feet of political leaders. As citizens, we need to think about the role that politicians can play in exacerbating the diffusion of political rumors and their acceptance among the American public, and we need to take responsibility for whom we put in power. It is the job of our leaders to stand up and challenge unsubstantiated rumors and outright falsehoods, even when the targets of such rumors are their political adversaries. Politicians have tremendous power to lead and shape the information environment. Our leaders can choose to amplify conspiracy theories or to tamp them down. We have seen what happens when they take the former path; to sustain our democracy, they need to forgo short-term political calculations and take the latter road. In chapter 6, I assess how the content and tone of elite discussions about rumors affect mass opinion. This chapter provides suggestive observational evidence that elites can shape mass belief about rumor and misinformation. I then explore the dynamics of these processes using experiments wherein I vary the partisan tone and content of rumors and their corrections. Though my empirical findings are inconclusive, they do suggest that politicians—and Republican politicians in particular—have contributed to and exacerbated the problem of political rumors in modern society.

2

Rumors in the Political World

Even a casual observer of politics can tell that political rumors are alive and well. There is no better example of this than the meteoric rise of the right-wing QAnon movement in 2020. QAnon is a sprawling and constantly evolving web of conspiracy theories alleging—among other things—that the world is run by a cabal of cannibalistic, Satan-worshipping pedophiles, consisting of top Democratic politicians, high-ranking government officials, celebrities, and religious leaders. QAnon adherents allege that former US president Donald Trump was specifically recruited by the military to bring members of this cabal to justice, culminating in a day of reckoning known as "the Storm" and characterized by mass arrests and executions. But QAnon is not just one theory; though the basic tenets of QAnon have remained stable over time, different narratives and beliefs have been associated with this movement at different points in time. Indeed, QAnon has frequently assimilated other, similarly outlandish conspiracies into its broader meta-narrative, even including claims about the true nature of the assassination of John F. Kennedy.

The origins of QAnon can be traced back to an October 2017 post on 4chan, an online message board. The anonymous poster behind the initial message, now known simply as "Q," claimed to be a high-ranking government official with access to insider information about the Trump administration's war against the global cabal. In the years since this initial message, Q posted thousands of cryptic messages, known as "Q drops," containing coded predictions about future events. These messages then get dissected and disseminated by networks of followers on Facebook, Twitter, YouTube, and other social media platforms.

From these humble beginnings, word of QAnon has spread through the larger information ecosystem. During the 2020 US presidential campaign and into 2021, it was difficult to avoid discussion of QAnon. Outlets ranging from legacy media organizations, such as the *New York Times* and the *Wall Street Journal*, to gossip websites like TMZ ran stories about the movement.[1] The Capitol Insurrection on January 6, 2021, made a minor celebrity of Jake Angeli, a rioter with a horned fur headdress and red, white, and blue war paint known better as "Q Shaman" or the "QAnon Shaman." The public profile of stories about QAnon, and the constant coverage of the theories at the heart of the movement, clearly had a large impact on the public consciousness; polls by the Pew Research Center found that public awareness of QAnon increased considerably from early to late 2020, with nearly half of Americans indicating that they had heard at least a little about QAnon in September 2020, compared with less than a quarter of Americans just seven months earlier.[2]

The larger QAnon narrative is composed of a series of claims, such as the direct involvement of leading Democratic Party officials in child trafficking, that are patently false and have been widely discredited. But despite this fact, significant portions of the US population are unwilling to dismiss QAnon out of hand. An October 2020 Yahoo News/YouGov poll found that just under 40 percent of registered voters who had heard of QAnon were at least partially unsure whether its assertions are true or not, with less than 20 percent of Trump supporters indicating that QAnon presents an extremist conspiracy theory with no basis in fact. Indeed, among those Trump supporters who indicated they had heard of QAnon, a full 50 percent said they believed that "top Democrats are involved in elite child sex-trafficking rings," with an additional 33 percent indicating they were "not sure" whether this statement was true or false. In short, stated belief in QAnon has risen to alarmingly high levels—especially among supporters of Trump.

The QAnon conspiracy theory has swiftly moved from a fringe belief to a mainstream phenomenon. As its reach has expanded, the conspiracy theory has acquired further legitimacy due to support from prominent politicians, including Donald Trump, who have repeatedly refused to denounce the movement and have publicly described QAnon supporters as patriots that "love our country."[3] Vocal proponents of the conspiracy theory, including Marjorie Taylor Greene and Lauren Boebert, have likewise run for—and subsequently won—seats in Congress.[4]

The dramatic rise of QAnon is not only deeply troubling but also potentially dangerous given its potential to radicalize individuals into violence. However, to understand why people believe QAnon–and how to undermine its influence—we need to better understand political rumors more generally. That is the task of this chapter.

I begin by diving into the history of rumors in the United States to situate the recent wave of rumors within their historical context. Though the current state of rumors may seem inexplicable, they are, in fact, only the most recent manifestation of patterns of political communication that extend back to the early days of the American Republic.

I next consider the general phenomenon of political rumors, addressing two important questions: What is a rumor? And where do rumors come from? The Merriam-Webster dictionary defines a rumor as "a statement or report current without known authority for its truth." But rumors about politics are not simply unverified conjectures; they may also contradict widely available and accepted evidence. For a statement to be fact, the evidence presented in its favor must stand up to expert scrutiny. Political rumors are therefore characterized not only by the *absence* of available evidence to support them but by credible evidence that contradicts the rumor.

I next consider the means by which rumors spread through society. I begin by defining four critical groups of citizens to better understand how citizens engage with rumors: the creators, the believers, the disbelievers, and the uncertain. Each of these groups has distinct characteristics that play a unique role in the existence and spread of rumors.

Finally, I consider the state of political rumors in the present day. Though rumors have a long history in the United States, the development of the modern media environment has shaped and changed the ways through which information flows across society. I therefore conclude the chapter with a discussion that situates the spread of political information—rumors being a particularly insidious form of such information—in an understanding of current social and mainstream media. I place special emphasis on the important distinctions between selective exposure, or the willful seeking of information of a particular slant, and incidental exposure, or the acquisition of information by happenstance. These modalities inform the modern-day spread of rumors, setting up the empirical analyses in the chapters that follow.

Historical Overview: Rumors in US Society

There may be great interest in rumors today, but the existence of rumors and conspiracy theories is nothing new in the American experience. In fact, as Olmsted demonstrates, their history dates back to at least the eighteenth century, when British settlers told tales of the pope sending swarms of priests to aid the Catholic French and Spanish empires in destroying their nascent colonies.[5] During the Revolutionary War era, even the founding fathers spread rumors to meet political ends: According to Dowd, in an attempt to stimulate French support for the American cause, Benjamin Franklin spread rumors of British-instigated brutalities by Native Americans against the colonial forces.[6] As Olson argues, "American conspiracy theories have always existed. Though the villains in these theories may change over time, the theories themselves are, in fact a normal part of American history and politics."[7] Widespread acceptance of unwarranted beliefs among the mass public is not novel.

Scholars have long been interested in these tales, and rumors have been a topic of social science research for over a hundred years.[8] Allport and Postman's classic analysis of rumors grew out of an investigation of rumors concerning waste and special privileges in rationing programs during World War II.[9] Similar rumors have also repeated throughout history, returning and resurfacing in different context, in a pattern that Bysow terms "diving rumors."[10] Fine and Ellis document several such rumors in their book, *The Global Grapevine*, including stories about food contamination and immigrant invasion that occur again and again in the American consciousness. Such rumors never fully evaporate; rather, they reappear in different forms over time.

Given this long history on the American political scene, why has there been a resurgence of interest in rumors and conspiracy theories today? Are rumors actually growing more common? Have we reached a turning point where seemingly preposterous conspiracy theories like QAnon now guide mainstream political discourse and command elite endorsements? More generally, is it the case that, as *Politico* claimed in a 2020 article, America is "living in the golden age of conspiracy theories"?[11]

THE RISE OF RUMORS?

Political rumors have received renewed attention in recent years amid growing concerns about the emergence of pernicious forms of misinformation, like "fake news."[12] In the wake of the 2016 US presidential election, scholars and pundits alike have increasingly voiced anxiety about the proliferation of misinformation in all its forms. Moreover, over the past several decades, the exponential growth of the journalistic fact-checking industry has shone a spotlight on viral misinformation.[13] Such heightened attention to the correction of misinformation has potentially made the challenge of misinformation especially salient in the current day and age—even if it is not the case that the absolute number of rumors and conspiracy theories has changed over the years in meaningful ways.

Indeed, a long-term view of the evidence demonstrates that the modern-day prevalence of rumors is not unique, or even especially unusual, in American history. Examining one hundred years of letters to the editor published by the *New York Times* for mentions of conspiracy theories, Uscinski and Parent make the case that the early twenty-first century is not, in fact, a particularly conspiratorial time.[14] Reaching back to the nineteenth century, they catalog rumors that range from the innuendo that the same Republicans who conspired to fix the 1888 election had their eyes on the 1892 election, to allegations that US financiers brought about World War I to further their financial interests, to claims in the 1950s that American scientists were trying to find methods to control the weather to take over enemy territory. In fact, by Uscinski and Parent's accounting, both the 1890s and 1950s were times of greater traffic in conspiracy theories than the present day. Olmsted brings a similar historical focus to the outgrowth of conspiracy theories in the twentieth century, dating back to World War I.[15] According to Olmsted, changes in the role of the federal government altered the nature of conspiratorial thinking over the course of the century. The consolidation of power at the federal level, combined with a willingness of government officials to engage in actual conspiracies, such as the Bay of Pigs invasion and the Watergate break-in, fostered greater conspiratorial thinking within the mass public. That is, once it became known that the government was engaging in *some* conspiracies, it became easier for some citizens to believe even outlandish conspiracy theories. Despite declarations that the United States is in an unprecedented era of misinformation, rumors, and conspiracy theories, these phenomena are clearly not new.

What Is a Rumor?

Across the social sciences, scholars have defined the term "rumor" in a variety of ways, but two common themes emerge across works and disciplines. First, rumors are characterized by their *lack of evidence*. Ellis and Fine argue that a "rumor is an expression of belief about a specific event that is supposed to have happened or is about to happen. This claim may pique our interest, but [it] lacks what the larger political system considers secure standards of evidence."[16] Similarly, in another commonly cited definition, DiFonzo and Bordia point to the unsubstantiated basis of evidence for the claim, stating that rumors are "unverified and instrumentally relevant information statements."[17] Second, rumors are not fringe beliefs concentrated among a small set of citizens; instead, they acquire their power through *social transmission*. For example, Sunstein refers to rumors as "claims of fact—about people, groups, events, and institutions—that have not been shown to be true, but that move from one person to another and hence have credibility not because direct evidence is known to support them, but because other people seem to believe them."[18] Likewise, Weeks and Garrett designate rumors as "unverified stories or information statements people share with one another."[19]

In sum, rumors consist of statements that are unverified and spread through social transmission (whether online or offline). Both of these components are important for understanding the nature of rumors and how they capture public attention.

STANDARD OF EVIDENCE AND EVIDENCE OF STANDARDS

Rumors often spread despite being unsupported by expert consensus or concrete evidence.[20] Though rumors might occasionally turn out to be true,[21] the vast majority are false or misleading. What characterizes rumors—and makes them like other forms of misinformation—is that they arise not solely from a *deficiency* of facts but also from the *presence* of unsubstantiated beliefs. That is, rumors are not just unverified, but they often contradict widely accepted evidence. As a result, to borrow a term from Hochschild and Einstein,[22] rumors stick because those who believe them are "actively misinformed" about the state of the world. This view is likewise consistent with Hofstadter's notion of the "paranoid style" of political thinking: What best characterizes the evidentiary foundation of such thinking is not the "absence of verifiable facts . . . but rather the curious leap in imagination that is always made at some critical point in the recital of events."[23]

In this way, rumors are akin to conspiracy theories. Conspiracy theories offer a "proposed explanation of some historical event (or events) in terms of the significant causal agency of a relatively small group of persons—the conspirators—acting in secret."[24] The proponents of these theories respond to contrary evidence "not by modifying their theory, but instead by insisting on the existence of ever-wider circles of high-level conspirators controlling most or all parts of society."[25] In other words, conspiracy theories can be considered a distinct subclass of rumors focused on the nefarious machinations of powerful individuals. For the remainder of the book, I use the term "rumor" to encompass a wide variety of unconfirmed and unsubstantiated claims, including, but not limited to, conspiracy theories. This approach is consistent with Ellis and Fine's contention that "conspiracy theories are not precisely rumors, but they are constructed out of rumors."[26] Regardless of their details, both rumors and conspiracy theories—like other forms of misinformation—involve claims that lack a reasonable evidentiary basis.

But how can we determine what constitutes a "reasonable" evidentiary basis? What information would it take to effectively dispute a rumor? The fact that rumors rest on unverified and sometimes even unverifiable statements creates a larger epistemological problem. Often, we cannot say that a given rumor is false with absolute confidence. As Weeks and Garrett note, rumors "may ultimately be proven true or false, but their defining feature is that they circulate without confirmation."[27] After all, it is possible that the evidence supporting a rumor exists somewhere but has not yet emerged. The veracity of rumors dwells in the realm of uncertainty.

Take the Watergate scandal as an example. In early 1973, the notion that Richard Nixon actively sought to cover up the events surrounding the break-in of the offices of the Democratic National Committee was dismissed as mere speculation. But the narrative shifted suddenly, following the release of the "smoking gun" tape in 1974, which proved that Nixon directed his chief of staff H. R. Haldeman to have the CIA interfere with the FBI's investigation. After this evidence came to light, claims about the Nixon administration's maleficence transformed from rumor to widely accepted fact. In contrast, in the case of the 9/11 "truth movement"—a contention that the September 11 attacks on the World Trade Center and Pentagon were the work of a US government conspiracy rather than a terrorist attack by al-Qaeda—no evidence has emerged in favor of these fringe beliefs, even after two decades. As a result, whereas the initial Watergate rumor ultimately achieved mainstream credibility, the 9/11 conspiracy remains confined to the realm of speculation. Can we say with absolute certainty, though, that damning evidence of the Bush administration's involvement in the events of 9/11 will never emerge? A discussion like this could easily slip into an endless debate over the meaning of "truth." It may be difficult to conclusively disprove a rumor, but surely evidence must count for something.

To avoid such a morass, I step back from a discussion of absolute truth to employ the same standard that Sunstein and Vermeule use to evaluate conspiracy theories. In their view, the most important criterion for labeling conspiracy theories is whether such theories are supported by available information. They argue that conspiracy theories are unjustified "not in the sense of being irrationally held by those individuals who hold them, but from the standpoint of the information available in the society as a whole."[28] Conspiracy theories—and rumors more generally—cannot be considered "warranted beliefs."[29] This interpretation is consistent with longstanding social science interpretation of rumors. In the mid-1940s, Allport and Postman argued that a central feature of rumors is that they are passed along "without secure standards of evidence being present," and in the 1970s, Rosnow posited that rumors are "constructed around unauthenticated information."[30]

The Watergate case illustrates the ways in which the evidentiary basis of rumors can evolve over time, but rumors and conspiracy theories often extend beyond single claims about individual events. In particular, as the example of QAnon illustrates, evaluating conspiracy theories requires the adoption of an increasingly fluid notion of falsifiability—one that encompasses elaborate and far-ranging schemes. Along these lines, Uscinski and Parent propose a framework for distinguishing actual conspiracies and conspiracy theories. For these authors, a conspiracy plausibly exists if the base of evidence provided in support of that conspiracy crosses some threshold that is set and determined by "properly constituted epistemic authorities."[31] Such authoritative evidence emerges when it is considered by experts in a way that makes transparent the evidence and the decision rules used to come to a conclusion.[32] Uscinski and Parent then go on to outline six logical tests to sort conspiracy fact from fiction as best one can. For example, they suggest probing the falsifiability of a particular theory by asking two questions: "What evidence would falsify such a theory?" and "what else would be true if I applied such a standard to other beliefs?" As they argue, if there is no evidence that could falsify a given theory, or if every theory could be deemed "true" if the same standards are applied, we may have moved from the realm of theory to theology. But the details of their method are less important than their guiding principle: for a conspiracy theory to be true, it must stand up to expert scrutiny and conform to available evidence.[33] A similar logic can be applied to the study of rumors more broadly. Over the course of this book, I adopt these same definitional standards when evaluating political rumors and the misinformation embedded in such beliefs. That is, I assume that political rumors involve claims that are not, on balance, supported by the best publicly available evidence that has been confirmed by experts. Rumors may purport to rest upon evidence, but that evidentiary base is nothing more than a mirage.

SOCIAL TRANSMISSION

In addition to lacking concrete standards of evidence, rumors are defined by their ability to spread rapidly through society. As Sunstein notes, rumors gain credibility because other people seem to believe them, or at least do not outrightly reject them.[34] Rumors do not simply represent fringe beliefs among a small segment of the citizenry. Instead, they acquire their power through widespread social transmission and repetition.[35] Thus, to become a rumor, an unsubstantiated claim needs to have a captive audience—a base of believers. Rosenblum and Muirhead make this point explicitly in their book, *A Lot of People Are Saying: The New Conspiracism and the Assault on Democracy*. For them, rumors—what they term the outgrowth of the "new conspiracism"—impose their own reality not through evidence but through repetition.

A rumor is therefore not merely an idea confined to a small subset of disconnected individuals. Indeed, rumors quickly infect the entire information environment. As rumors ricochet around the public, people beyond the core group of true believers are incidentally exposed. This element of social transmission is what makes rumors an especially powerful—and tenacious— form of misinformation. As I discuss in chapter 4, the more familiar a rumor seems (and the more often it is repeated), the more difficult it is to correct. Rumors rest on a foundation of believers, but they create uncertainty in their wake. In other words, what makes a rumor a rumor is not simply the content of its claims and its resulting acceptance by individual citizens, but rather the larger social matrix in which it is imbedded.

Pebble in the Pond

The nature of the social matrix in which rumors abound has far-reaching consequences for understanding the spread and reach of rumors in society. Once introduced, rumors can take on a life of their own. The dissemination of a rumor is thus not a singular event but an ongoing process.

The spread of belief in a rumor among the mass public may be conceptualized as a series of circles of dwindling strength, radiating out from the core

FIGURE 2.1. Pebble in the Pond Metaphor for Rumor Belief

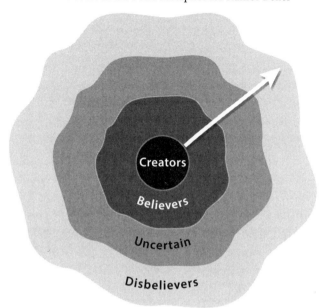

where the rumor originates, and shaping convictions along the way. A pebble dropped into a pond creates ripples that can spread throughout the entire surface of water, with force fading from the initial point of impact. Similarly, a single rumor, introduced by a motivated individual or group, can perturb the broader information ecosystem. From the initial point of impact, the rumor spreads, with impact of the rumor on belief diminishing in intensity as it moves from the core throughout the citizenry.[36] Figure 2.1 illustrates this analogy, depicting the citizenry as separated into a continuum of four groups based on the impact of the rumor on their beliefs: creators, believers, disbelievers and—between the latter two groups—the uncertain.[37]

Rumor transmission begins with a core group of individuals—"creators," in my parlance—who first start to manufacture and circulate a particular rumor. These creators drop the metaphorical pebble that begins the diffusion of rumors and misinformation. While some rumors seem to spring up spontaneously, many gain strength through the direct actions of those actors whom Cass Sunstein has called "conspiracy entrepreneurs" and Ted Goertzel has labeled "first-tier" conspiracy intellectuals.[38] Some of these individuals or groups may sincerely hold fanatical beliefs, whereas others may be motivated by political or economic gain.[39] Returning to the example that introduced this chapter, the origins of QAnon can be traced back to the work of Q, the eponymous figure whose mysterious "Q drops" on obscure online forums provide the fodder for this movement. Though Q's identity and underlying motives remain unknown, this individual (or group of individuals) is undeniably responsible for the birth of this movement. Regardless of its ultimate goals, this creator (or group of creators) serves as the initial instigator of political rumors.

Even if creators are distinct from the broader mass public, they can still have great influence on the beliefs of the citizenry. I consider the role of the creators more explicitly in chapter 6, but I will preview my argument here. The group of creators is typically small; they almost always comprise a trivial portion of the overall population.[40] What is most worrisome for a democracy is not the absolute size of the creator group but rather the resulting ripples of belief that spread from them through the rest of the mass public. To return to the metaphor of the pebble in the pond, once creators drop the stone in the water, they set a series of larger events into motion. Rumors diffuse from this core, and citizens' beliefs in these rumors correspondingly reverberate, diminishing in intensity as rumors radiate outward from the creators to the mass public. These ripples of misinformation may eventually fade, but they can still do great damage to democracy in their wake.

The strongest effect of these radiating beliefs is found among the group of individuals situated on top of the largest ripple within the first ring of the mass public: the believers.[41] Believers lie outside the circle of creators in that they do not manufacture rumors themselves. Rather, believers accept the narrative and conclusions of a particular rumor. That is, they are the individuals who actively endorse a rumor. For example, believers include the "birthers" who think that Obama is not actually a citizen of the United States, the "truthers" who contend that the events of 9/11 were the result of a government conspiracy, and the QAnon adherents who believe that Democrats are operating elite child sex-trafficking rings.[42]

In contrast, the weakest rumor beliefs are found among the "disbelievers," who lie within the outermost ring of the mass public. Disbelievers decisively reject rumors out of hand. Rumor rejection is a normatively desirable outcome; a well-informed citizenry requires individuals to espouse warranted beliefs that cohere with openly available evidence. This does not mean, however, that the disbelievers necessarily arrive at their beliefs through pure logic and reasoning. As I will discuss in the next chapter, people can renounce rumors on the basis of personal or partisan interests. Regardless of their motivations, however, what is important for the present conceptualization is the outcome: disbelievers evaluate rumors and, for whatever reason, find them unjustified. Put another way, once the ripples generated by the creators reach the disbelievers, the power of the rumor has faded completely.

In between the believers and the disbelievers on the continuum lie the "uncertain" group. These are individuals who have been exposed to rumors—whether through political discourse, their social media feeds, or just casual conversations—but have not decided whether they believe the rumor is true. For these individuals, maybe Obama was born in Kenya—or maybe he was not. Perhaps some top Democrats are involved in elite child sex-trafficking rings, or perhaps they are not. As I will discuss later in this chapter, the opportunities for such incidental exposure are magnified in the modern information environment. Though not often discussed in academic work on misinformation,[43] the uncertain group demarcates a boundary that is crucial for the functioning of democracy. They are not so close to the center of a rumor's initial point of impact that they hold firm in their belief, even in the face of corrective information. Nor are they so far conceptually from the source that the intensity of the rumor has fully dissipated. These individuals who say they are "not sure" or "don't know" if a given rumor is true are critical for understanding the power of rumors precisely *because* their beliefs are not completely immutable.

In the next chapter, I will present some suggestive findings indicating that these uncertain citizens at the middle of the continuum represent a some-what heterogeneous collection of individuals, composed of three groups: the disengaged, the skeptical, and the truly unsure. First, *disengaged* individuals are detached from political discourse and, as a result, do not possess even the inklings of a position on the veracity of a rumor. Others choose the "not sure" response because they are unwilling to dismiss rumors out of hand. These people are best thought of as *skeptical* consumers of political information—where there is smoke, their thinking goes, there could be fire. Finally, some people are simply *unsure* whether particular rumors are true or false. These three groups are often conflated in public opinion surveys. For instance, when presenting polling about QAnon beliefs, Morning Con-sult reports the proportion of respondents who either say "don't know" or express "no opinion" about whether QAnon's claims are accurate or inac-curate.[44] These two options, however, are not interchangeable. Disengaged respondents, on the one hand, may truly have "no opinion" because they lack the basic knowledge about QAnon needed to judge whether its tenets are accurate or not. Ambivalent respondents, on the other hand, may have heard some details about QAnon but do not feel comfortable making a judgment one way or the other, choosing instead to signal their uncertainty via a "don't know" response. When we think about this uncertain group—the middle ground between acceptance and rejection—it is thus important to recognize that there is a mix of different types of individuals in these groups.

Though these three subgroups may begin with different motives, they ultimately neither accept nor reject the rumor. As I have argued elsewhere, we must pay careful attention to where the individuals who say they "don't know" stand: Such responses do not "indicate the lack of articulated political concerns or political thought, but rather the lack of political thought structured enough to easily form a summary evaluation in response to the survey question."[45] Here, uncertainty could arise due to a lack of information, yet it could also be a function of skepticism or ambivalence about the underlying claims. Empirically, it may be difficult to parse out these different types, but whatever the reason behind their indecision, the uncertain individuals will neither accept nor reject rumors.

This conceptualization of the uncertain group as those individuals who "don't know" or are "not sure" about a rumor's veracity marks a notable departure from previous approaches to studying political misperceptions. For example, in their differential informedness model, Li and Wagner treat "don't know" responses as solely indicative of being *uninformed* about a particular topic.[46] In contrast, I argue that this group of "don't know" respondents does not just comprise individuals who are ignorant about politics but also those who have not yet made up their minds about whether a rumor is true or not (either due to general skepticism or genuine ambivalence). Because rumors thrive in ambiguous environments, the presence of *any* uncertain individuals, regardless of their reasons for uncertainty, is cause for concern. Any position short of outright rejecting a rumor—even a "don't know" or "not sure" response—may enhance a rumor's credibility and is thus normatively undesirable.

We can see the practical consequences of a large uncertain group in some media reporting of polls concerning political rumors. While the focus of such reporting is often on the percentage of the public that accepts a rumor, in other cases, the rate of the "not sure" responses is reported alongside rumor acceptance. This latter focus frames the problem as one of confusion or tacit acceptance, thus heightening apparent belief in the claim. Consider, for instance, the report of public beliefs concerning Obama's citizenship after the release of his birth certificate in April of 2011. A month later, Gallup led a press release of their poll with the following headline: "Obama's Birth

Certificate Convinces Some, but Not All, Skeptics: Less than half of Republicans still say he was definitely or probably born in the U.S."[47] This framing served to magnify the false controversy concerning Obama's place of birth. The presence of a group of birthers alone might not be enough to diminish the authority of the Obama presidency. But when the media reports that a sizable portion of the American citizenry does not know if a given rumor is true or not, Obama's legitimacy—and by association the legitimacy of his administration more broadly—is threatened.

Importantly, the rings of belief presented in figure 2.1 are not intended to represent fixed categories. Rather they are general groupings along a continuum. But the middle space that the uncertain respondents occupy is important. A "not sure" response indicates that the respondent is not prepared to disavow a given rumor. As I discuss in the chapters that follow, these people are key to understanding and ultimately diffusing the power of rumors. The uncertain group is often large, but under some circumstances its members can be persuaded more easily to reject rumors than the believers.

Of course, this is not to say that believers can never be converted to disbelievers. Yet it must be recognized that believers' minds are extremely hard to change. Targeting corrective efforts at this group can be a Sisyphean task. Equal energy should be put into efforts designed to move the "uncertain." Under the right circumstances, individuals in the latter group can be persuaded to move to the outermost circle of belief, becoming disbelievers. By focusing on influencing the beliefs of this group, we may be able to short-circuit the social transmission of rumors, thereby reducing the spread of misinformation.

Rumors in the Modern Day

Having identified and classified the different groups of people who engage with rumors, I consider how rumors spread in the present day, taking into consideration how the information environment has changed with the development of offline and online media.

As noted above, research has demonstrated that rumors are not uniquely rampant today; this is not to say that recent concerns about rumors and misinformation are necessarily overblown. While detailed discussion of this matter is beyond the scope of this book, it is clear that the development of mass media over the last century has transformed the way that information diffuses through society. Many of these changes predate the mass use of the internet. But the rise of the internet has almost certainly facilitated the diffusion of rumors across all facets of society. Given that rumors acquire their power through transmission and repetition, these changes have important implications for our understanding of rumors.

Writing in the wake of World War II, Allport and Postman argued that the primary mode of rumor transmission was word of mouth.[48] During this time, the US government's Office of War Information (OWI), which was tasked with monitoring civilian morale and collecting data on the public's attitudes and behavior concerning the war, took this idea to heart. Throughout the war, the OWI engaged field representatives to collect information about rumors from community-based correspondents to be sent to the Bureau of Public Inquiries of the OWI.[49]

The nature of rumor transmission evolved in subsequent decades. The spread of various theories surrounding the assassination of John F. Kennedy after his death was aided by grassroots citizen groups and alternative media in an environment that, as Olmsted notes, led to "the dispersion of cultural authority to challenge the government's narrative."[50] By the 1960s, there were simply more pathways through which information about rumors could spread through society than had existed in the previous decades. The rise of the internet in the last twenty-five years has almost certainly accelerated this trend.[51] As Olmsted argues in her comprehensive history of conspiracy theories in the United States, "The Internet further leveled the playing field for proponents of alternative conspiracy theories. Anyone in the world could broadcast a personal theory to a potential audience of billions and form a virtual community with fellow skeptics."[52] Today, anyone can publish on the web, instantly acquiring a degree of credibility regardless of the quality of information they provide.[53] Political rumors themselves may not be larger in scope in terms of their content and importance to political life than in previous times, but the way those rumors spread today may be different in kind. As the rapid rise in awareness of the rumors at the core of the QAnon conspiracy suggests, it is much easier today for would-be conspiracy theory entrepreneurs—the creators who toss rumors into the information ecosystem like pebbles in a pond—to find a captive audience than it was in the past.[54]

The nature of the internet also facilitates communication between potential rumor believers.[55] As Uscinski and Parent note, finding information about rumors and conspiracy theories on the internet often requires some initiative.[56] For those so inclined, the internet is a resource that can fuel flights of fancy to a far greater degree than was true for previous generations. More than ever before, individual believers can find each other and build a community. These communities can foster conversations and interactions that not only reinforce the views of the believers but can spill over into the broader public as well. In particular, the conversations of the believers may become visible to those on the sidelines—people who might not independently subscribe to rumors but are affected by the information flow such conversations leave in their wake. Some rumors have even attracted wide media coverage, thereby exposing a much larger audience to their content. Returning to an earlier example, the QAnon conspiracy has received ample coverage by mainstream media outlets since it first emerged in 2017.[57] Even though these outlets clearly flag this conspiracy theory as false, they nonetheless broadcast details about it to individuals who might not otherwise encounter this information on their own.[58] It is this incidental exposure to rumor discourse that can foster the "uncertain" group described above by introducing doubt through the mere mention of such rumors. Such individuals do not fully reject these questionable claims no matter how unbelievable they appear to be.

In this way, the dissemination of rumors through society may follow a two-step flow of communication.[59] In this first step, rumor creators can reach potential believers—and believers can find each other. This enhanced ability for creators and believers to connect creates centers of discourse on the internet, which can generate hubs of rumor diffusion. Selective exposure to particular types of political and conspiratorial rhetoric can foster self-reinforcing bubbles in which rumors can breed. In this first step, creators cultivate rumors, which believers absorb and accept. However, even if creators and believers only constitute a small number of individuals, they can broadcast rumors and conspiratorial information outward into the larger media environment. Through this second broadcasting step, the discussions within communities of rumormongers can infect the entire information ecosystem and spread rumors to the uncertain—those individuals who do not actively seek out information about rumors but still come across it. This incidental exposure can amplify the spread of rumors and misinformation through society.

SELECTIVE EXPOSURE TO RUMORS

One commonly voiced concern is that the internet breeds conspiracy.[60] For example, in 2004, a *Washington Post* article entitled "Conspiracy Theories Flourish on the Internet" declared that "American history is rife with conspiracy theories" but noted that, in an internet age, "urban legends have become cyberlegends, and suspicions speed their way globally not over months and weeks but within days and hours on the Web."[61] More recently, a *New York Times* columnist likewise speculated that "QAnon . . . and other conspiracy theories may be part of a larger authority crisis created by the internet."[62] Moreover, the internet does not just enable rapid transmission of rumors and conspiracy theories. As noted in the previous section, it also provides venues for rumor proponents to convene and converse. In an era where people can increasingly self-select the media they consume, individuals seeking out other conspiracy-minded people can find each other online. Numerous scholars and political observers suggest that the greater range of options from which to choose media may cause individuals to retreat into increasingly narrow news silos—dubbed "me channels," "the daily me," "echo chambers," or "filter bubbles."[63]

This argument is not simply about the current political moment. Rather, it arises, in part, from a more general concern about the potential dangers of self-selected media in an environment of increased choice. For instance, Prior describes how cable television changed the way people consumed political news in the 1970s and 1980s.[64] When television consisted primarily of the three major news networks, people would watch nightly news shows not because they wanted to, but because there was simply nothing else on television in the early evenings. With the advent of cable television, consumers' media choices skyrocketed; this newly expanded menu of channels ensured that people could handpick content that matched their consumption preferences. For most Americans, these preferences led them to sports and other forms of nonpolitical entertainment. But some sought out highly partisan news, which led to the development of specialized outlets, like the Fox News Channel, where people could immerse themselves in media that reflected more targeted political interests. If individuals increasingly seek out media that affirm their views, while avoiding contradictory content, they may be exposed to a distorted picture of the world. These so-called echo chambers have the potential to foster extreme beliefs by insulating individuals from alternative perspectives.[65]

The possible emergence of online echo chambers has important implications for the study of rumors. The internet and social media have made it easier for true believers—the creators and believers of rumors—to engage with each other.[66] Compare, for example, Olmsted's characterization of the development of the Kennedy assassination rumor industry to more recent phenomena. In the 1960s, communication about rumors concerning the assassination took place through newsletters and occasional conventions.

Now, rumor adherents can simply go to the appropriate online forum—whether that be a subreddit, a Facebook group, or something altogether more obscure—to learn more about particular rumors and find like-minded individuals. These social media interactions can breed conspiratorial thinkers. Vicario and colleagues find, for example, that social media users congregate in homogeneous and polarized communities of interest around information related to conspiratorial narratives.[67] Put simply, it is far easier today for believers to form self-reinforcing networks than in the past. These communities are fertile swamps in which rumors can breed and grow.

Clearly, the existence of these communities is potentially dangerous in theory. But just how dangerous these communities are in practice depends on the nature and extent of their membership. While a great deal of ink has been spilled warning about the dangers of echo chambers—especially those that traffic in extreme ideas—a large volume of recent work suggests that these one-sided information environments are far less pervasive than the conventional wisdom presumes.[68] Guess and colleagues summarize the state of the literature well, writing, "behavioral data shows that tendencies toward selective exposure do not translate into real-world outcomes as often as public discussion would suggest. . . . [M]uch of the public is not attentive to politics and thus unlikely to be in an echo chamber of any sort. Moreover, among those who do consume more than a negligible amount of political news, most do not get all or even most of it from congenial media outlets."[69] In general, some individuals exhibit a tendency toward politically agreeable news consumption, but to a much lesser extent than commonly believed. Consider, for example, data drawn from Nguyen and summarized by Guess and colleagues.[70] In April 2017, they find that only about 10 million people visited Breitbart, a far-right outlet. In contrast, the *Washington Post* and the *New York Times* attract 70 to 100 million unique visitors per month. Individual-level analysis of online behavior leads to similar conclusions regarding the limited ideological segregation in online news visits.[71] As Guess and colleagues conclude, "Most news is consumed from large mainstream sites and . . . even the audiences for niche partisan media are ideologically mixed."[72] Additionally, individuals are often exposed to news through intermediaries such as social network sites and search engines, which are shown to encourage more diverse online news diets.[73] It is important, however, to not assume the impact of an intermediary is consistent across platforms. Recent work has highlighted how different social media platforms can vary in their ability to shape individual news consumption behavior.[74] Thus, while the concept of echo chambers is based on a plausible theory of human behavior and may in fact exist among a small subset of users, in practice, such information bubbles are rare. Though online communities may comprise swamps of misinformation, few individuals traffic in such bogs. However, just because few people retreat to these narrow silos does not mean their behavior is inconsequential. Information can escape from silos and set a series of larger events into motion that foster rumor belief among the mass public.

INCIDENTAL EXPOSURE TO RUMORS

While most people across the political spectrum seem to have relatively moderate media diets—and there is a great deal of overlap in the media consumed by Republicans and Democrats—some people *are* enmeshed in one-sided media environments.[75] The echo chambers that do exist are confined to a small group of highly partisan consumers, but these people drive a disproportionate amount of traffic to ideologically slanted websites. Thus, while the aggregate picture regarding the prevalence of insulated information communities might be relatively rosy, the mere fact that the beliefs and rhetoric of the members of these communities is so extreme has the potential to affect broad swaths of the public. After all, discussion of rumors in these communities does not necessarily stop at the edge of those groups; individuals may be incidentally exposed to such discussions through interpersonal conversations or via social commentary on their news feeds.[76]

We therefore need to be concerned about the rhetoric emerging from echo chambers. Social media are designed to enable people to stay connected and learn about their friends and acquaintances. If individuals are directly connected to people who occupy siloed information bubbles, they may be incidentally exposed to news and rumors via social media. And even if individuals do not directly seek out this information, this content may nonetheless appear in their social interactions on the internet and expose them to rumors they might not otherwise encounter. Mainstream media can then amplify this content even further by providing coverage of particular rumors without concern for their credibility.[77] These patterns of incidental exposure to rumors online or in mainstream media can prolong a rumor's longevity by keeping it in the public consciousness.

There are ample opportunities for individuals to become exposed to political rumors, and increasingly so as more and more information is hosted online and centralized on social media platforms.[78] Experimental research shows that even incidental exposure to online news increases recognition and recall of that information, so merely being exposed to information in the modern day can shape how people think about politics and undermine trust in democratic governance.[79] Additionally, other research shows not only that incidental exposure to online news and political information increases knowledge in presidential candidates' policy positions, but also that the least politically interested gain the most from this type of exposure.[80] There is broad agreement that the changing media environment is increasingly providing opportunities for individuals to encounter news over social media without intending to do so.[81]

Consider, for example, Settle's study of the political consequences of Facebook's News Feed. Settle argues that Facebook—and, by implication, social media more generally—serves to spread political information through a system of comments, likes, and links to external content.[82] As she notes, interactions on Facebook take place in an environment where "politically informative expression, news, and discussion . . . is seamlessly interwoven in a single interface with non-political content."[83] The consumption of political information is not limited to posts that are obviously about politics. Just scrolling through the News Feed gives users a glimpse into the larger world around them because, as Settle argues, "The volume of information that is politically informative is much larger than the volume of information that is explicitly political."[84] This information can come directly from personal connections, but engagement with the posts of acquaintances and friends of friends can also transmit politically relevant information. For instance, some posts on Facebook can signal political positions or convey politically relevant information that could be true or false. People on social media are therefore immersed in an informational network that contains signals that are relevant for navigating the political world. As Settle concludes, "for most people, the cycle of News Feed consumption and engagement involves encountering political information while seeking social information."[85]

More recent data underscore the importance of social media in transmitting political information. Polling conducted by the Pew Research Center for the People and the Press in the summer of 2020 indicates that almost one-fifth of Americans got their political news primarily from social media, the second-most common source after news apps or websites and ahead of cable television.[86] These individuals differed from other news consumers in a number of ways. Most importantly, they were less likely to closely follow major news stories and were also less knowledgeable about current events in the political sphere—consistent with the "disengaged" group of citizens I described earlier.[87]

This combination of low knowledge and high levels of social media use is especially perilous. A July 2020 Pew poll found that individuals who primarily get their news from social media reported extremely high exposure to rumors—specifically, the conspiracy theory that powerful people intentionally planned the COVID-19 pandemic. Awareness of the rumor was much higher for this group than for any other media consumption group: about a quarter said they had heard "a lot" about this conspiracy theory, while over 80 percent had heard at least "a little" about the conspiracy.

In sum, even incidental exposure to rumors can be potentially dangerous. Self-reinforcing communities where rumors arise can produce crosstalk on social media. As rumors pass from believer to believer, there are increased opportunities for those on the sidelines to become activated as well. Individuals who are incidentally exposed might not become firm believers themselves, but exposure to such rhetoric could affect those who are generally less engaged with the political world—the kinds of people who, through chance exposure, might become members of the "uncertain" group. It is these individuals who, as I will detail in the chapters to follow, are critical for the success or failure of rumor campaigns in the mass public.

Conclusion

Rumors may not be larger in scope than in previous eras, but the spread of rumors may be different in kind. It is much easier for those who believe in a rumor to create a self-reinforcing community than in the past, and these hubs of rumor belief can distort the broader information environment through the incidental exposure of broader segments of the mass public. As individuals increasingly encounter rumors online—both intentionally and inadvertently—there is a greater risk that a sizable number of citizens will actively endorse—or, at the very least, not reject out of hand—a given rumor. The mere existence of centers of belief in the modern information environment can thus have a profound effect on the prevalence of inaccurate and unsubstantiated beliefs in society.

When tracing a rumor's political and social impact, it is important to distinguish between four broad groups: the creators, the believers, the disbelievers, and the uncertain. The distribution of individuals across these groups has important implications for the effect of any given rumor. Recall that in the previous chapter I presented data showing that it is not the case that a small number of people believe a lot of rumors, but rather that a large number of people believe at least one rumor. So regardless of whether people consider themselves politically sophisticated, it is likely that they actively or tacitly endorse one rumor or another. It is therefore critical for scholars and practitioners alike to understand the antecedents of membership in each group for particular rumors. Why do some people categorically reject or accept a rumor while others remain unsure? To understand how we can persuade someone to reject a rumor, we first must understand when and why certain individuals are more or less likely to accept a given rumor in the first place. The next chapter focuses on this question by exploring the roots of rumor acceptance and rejection, and—equally important for the functioning of politics—positions in between.

3

The Roots of Rumor Belief

Who are the people who comprise the uncertain and the believers? Why do they have the beliefs they do? Over the last decade, I have collected a great deal of survey data to answer these questions. This chapter uses these data to trace the nature of belief in misperceptions among the public in misinformation that arise from particular political rumors.

I begin by exploring the nature of the believers. Specifically, I answer a question that may already be on the minds of readers: do people actually believe political rumors, or are such expressions of belief just empty words they tell survey interviewers? I will present experimental evidence supporting the contention that the failure to reject particular political rumors out of hand stems from genuine belief in these rumors on the part of the respondents.

Having established that the vast majority of believers who endorse rumors actually believe those rumors, I move to the business of exploring the nature of judgments concerning the veracity of rumors. I first detail the degree to which members of the mass public fall into the different categories along the continuum of belief—believers, disbelievers, and the uncertain— for various rumors across the political spectrum. These rumors span a broad range, from beliefs about President Obama's citizenship to conspiracies surrounding illegal immigrants voting in presidential elections. I then examine the personality and political correlates of rumor belief in the mass public. While there are certain factors that lead individuals to lend plausibility to particular rumors regardless of their content, in today's polarized world, rumor rejection is also in large part a function of political attachments. Thus, the mechanism at work is the interaction of conspiratorial dispositions and partisan motivation: it is those political partisans prone to conspiratorial thinking who are also the least likely to question the veracity of rumors impugning their political adversaries. Rumor belief is the toxic marriage of political beliefs and conspiratorial orientation.

Rumors: Endorsement of Belief or Expressive Response?

Before diving into an examination of the nature and structure of rumor acceptance and rejection, I begin by digging more deeply into the position of the believers. Specifically, I address a more basic question that has bearing on the analysis that follows. People may say that they believe rumors (or that they are "not sure" if particular rumors are true), but when offering such responses, do they truly believe what they say?

Perhaps they do not. After all, people may endorse a rumor instrumentally to send a signal about their support (or lack thereof) for political figures and policies. In other words, people may answer rumor questions sincerely (albeit incorrectly), or they could instead use surveys as a vehicle to express more basic political judgments about politicians and policies they oppose.[1]

Some commentators have argued that the latter is a far more likely state of the world than the former. For instance, Gary Langer, former chief pollster for ABC News, contends that "[s]ome people who strongly oppose a person or proposition will take virtually any opportunity to express that antipathy . . . not to express their 'belief,' in its conventional meaning, but rather to throw verbal stones."[2] Langer's position is consistent with the notion that people may engage in partisan cheerleading when responding to survey questions—giving answers that support their chosen "team."[3] In this view—for many respondents—an expression of support for rumors surrounding Obama's birthplace or voter fraud in Ohio is a purely instrumental response, representing nothing more than simple "cheap talk."[4]

From a practical standpoint, the question is how we can distinguish between these two forms of affirmation of belief in a rumor—the difference between genuine conviction and a cheap-talk response. I take "genuine belief" to mean that respondents make no conscious or active effort to deceive the surveyor when answering a question, so the opinion expressed by the respondent is the same as the opinion formed by the respondent.[5] Conversely, a cheap-talk expressive response involves impression management when reporting the survey response—a conscious decision to willfully misrepresent one's personal beliefs.[6]

The distinction here is not merely semantic. These two forms of rumor acceptance—an expression of genuine belief against a purely expressive response—have very different implications for our understanding of the public will and the functioning of democracy. On the one hand, if acceptance of political rumors represents genuine internalization of misinformation—the belief in information that is factually incorrect—expressions of rumor support undermine the foundations of a democratic society, as discussed previously. On the other hand, if rumor support is merely cheap talk, then responses to rumor questions are simply another symptom of polarized political rhetoric, not a sign of a misinformed electorate.

To distinguish empirically between the prevalence of deep-seated genuine political beliefs and ephemeral and empty partisan badmouthing, I conducted a series of experiments, which are reported more fully in "Rumors and Health Care Reform: Experiments in Political Misinformation."[7] I focused on the response behavior of individuals who belong to those groups who have the most to gain through expressive responding and, as a result, are particularly motivated to dissemble in the survey interview. For example, Republicans might "throw verbal stones" by disparaging former President Obama. We could reduce partisan-motivated answers by altering the costs and benefits of the opinion expression stage of the survey response process in one of two ways: we could *increase the costs* of giving an expressive response by providing incentives for reporting genuine beliefs, or we could design a survey instrument to *decrease the benefits* of that expressive response.[8] These alterations to the cost-benefit calculus of expressing rumor beliefs may enable us to more accurately determine what people truly believe, rather than what they are willing to say in the context of a survey interview.

I designed several experiments that used different methods to reduce expressive responding on whether Obama is a Muslim and whether people in the federal government knowingly allowed the 9/11 attacks to happen. These experimental methods work by altering the calculus on both the cost and benefit sides of the equation for those respondents most motivated to cast aspersions on the political figures mentioned in the rumors. It is these people—in this case Republicans considering rumors about Obama's religion and Democrats considering rumors about 9/11—who would be most motivated to misrepresent their true beliefs.

Each method used a different logic, design, and sample to separate expressive responses from true beliefs. All of the methods have proven effective at influencing response patterns in other contexts. One method asked the respondents to set aside their personal feelings when answering the question, thereby encouraging them to focus on factual information and to remove expressive responses from the scope of acceptable considerations. Another method acknowledged the central problem more directly by stating that people sometimes endorse statements they do not actually believe to criticize the people mentioned in the statements, and then asked respondents to avoid such behavior. The third method provided an incentive for respondents to avoid expressive responding by allowing them to complete the survey much faster while still giving them full pay if they avoided expressive responses. To avoid the risk that true believers would simply guess the desired answer only for the sake of securing the reward, it also estimated a baseline of how many respondents would give any response in return for an incentive. The final method employed a list experiment design that presented the subjects with a list of statements that randomly included or omitted the rumor of interest. Respondents then provided only the number of items on the list that they endorsed or rejected. Comparing the mean number of endorsed items across the two versions of the list can identify the proportion of respondents that support or oppose the rumor. Taking this indirect approach cloaks the real topic of interest and reduces the benefits of expressive responses since respondents provide only an aggregate tally rather than endorsing any particular statement criticizing a person they dislike.

Each of the studies is imperfect on its own, but taken together the diverse evidence points to one common conclusion: People by and large say what they mean.[9] My estimates of the total proportion of rumor endorsements that are sincere are at least 85 percent. Thus, there is little evidence of expressive responding on the question of whether Obama is a Muslim among Republicans or among Democrats on whether members of the government were involved in 9/11. Granted, these are only two questions among many. But because these questions are exemplars of the larger class of political rumors, these results speak to the broader question of the sincerity of beliefs in rumors across the ideological spectrum. Moreover, these are also "easy cases" for the expressive argument. If people do not jump at the opportunity to criticize prominent and polarizing politicians such as Bush and Obama, it seems less likely that they would in the context of other rumors. Consistent with these results, Peterson and Iyengar ran incentive experiments with a broader class of political rumors and information questions, and they found that partisans sincerely adopt inaccurate beliefs that cast their party in a favorable light.[10] The results imply that expressive responses to rumor questions from across the political spectrum are relatively rare. The believers genuinely hold those beliefs they say they do.[11]

TABLE 3.1. Overview of Surveys

Timing	Source	Sample Size	Waves
July 2010	YouGov	800	1
Oct. to Nov. 2010	Cooperative Congressional Election Study (CCES)	1,000	2
May 2011	YouGov	1,000	1
July 2012	YouGov	1,000	1
Sep. 2012 to Jan. 2013	American National Election Study (ANES)	2,054	2
May 2013	YouGov	1,000	1
Oct. to Nov. 2014	Cooperative Congressional Election Study (CCES)	1,000	2
May 2015	YouGov	1,000	1
December 2017	YouGov	1,000	1
April 2019	YouGov	1,000	1
December 2019	YouGov	1,000	1

Exploring Political Rumors

The next step in understanding the power of political rumors is to examine the structure of mass beliefs regarding those rumors. In the previous chapter, I categorized the mass public into three groups that vary on the degree to which they believe a rumor: the believers, the disbelievers, and the uncertain. Here I use survey data to examine these groups across different rumors. To begin this exploration, I draw upon the results of multiple surveys that I commissioned to measure belief in specific political rumors. I also explore the independently administered 2012 American National Election Study (ANES) survey, which included questions I was involved in designing.[12] Table 3.1 presents an overview of these eleven surveys.

As described in the first chapter, I conducted an internet sample survey in July 2010 through YouGov to measure acceptance of seven rumors (table 3.2).[13] As a reminder, this table consists of a series of four Democratic-leaning, two Republican-leaning, and one nonpartisan rumor question.[14]

In subsequent surveys over the years, I asked about a varying set of rumors. For instance, I included questions that measure the belief that the Republicans stole the 2004 presidential election through widespread voter fraud in Ohio, that Russia tampered with the 2016 presidential election results in support of Trump, that millions of noncitizens voted in the 2016

TABLE 3.2. Responses to Rumor Questions, July 2010

Question	Rumor Target	Endorse Rumor (%)	Reject Rumor (%)	Not Sure (%)
Do you believe that Barack Obama was born in the United States of America?	Democrat	27	55	19
Do you think the changes to the health care system that have been enacted by Congress and the Obama administration creates "death panels" which have the authority to determine whether or not a gravely ill or injured person should receive health care based on their "level of productivity in society"?	Democrat	33	46	22
Do you think that Senator John Kerry lied about his actions during the Vietnam War in order to receive medals from the US Army?	Democrat	35	34	31
Do you think the changes to the health care system that have been enacted by Congress and the Obama administration require elderly patients to meet with government officials to discuss "end of life" options including euthanasia?	Democrat	26	46	28
Do you think the FBI and the CIA make sure that there is a steady supply of guns and drugs in the inner city?	Republican	15	63	22
Do you think that people in the federal government either assisted in the 9/11 attacks or took no action to stop the attacks because they wanted the United States to go to war in the Middle East?	Republican	18	64	18
Do you believe that a spacecraft from another planet crashed in Roswell, New Mexico, in 1947?	Neutral	22	45	33

Note: Percentages are rounded. For all items except for the Obama citizenship question (which was reverse-scored), "Yes" responses are coded as rumor endorsement, and "No" responses are coded as rumor rejection.

Source: YouGov, July 2010.

presidential election, and that there exists a "deep state" in the US government. In this chapter, I primarily draw on the July 2010 survey data because they have the richest set of measures of belief in conspiracy theories and its antecedents, but I will also refer to the other surveys throughout this chapter to explore change and continuity in belief over time.[15]

As the presentation of the July 2010 survey results in table 3.2 demonstrates, the questions vary in the degree of rumor acceptance, from 15 percent on the guns and drugs question to 35 percent on the question about Kerry's war conduct. While the Kerry question is the only rumor endorsed by a plurality of respondents, the relatively high "not sure" rates across all the questions indicates that the uncertain group represents a substantial portion of the public. On the whole, respondents were not prepared to reject the rumors out of hand—only the Obama citizenship and the two Republican-targeted rumors were rejected by a majority of respondents. Tables 3.3, 3.4, and 3.5 demonstrate that subsequent surveys over the years paint a similar pattern of aggregate rumor belief.

The rumor questions on several of my surveys were asked in a branching format. Respondents were first asked if they accepted the rumor, rejected the rumor, or were not sure about the validity of the rumor. These options were designed to sort respondents into the three groupings of belief introduced in the previous chapter: the believers, the disbelievers, and the uncertain. I then probed the strength with which the believers and disbelievers held their belief—namely whether they accepted or rejected the rumor "strongly" or only "somewhat." Respondents who initially said they were not sure of their stance were asked what they would say if forced to choose (they were again given a "not sure" option).[16] These follow-up questions were designed to allow me to assess finer-grained distinctions in the strength of rumor belief.

Recall that table 3.2 presents the responses for the initial three-option branch of the July 2010 survey. For every question except the one about Obama's citizenship, the "reject rumor" response signals the rejection of a rumor (the disbelievers). The "endorse rumor" response signals the acceptance of a rumor (the believers). And a "not sure" response signals ambivalence about the veracity of a rumor (the uncertain). Seven-point scales constructed from both the initial branch and the follow-up questions about the strength of belief are presented below in figure 3.1. These scales represent rumor belief as a continuum of strength, instead of a discrete three-category measure. In that figure, high scores indicate greater levels of rumor rejection. Respondents who strongly accept the rumor are placed at 1, those

TABLE 3.3. Responses to Rumor Questions over Time, October–November 2010

Question	Rumor Target	Wave 1, October			Wave 2, November		
		Endorse Rumor (%)	Reject Rumor (%)	Not Sure (%)	Endorse Rumor (%)	Reject Rumor (%)	Not Sure (%)
Do you believe that Barack Obama was born in the United States of America?	Dem.	28	53	20	27	53	21
Do you think that Senator John Kerry lied about his actions during the Vietnam war in order to receive medals from the US Army?	Dem.	—	—	—	25	28	47
Do you believe that the United States government provides illegal immigrants with special benefits, such as houses, cars, or tax breaks?	Dem.	50	34	16	—	—	—
Do you think that illegal immigrants are the primary carriers of diseases such as AIDS, leprosy, and swine flu into the United States?	Dem.	19	62	19	22	57	21
Do you think that people in the federal government, such as George Bush and Dick Cheney, either assisted in the 9/11 attacks or took no action to stop the attacks because they wanted the United States to go to war in the Middle East?	Rep.	22	59	19	—	—	—
Do you think the Republicans stole the 2004 presidential election through voter fraud in Ohio?	Rep.	23	44	32	23	47	30
Do you believe that a spacecraft from another planet crashed in Roswell, New Mexico, in 1947?	Neutral	17	47	37	—	—	—

Note: Percentages are rounded. For all items except for the Obama citizenship question (which was reverse-scored), "Yes" responses are coded as rumor endorsement, and "No" responses are coded as rumor rejection.

Source: CCES, October/November 2010.

TABLE 3.4. Responses to Rumor Questions, December 2017

Question	Rumor Target	Endorse Rumor (%)	Reject Rumor (%)	Not Sure (%)
Do you believe that Barack Obama was born in the United States of America?	Democrat	18	61	20
Do you think Barack Obama is a Muslim or not?	Democrat	25	49	25
Do you think that the United States government provides illegal immigrants with special benefits, such as houses, cars, or tax breaks?	Democrat	44	39	17
Do you believe that 3–5 million noncitizens voted in the 2016 presidential election through widespread voter fraud, or not?	Democrat	27	38	35
There's been talk of what some people call a "deep state," meaning military, intelligence, and government officials who try to secretly manipulate government policy. Do you think there is such a thing as a deep state in this country, or is it just a conspiracy theory?	Democrat	41	24	35
Do you think that people in the federal government, such as George Bush and Dick Cheney, either assisted in the 9/11 attacks or took no action to stop the attacks because they wanted the United States to go to war in the Middle East?	Republican	21	56	23
Do you think that Republicans stole the 2004 presidential election through voter fraud in Ohio?	Republican	16	39	45
Do you believe that Russia tampered with vote tallies to help Donald Trump?	Republican	37	38	25
Do you believe that a spacecraft from another planet crashed in Roswell, New Mexico in 1947?	Neutral	21	37	42

Note: Percentages are rounded. For all items except for the Obama citizenship question (which was reverse-scored), "Yes" responses are coded as rumor endorsement, and "No" responses are coded as rumor rejection.

Source: YouGov, December 2017.

TABLE 3.5. Responses to Rumor Questions, April 2019

Question	Rumor Target	Endorse Rumor (%)	Reject Rumor (%)	Not Sure (%)
Do you believe that Barack Obama was born in the United States of America?	Democrat	26	57	17
Do you think Barack Obama is a Muslim?	Democrat	28	54	19
Do you think that the United States government provides illegal immigrants with special benefits, such as houses, cars, or tax breaks?	Democrat	38	43	19
Do you believe that 3–5 million noncitizens voted in the 2016 presidential election through widespread voter fraud?	Democrat	36	38	27
There's been talk of what some people call a "deep state," meaning military, intelligence and government officials who try to secretly manipulate government policy. Do you think there is such a thing as a deep state in this country ["Yes" column], or is it just a conspiracy theory ["No" column]?	Democrat	44	30	26
Do you think that people in the federal government, such as George Bush and Dick Cheney, either assisted in the 9/11 attacks or took no action to stop the attacks because they wanted the United States to go to war in the Middle East?	Republican	22	55	22
Do you believe that Russia tampered with vote tallies to help Donald Trump?	Republican	40	42	18
Do you think that one man was responsible for the assassination of President Kennedy ["Yes" column], or do you think that others were involved in the conspiracy ["No" column]?	Neutral	24	50	26
Do you believe that a spacecraft from another planet crashed in Roswell, New Mexico, in 1947?	Neutral	22	40	38

Note: Percentages are rounded. For all items except for the Obama citizenship question (which was reverse-scored), "Yes" responses are coded as rumor endorsement, and "No" responses are coded as rumor rejection.

Source: YouGov, April 2019.

FIGURE 3.1. Distribution of Beliefs on Rumor Questions Seven-Point Belief Scale, July 2010

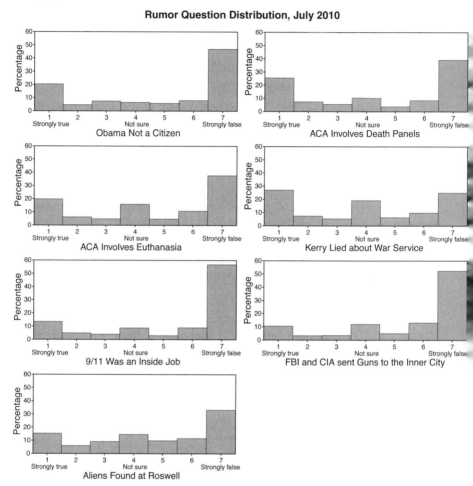

Note: The graph shows the distribution of rumor belief for various rumor items (refer to table 3.2) using a seven-point response scale of rumor belief. The scale runs from 1 (where a respondent strongly accepts the rumor) to 7 (where the respondent strongly rejects the rumor). *Source*: YouGov, July 2010.

who strongly reject the rumor are at 7, those who indicate that they are "not sure" in both the initial branch and the follow-up are put at 4, and other patterns of responses comprise the intermediate points. For example, respondents who initially say that they are not sure about the veracity of a rumor, but then say they would accept that rumor if forced to choose are scored as a 3. Respondents who say they accept the rumor, but do so only somewhat are scored as a 2. Although the branching format does allow for some finer-grain measurement of the degree to which respondents subscribe to the various rumors, figure 3.1 clearly shows that the first branch—acceptance, rejection, or uncertainty—sorts the respondents well into primary categories of belief implied by the analogy of the pebble in the pond. Very few citizens weakly endorse or oppose particular rumors. This pattern of results is consistent for the other surveys, as detailed in the appendix.[17]

GETTING TO KNOW THE "DON'T KNOWS"

The individuals who comprise the uncertain group are critical for understanding the nature of belief in rumors. These individuals do not tenaciously hold to their beliefs in a rumor. But they do not reject that rumor either.

For some people, the "not sure" response certainly reflects a degree of disengagement from the substance of the rumor. We can see some evidence of this phenomenon at the aggregate level by comparing responses across the different questions. Figure 3.1 demonstrates that the rumor questions vary considerably in the distribution of underlying uncertainty. Responses to the Obama citizenship question are clearly bifurcated—respondents either strongly accept or strongly reject the rumors. Other questions, such as Kerry's war record and the health care rumors show a more dispersed distribution of responses, indicating greater degrees of indeterminacy. Table 3.3, with the somewhat different set of questions asked in late 2010, shows a similar pattern of responses. For one of the items—the question relating to the provision of special benefits to illegal immigrants—a majority accepted the rumor, but the distributions of the other items are very much in line with the July 2010 survey results.

At the same time, these "not sure" responses are also surely different in kind than the types of "don't know" responses often found on public opinion surveys.[18] Indeed, qualitative evidence indicates that, for a significant proportion of the respondents, a "not sure" response is more an expression of ambiguity or skepticism than of uncertainty, as alluded to in the previous chapter. In the spring of 2015, I asked the Obama citizenship and 9/11 questions described above. But I also asked a follow-up question inquiring why individuals believe what they do about the rumor in question. Many of the respondents who said they were not sure the rumors were true expressed doubt about the true state of political reality. For example, many Republicans who said they were not sure whether Obama was born in the United States stated that they believed that Obama had something to hide, and they referenced specific pieces of evidence to suggest Obama was born elsewhere. One respondent wrote that the "not sure" response was chosen because of "the in-depth research putting doubt on the validity of his birth certificate."

Another wrote, "The people who tried to prove he was born in the USA were less than convincing. The people who claimed he was not had more facts on their side." "I think he has a very shady past," concluded another. Similarly, only a few Democrats who said they were unsure if Bush and Cheney were aware of the 9/11 attacks beforehand said that they did not have enough information to decide. Quite a few uncertain Democrats gave rationales similar to those Democratic respondents who outright accepted the rumor, referencing the Bush administration's political or financial motives for inaction.[19] For instance, one respondent wrote, "G. W. Bush said he needed a war to give him more power in his term. There are some strange things that happened afterwards that seem as if there is more to it than known. Not to mention G. W. Bush ignored warnings as he came into office and did nothing to prevent it." Despite not accepting a rumor, they are not willing to reject the arguments supporting that rumor either. Thus, as argued in the last chapter, any position short of outright rejecting a rumor—even an expression of uncertainty about its veracity through a "don't know" or "not sure" response—could enhance the credibility of rumors. A "not sure" response, after all, indicates that the respondent is not prepared to disavow a given rumor.[20]

THE STABILITY OF RESPONSES

The responses to the rumor questions appear to be more than simply off-the-cuff reactions to, admittedly, somewhat bizarre questions. As discussed above, I have direct evidence that expressions of support for the rumors were sincere; most people who say they believe rumors truly believe them. Panel data from the 2010 CCES survey provides further evidence that expressions of rumor acceptance and rejection are not transitory. Over time, the belief about political rumors that people state in surveys—whether that belief is acceptance or rejection—is quite stable.

I repeated three questions across the two waves of the 2010 CCES—two Democratic-based rumors and one a Republican-based rumor.[21] Specifically, the first rumor concerns Obama's citizenship, the second addresses beliefs about illegal immigrants, and the third questions whether the Republicans stole the 2004 presidential election through voter fraud in Ohio. The aggregate distribution of the responses was extremely stable for each question across both waves (see table 3.3). This aggregate stability extended to the individual level. In table 3.6, I show the cross-tabulation of responses across the October 2010 and November 2010 waves, for the initial branch of the questions.[22] About 80 percent of respondents gave the same answer to

TABLE 3.6. Belief Stability in Rumor Questions, October–November 2010

Obama Is a Citizen (Reverse Score)

Democrat-Targeted Rumor

October	November		
	Yes (%)	No (%)	Not Sure (%)
Yes	90	4	18
No	2	85	16
Not Sure	7	11	66

Republicans Stole the '04 Election

Republican-Targeted Rumor

October	November		
	Yes (%)	No (%)	Not Sure (%)
Yes	81	4	11
No	7	79	14
Not Sure	12	16	75

Immigrants Are Disease Carriers

Democrat-Targeted Rumor

October	November		
	Yes (%)	No (%)	Not Sure (%)
Yes	71	3	10
No	17	89	39
Not Sure	12	8	50

Note: Percentages are rounded.

Source: CCES, October/November 2010.

the rumor items in both waves, even though the surveys were conducted, on average, one month apart. Moreover, the stability was particularly high among respondents who accepted or rejected the rumor; to the extent that there is significant movement in responses, it occurs among respondents who said they were not sure about the veracity of particular rumors. Using the follow-up questions to compute seven-point scales yields a similar picture regarding belief stability between waves: the Obama items are correlated at .90, the voter fraud questions are correlated at .84, and the immigration item is correlated at .74. These numbers are extremely high compared to the stability of other survey questions over a similar length of time.[23]

Determinants of Rumor Belief Holding

The previous section describes the distribution of beliefs in particular rumors across the mass public, presenting the composition of the base of belief across various rumors—the disbelievers, the believers, and the uncertain. Overall, the aggregate patterns of rumor belief holding suggests that public belief in political rumors is by no means universal. Nevertheless, taken together, the believers and the uncertain comprise a large portion of the public. Moreover, these levels of rumor acceptance are remarkably stable over time.

However, just because a given portion of the public is willing to endorse different statements that are factually unsupported does not mean that these statements constitute evidence of a particular way of thinking about the world among a fixed subset of citizens. After all, aggregate distributions can conceal important individual-level heterogeneity in willingness to accept or reject particular rumors. It is therefore important to peek under the hood of these aggregate numbers and look at beliefs regarding rumors from across the ideological spectrum.

These findings indicate the likely importance of personal characteristics in informing whether and to what extent individuals accept or reject political rumors. In addition, it leads to a more general question that has profound implications for the functioning of the democratic system: given how widely rumors and political misinformation have spread through modern society, what determines whether particular individuals are attracted to particular rumors?

I contend that rumor acceptance is a combination of specific rumor content and individual disposition. The failure to categorically reject a rumor is a function of the generalized propensity of a person to adopt a conspiratorial orientation and is shaped by the content of the rumors vis-à-vis the political beliefs of a given individual.[24] Put another way, while there are true believers who are likely to accept any rumor no matter its content, when it comes to rumor acceptance, where one stands also depends heavily upon where one sits. It is this marriage of conspiratorial orientation and political content that shapes the pattern of rumor belief in the mass public.

GENERALIZED RUMOR ACCEPTANCE

Writing about conspiracy theories, journalist Jonathan Kay argues that "people come to their paranoias for all sorts of complicated reasons."[25] This may be true, but there are certain patterns to this type of thinking. While there are some kinds of people who will reject outlandish information out of hand, there are other individuals who tend toward a conspiratorial mindset and would be more inclined to accept the types of beliefs that Thompson terms "counterknowledge," among them rumors that paint government figures in a poor light.[26]

Social scientists in a variety of fields have long studied these tendencies toward conspiratorial thinking. Allport and Postman's foundational work on rumors in the 1940s made an early attempt to identify the kinds of individuals who would grasp onto misinformation, arguing that "those who are suggestable toward rumor are people whose minds are in some respects 'over-stuck.' Into their rigid compartments of explanation and prejudgment congenial rumors are greedily absorbed."[27]

More recently, there has been a great deal of work in psychology that seeks to uncover the roots of susceptibility to conspiracies, and this work spans a wide range of approaches. Some scholars seek to measure the kinds of thinking that lead to a conspiracist ideation. For instance, Goertzel argues that interpersonal differences in anomie—a lack of interpersonal trust and a sense of alienation from a group or society—is related to the degree to which individuals subscribe to various conspiracy theories.[28] In a similar vein, Douglas, Sutton and Cichocka conclude that "conspiracy belief appears to stem to a large extent from epistemic, existential, and social motives."[29] At a more granular level, Bruder and colleagues propose a "conspiracy mentality questionnaire," which includes items tapping a general tendency toward conspiratorial thinking, such as agreement with the phrase, "I think that there are secret organizations that greatly influence political decisions."[30] Other scholars measure susceptibility to general conspiratorial thinking by assessing support for a broad range of *specific* conspiracy theories. For example, Lewandowsky and colleagues gauge conspiracist ideation through support or rejection of six different conspiracy theories, ranging from the notion that the moon landing was faked to the belief that Princess Diana was assassinated.[31] Brotherton and colleagues cast an even wider net, calculating support through a list of 75 conspiracy theories.[32]

Political scientists have taken up this mantle as well. Oliver and Wood measure support for conspiracy theories as a function of two factors. The first factor taps the predisposition toward making causal attributions to unseen intentional forces, such as the supernatural and cabals. The second measures subscription to Manichean tendencies—the draw toward "melodramatic narratives as explanations for prominent events, particularly those that interpret history relative to universal struggles between good and evil."[33] Employing a similar strategy, Uscinski and Parent use three items to capture general predispositions toward conspiratorial thinking, with the general flavor of the items resembling those contained in the Bruder and colleagues scale.[34]

These different measures take a variety of theoretic approaches, ranging from a search for the general factors that lead individuals to accept political rumors to the measurement of subscription to a broad range of specific conspiracy theories.[35] The measures also employ a variety of empirical methods. But at the core, all these scholars are working to capture variation in some general tendency to accept conspiracies and rumor as truth.[36] This is my goal here as well.

For my purposes, identifying the single best measure is not as important as having *some* measure of such a tendency toward belief in conspiracies and rumors of all types.[37] With such a measure in hand, I can account for the fact that some individuals are more susceptible than others to the conspiratorial thinking that leads to the acceptance of political rumors, and can better focus on the *political* roots and consequences of rumors.

I employ slightly different scales in different studies, but in every study, I include some measure of the precursors to conspiratorial orientation. In particular, I use two scales to measure the conspiratorial ideation that leads some individuals to more readily accept political rumors.[38] Both of these scales were drawn from measures used in McClosky and Chong's study of left-wing and right-wing radicals in the late 1970s.[39] I generated these scales when I first began my research into political rumors in 2009. My hope was to find measures that could capture identical patterns of extremist thinking on *both* the left and the right. As a result, these scales serve my purpose by measuring a general disposition toward accepting conspiracy theories. I make no claim that they are superior to other measures in use in the literature. But because I have been asking such questions for over a decade, they meet my purpose across the surveys I analyze here.

The first of these measures is a concept that reflects intolerance of ambiguity in thinking in general. McClosky and Chong asked a series of questions to measure subscription to "far left" and "far right" principles. Having identified the core members of these groups in their surveys, they then examined the underlying correlates of these beliefs. McClosky and Chong found that members of the Far Left and the Far Right were similarly intolerant of ambiguity. Such intolerance is similar in spirit to the Manichean narrative worldview discussed by Oliver and Wood, and this melodramatic worldview is readily compatible with conspiratorial explanations for ambiguous events.[40] In other words, people who score high on the dogmatic-thinking scale tend to view the world in stark degrees of black and white and, therefore, are more likely to accept fanciful accusations about political figures and events, no matter the nature of their political attachments.[41] Thus, a properly constructed scale should identify individuals who would be more willing to accept rumors on the *both* the left and the right.[42]

To this end, I created a scale—which I call "dogmatism"—using items McClosky and Chong grouped under the heading "Intolerance of Ambiguity." I selected items that had majority agreement from both the "far left" and "far right" subsamples. I also tried to find items that had roughly equal levels of agreement between the two groups. Such a task was easier said than done, because many of the items examined by McClosky and Chong were quite skewed, with extremists of the Left rejecting items that were widely embraced on the right and vice-versa. In the end, I chose three questions. These items, presented in table 3.7, are, by design, largely divorced from the political world. While one of the questions makes reference to "important public issues," the other items are free of political content and tap the need to take a firm stance on a variety of beliefs.[43]

The second scale I designed, which I call "political disengagement" was also drawn from the McClosky and Chong items but was more directly political in nature. Specifically, I sought to create a scale that measures the degree to which individuals are distrusting of politicians and the political system in general.[44] This concept is distinct from the more general form of political trust, measured in the National Elections Study. As a result, the content of these items is different—and far more cynical—than the typical "trust in government" items.[45]

McClosky and Chong found that members of the Far Left and the Far Right had similarly low levels of trust in the political system. While the current political landscape is certainly different from that of the late 1970s, as with the dogmatism measure, I hoped that the political disengagement scale might enable me to identify those respondents who would be more willing to accept rumors on both the left and the right. After all, distrust of the political system breeds a willingness to believe negative information about the people and institutions that make up that system, regardless

TABLE 3.7. Measures of Conspiratorial Disposition

DOGMATISM ITEMS

1. On important public issues, I believe you should:

    a. Always keep in mind that there is more than one side to most issues.

    b. Either be for them or against them and not take a middle course.

2. Which is better:

    a. To remain undecided.

    b. To take a stand on an issue even if it's wrong.

3. When it comes to the really important questions about religion and philosophy of life:

    a. It doesn't especially bother me to leave them undecided.

    b. A person must decide them, one way or the other.

POLITICAL DISENGAGEMENT ITEMS

1. Politicians do not care much about what they say, so long as they get elected.

2. The best way to get elected is to put on a good show.

3. The people think they govern themselves, but they really don't.

Note: Scales are adapted from McClosky and Chong, "Similarities and Differences." For the Political Disengagement scale, respondents were asked to rate their level of agreement/disagreement on a five-point scale. For the Dogmatism scale, the respondents were forced to select from a binary response format. Each individual was assigned a political disengagement and dogmatism score by calculating the mean of all items they answered.

of the ideological affiliation of the target of the rumors. This scale essentially taps a core concept at the heart of conspiracy theory acceptance. As Sunstein and Vermeule note, to embrace conspiracy theories, "those who accept them must also accept a kind of spreading distrust of all knowledge-producing institutions, in a way that makes it difficult to believe anything at all."[46] The items to measure political disengagement are listed in the lower part of table 3.7. In addition the distribution of the dogmatism and political disengagement scales in my July 2010 sample is presented in figure 3.2.[47]

POLITICAL MOTIVATION

Though there are factors that increase the likelihood that some individuals will accept any political rumor regardless of its content, the distribution of political rumor rejection throughout the population indicates that it is not simply a conspiratorial disposition alone that leads to public acceptance

FIGURE 3.2. Distribution of Political Disengagement Scale and Dogmatism Scale, July 2010

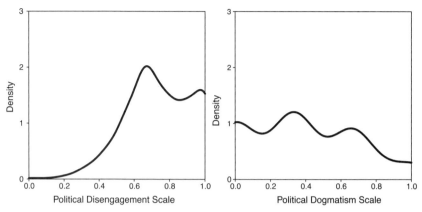

Source: YouGov, July 2010.

of seemingly fanciful rumors. Critically, the content of particular rumors matters as well. In addition to general processes of rumor acceptance and rejection, I therefore expect that the specific target of rumors will affect whether individuals will believe a given statement. In politics, identity is central. The particular political beliefs of the respondent—most notably their partisanship or other markers of group affiliation—should make a great difference in whether an individual will cling to fanciful beliefs.

Partisanship is an especially powerful force in the realm of rumor. The introduction of political concerns changes the nature of information processing in important ways. Most importantly, adding measures of political identity to the mix exacerbates the tendency for citizens to engage in motivated reasoning.[48] As Taber and Lodge note, ordinary citizens are goal-directed information processors—they perceive new information in light of their preexisting views.[49] Thus, when presented with a balanced set of arguments, respondents evaluate attitudinally congruent arguments as stronger than attitudinally incongruent arguments. Democrats tend to discount information that supports Republican positions (and vice versa), which means that some citizens may be more likely to believe particular rumors because they are motivated to cling to beliefs that are compatible with their partisan or political outlook.[50] As Kahan notes, this brand of motivated cognition is a form of information processing that facilitates the ability of individuals to form and maintain beliefs that signify their loyalty to groups to which they feel strong attachments.[51] Thus, a Republican who is suspicious of Obama might endorse the death panel rumor—and genuinely believe that rumor—because they want to embrace reasons for their opposition to his policy. Another strand of literature argues that conservatives are more likely than liberals to engage in partisan-motivated reasoning. I discuss this research in depth in chapter 5.

Even a casual glance at the pattern of rumor acceptance and rejection reveals the large partisan split in patterns of belief. Recall the discussion of the partisan differences over the rumors concerning Obama's citizenship and Republican vote fraud in the 2004 election. In both of those cases, partisans of a particular stripe were less likely to reject rumors about politicians of the opposite party than were their counterparts across the aisle. Such patterns are systematic: When it comes to rumors, partisanship colors everything political.

Figure 3.3 presents the partisan differences in rumor rejection rates for five items I asked in multiple surveys over the last ten years. Two of these rumors target Democratic politicians and policies, while two others implicate Republicans. The final item concerns the question of whether an alien spacecraft crashed in Roswell, New Mexico—a nonpartisan (if not nonpolitical) rumor. The figure demonstrates that each of these three sets of items behave quite differently. While the partisan differences wax and wane somewhat, figure 3.3 provides evidence of an enduring chasm in the willingness of Democratic citizens to implicate Republican politicians and policies relative to Democratic actors and actions (and vice versa). However, the stark differences found on the other questions do not emerge in the case of beliefs about alien life; the partisan gap on the Roswell rumor is essentially zero.

At the most extreme, we can even see the trace of partisan loyalties in the responses that partisans give to obscure—and even made up—political rumor questions. In 2012 and 2013, I asked respondents if they believed two statements about actions taken by the government. In both cases, the rumors were invented and far-fetched. One was an obscure rumor concerning the effect of the vapor trails left by airplanes. The other was a statement about compact fluorescent light bulbs that was constructed by Oliver and Wood.[52] I conducted an experiment with each of the rumors. One-half of the respondents were presented a conspiracy attributed to Democrats, and the other half was presented a conspiracy attributed to Republicans. I counterbalanced the order of these items so that each respondent was presented with one rumor attributed to Democrats, and the other to Republicans. This experiment allows us to assess the effect of group labeling alone on rumor acceptance rates.

FIGURE 3.3. Partisan Differences in Rumor Rejection Rates over Time, 2010–2019

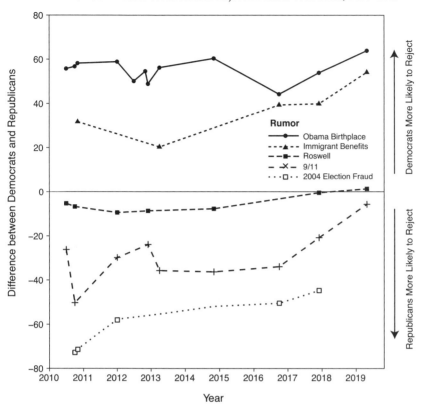

Note: This graph shows the partisan differences in rumor rejection rates for five survey items asked in multiple surveys from 2010 to 2019. The difference is calculated by subtracting the average rumor rejection rate for self-identified Republicans from that of self-identified Democrats.

Specifically, I asked respondents their agreement with the following statements:

1. [Democrats/Republicans] in the government are mandating the switch to compact fluorescent light bulbs because such lights make people more obedient and easier to control.
2. Vapor trails left by aircraft are actually chemical agents deliberately sprayed in a clandestine program directed by [Republicans/Democrats] in the government.

The results are presented in table 3.8. In the full sample, rumor acceptance rates rise above the single digits for only one question for one party—the

TABLE 3.8. Constructed Rumor Agreement Rates

Question	Rumor Target	July 2012			May 2013		
		Full (%)	Democrats (%)	Republicans (%)	Full (%)	Democrats (%)	Republicans (%)
Democrats in the government are mandating the switch to compact fluorescent light bulbs because such lights make people more obedient and easier to control.	Democrats	11	10	22	6	3	13
Republicans in the government are mandating the switch to compact fluorescent light bulbs because such lights make people more obedient and easier to control.	Republicans	3	5	1	5	5	5
Vapor trails left by aircraft are actually chemical agents deliberately sprayed in a clandestine program directed by **Democrats** in the government.	Democrats	—	—	—	6	6	9
Vapor trails left by aircraft are actually chemical agents deliberately sprayed in a clandestine program directed by **Republicans** in the government.	Republicans	—	—	—	4	5	2

Note: Percentages are rounded and indicate the degree of rumor acceptance in each subgroup. Rumor acceptance is coded as "True" responses; rumor rejection is coded as "False" responses. "Not sure" responses are excluded from the present analysis.

Source: YouGov, July 2012/May 2013.

fluorescent bulb rumor in 2012 for Democrats. But in every case except the fluorescent bulb rumor (Republican-targeted) in 2013, we see that partisans in the mass public are less inclined to believe the rumors about their own party than they are about rumors about the other party.[53] This difference, while small, is consistent.[54] Some might argue that such responses are little more than cheap talk disparaging the opposition party. But, as I discussed above, individuals mostly say what they mean when it comes to political rumors. And what partisans are clearly saying here is that they are less likely to reject rumors about the opposition party than they are rumors concerning their own party.

Returning to the set of rumors in actual circulation in the political world, the partisan pattern of responses to the rumor questions is readily apparent by looking at how responses to the individual rumor questions are structured *within* individuals. For this analysis, I use the continuous measures of rumor acceptance running from strong acceptance to strong rejection (with uncertainty in the middle), as captured by the seven-point scales discussed earlier in this chapter. Table 3.9 presents the correlations—the degree of correspondence—among the seven-point scales constructed from the items for the July 2010 surveys.[55] As expected, the questions on Democrat-based rumors are positively intercorrelated with each other, and those on Republican-based rumors are also positively correlated. At the same time these Democratic and Republican question clusters are negatively correlated (albeit weakly) with one another, indicating that while the different Democratic-based rumor questions are similar to each other, they are distinct from the Republican-based rumor questions (and vice versa).[56] And all the rumor questions are positively correlated with the Roswell rumor, regardless of their partisan valence. This same basic structure emerges among the items asked on the other surveys (see tables A6–8 in the appendix for details).

OTHER FACTORS

The combination of conspiratorial orientation—measured by dogmatism and political disengagement—and political content are the primary drivers of rumor acceptance and rejection. But, of course, these are not the only factors that lead individuals to embrace political rumors. It is not my intention to provide an exhaustive list of such factors. To hone in on the political content of rumors, I account for some other factors that affect the endorsement of political rumors of all types.[57] In addition to general conspiratorial

TABLE 3.9. Correlations among 7-Point Belief Scales, July 2010

Rumor (Partisan Target)	Obama Citizenship (Democrat)	Kerry (Democrat)	Death Panel (Democrat)	Euthanasia (Democrat)	9/11 (Republican)	FBI (Republican)
Kerry (Democrat)	.52**					
Death Panel (Democrat)	.63**	.59**				
Euthanasia (Democrat)	.52**	.50**	.69**			
9/11 (Republican)	-.13**	-.12**	-.11**	-.05		
FBI (Republican)	.01	.00	0.01	.06**	.53**	
Roswell (Neutral)	.07**	.04*	.04**	.03	.23**	.23**

Key	Partisan-Congruent	Partisan-Incongruent	Neutral-Partisan

Note: * = $p < .10$; ** = $p < .05$. The Democrat-targeted rumors include "Obama Citizenship," "Kerry," "Death Panel," and "Euthanasia." The Republican-targeted rumors include "9/11" and "FBI." The "Roswell" rumor is neutral (nonpartisan and nonpolitical).

Source: YouGov, July 2010.

orientation, there is reason to believe that there are certain traits that would lead to the rejection of political rumors across the board, regardless of the particular content of those rumors. Most notably, I examine the power of education and political awareness, as measured by political information levels (specifically the proportion of correct answers respondents give to factual questions about politics).[58] If political rumors are a form of misinformation, perhaps the solution for reducing their acceptance is more information. Later in the book, I consider experimental treatments designed to directly test the effect of new information on rumor acceptance. Here I posit that people who are better informed about the political world are, on average, less likely to accept political rumors. However, to the extent that political information measures engagement with political rhetoric, it could be that the relationship between information levels and rumor rejection is conditional on the political predilections of the respondent—a possibility I explore in greater detail in chapter 6.[59]

Determinants of Rumor Rejection

Based on my expectations regarding patterns of rumor holding, I created separate additive scales of rumor rejection for the Democrat-based rumors and the Republican-based rumors for the 2010 studies.[60] To create these scales, I use the continuous seven-point rumor acceptance measures (though using simple counts of the number of rumors accepted or rejected yields similar results). Specifically, the scales are created by averaging the seven-point rumor items described above.[61] The scales run from zero (where a respondent strongly *accepts* every rumor comprising the scale) to one (where the respondent strongly *rejects* every rumor in the scale).[62] The distribution of the scales is presented in figure 3.4.

Figure 3.5 plots the regression coefficients and 95 percent confidence intervals from a regression analysis of the correlates of rumor rejection for the July 2010 study. Negative coefficients indicate factors that are associated with greater acceptance of rumors, while positive coefficients are factors associated with greater rejection of rumors. I plot a dotted line at zero to facilitate interpretation of standard tests of statistical significance.[63]

As expected, the factors that predict a rejection of general conspiratorial thinking—here, low levels of dogmatism and political disengagement—are associated with rejection of political rumors across the ideological spectrum (though the relationship between the dogmatism scale and rumor

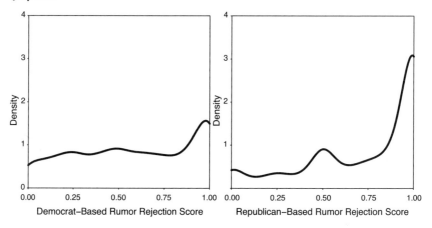

FIGURE 3.4. Distribution of Democratic Rumor Scale and Republican Rumor Scale, July 2010

Source: YouGov, July 2010.

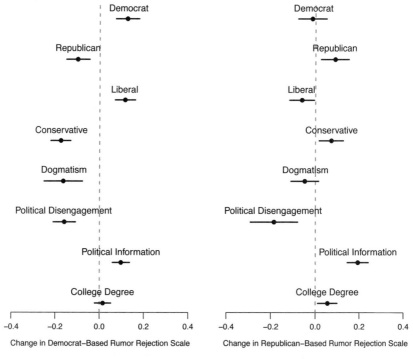

FIGURE 3.5. Predictors of Rumor Rejection, July 2010

Note: Figure shows the regression coefficients and 95 percent confidence intervals from an OLS regression analysis of the predictors of rumor rejection. Models are displayed for Democrat-targeted rumors (*left*) and Republican-targeted rumors (*right*). *Source*: YouGov, July 2010.

acceptance is considerably stronger for the Democratic-based rumors). Thus, as expected, there are a core group of factors that are associated with rumor acceptance, regardless of the partisan target of those rumors. Moreover, better-educated and better-informed individuals are more likely to reject rumors of all types.

At the same time, a person's political beliefs, namely their attachment to political parties, interact with the content of the rumor to shape patterns of acceptance and rejection. Republicans are more likely to accept Democratic-based rumors and reject Republican-based rumors.[64] The reverse is true for Democrats (though this relationship is somewhat weaker, especially for Republican-based rumors). Self-placement on the ideology scale yields a similar pattern of results. These results extend to the other rumor data I collected later in 2010, 2011, and 2017 as well as the 2012 ANES data (see figures A1–A3 and figure A7 in the appendix).

In sum, my expectations regarding the patterns of rumor holding are supported by the data. Clearly, there are conspiratorial inclinations—here measured through alienation from the political world and dogmatism—that foster subscription to *all* rumors. At the same time, the political content of the rumors matters critically. In particular, for rumors about Democratic politicians and policies—but also to a more limited degree for Republican positions—political affiliation shapes the kinds of fanciful statements that citizens will endorse.

INTERACTIVE EFFECTS OF DISPOSITION AND PARTISANSHIP

The main effects presented in the preceding section of this chapter are interesting, but, as I argued above, rumors find their greatest support among those citizens who are both conspiratorially inclined *and* have partisan attachments. The combination of these two factors—the disposition and the motivation—together should increase susceptibility to rumors.

I systematically examined the relationship between disposition and motivation by including interaction terms between the various dispositions that increase susceptibility to rumors and the political predispositions of the respondents, as indexed by their partisan attachment. Beginning with political alienation in the July 2010 study, I found that the large main effect of disengagement observed in figure 3.5 actually obscures a significant degree of heterogeneity. The interaction between partisanship and disengagement is highly significant. Figure 3.6 below presents the predicted results of an

FIGURE 3.6. Marginal Effect of Disengagement on Rumor Rejection by Partisanship, July 2010

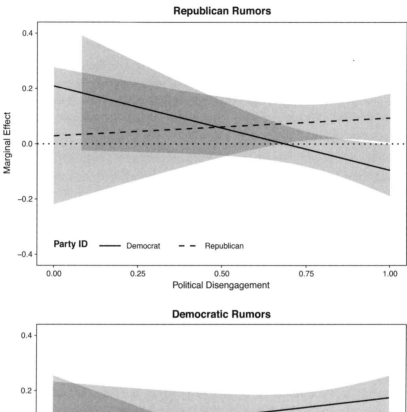

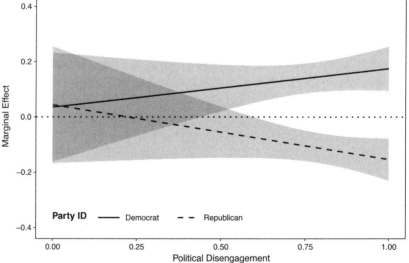

Note: The lines represent the marginal effects of political disengagement on rumor rejection for self-identifying Democrats and Republicans, estimated using OLS regression. The shaded areas represent 95 percent confidence intervals. Models are displayed for Republican-targeted rumors (*top*) and Democrat-targeted rumors (*bottom*). Higher scores indicate stronger belief in the accuracy of the statement. *Source*: YouGov, July 2010.

interactive regression. The gap between low and high disengagement among Republican identifiers on the Republican rumor scale is almost nonexistent. Yet highly alienated Democrat identifiers are much less likely to reject rumors about Republicans than are their ilk who score low on the disengagement scale. This pattern reverses itself for rumors about Democrats, yielding even stronger differences between Democrat and Republican identifiers. All told, it seems that—at least for political disengagement—the combination of motive and disposition induces rumor acceptance.[67]

The picture for the dogmatism orientation is similar in scope, if not size. As figure 3.7 demonstrates, for rumors about Democrats, we see the same interactive effect, albeit in a more muted form. While dogmatism on its own seems to decrease the tendency to reject rumors among both Democratic and Republican respondents, the effect of dogmatism is far larger among Democrats. Turning to rumors about Republican politicians, the differences in the relationship between dogmatism and rumor rejection is not statistically significant between the two parties, but it is in the expected direction. There is strong evidence that these results are not simple flukes of the data set. I replicated the same pattern of findings for the dogmatism measure in separate studies in 2010, 2011, and 2017.[68] Though the results for the Republican-based rumors were somewhat inconsistent, the interaction between partisanship and dogmatism always yield the same large, statistically significant relationship.

Conclusion

This chapter focused on identifying and characterizing the kinds of individuals who are unwilling to reject rumors out of hand—the believers and the uncertain. To understand why ordinary people fail to dismiss seemingly bizarre rumors, this chapter addressed three questions. First, do people actually believe these claims, or are they just willing to endorse anything that is critical of individuals or groups they dislike? Second, which claims find widespread purchase in public opinion, and how strong is the general belief in them? Third, why is there variation across individuals with respect to belief in certain rumors but not others?

The answers to these questions provide several lessons about the roots of misinformation on the modern political scene. First, the evidence here suggests that many people do genuinely believe seemingly outlandish claims. They are not simply engaging in partisan cheerleading, but instead express sincerely held beliefs. Moreover, these beliefs are relatively stable within

FIGURE 3.7. Marginal Effect of Dogmatism on Rumor Rejection by Partisanship, July 2010

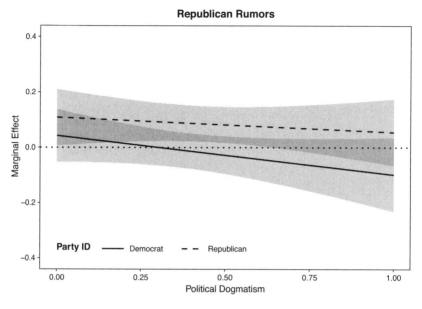

Note: The lines represent the marginal effects of dogmatism on rumor rejection for self-identifying Democrats and Republicans, estimated using OLS regression. The shaded areas represent 95 percent confidence intervals. Models are displayed for Republican-targeted rumors (*top*) and Democrat-targeted rumors (*bottom*). *Source*: YouGov, July 2010.

individuals over time, and they apply to rumors about both the political Left and the political Right.

Next, there are clear factors that predict subscription to some rumors and not others. Individual disposition toward conspiratorial thinking pushes people to accept rumors of all stripes. Disposition, though, is not the only important factor. This chapter demonstrates the enduring power of partisanship to shape beliefs concerning American politics. It is true that partisans from both sides of the aisle believe rumors, but attachment to a specific political party is critical to understanding individual-level variation in the rumors people believe. Republicans are less likely to reject rumors about Democrats and Democrats are less likely to reject rumors about Republicans. Finally, partisan motivation and personality dispositions have a cumulative influence; they interact to shape why people believe certain rumors but not others. Republican identifiers who are conspiratorially inclined are more likely to believe rumors about Democratic policies and politicians than Republicans who are not. The same is true for the way in which Democratic identifiers evaluate rumors about Republicans. Having examined the nature and structure of belief in rumors, and with a better understanding of mass beliefs about rumors and misinformation, I now turn to exploring the consequences of such beliefs in the political world—a task I take up in the rest of this book.

4

Can We Correct Rumors?

In the summer of 2009, stories swirled alleging that President Obama's health care reforms would include procedures to withhold care from certain citizens. The elderly, these rumors suggested, would have to meet with government officials to discuss "end of life" options like euthanasia.[1] On August 7, 2009, former Alaska governor and US vice presidential candidate Sarah Palin wrote on her Facebook page: "The America I know and love is not one in which my parents or my baby with Down Syndrome will have to stand in front of Obama's 'death panel' so his bureaucrats can decide, based on a subjective judgment of their 'level of productivity in society,' whether they are worthy of health care. Such a system is downright evil."[2] Within a week, 86 percent of the American public was aware of Palin's accusation.[3] Though these objectively false rumors were widely discredited, the controversy surrounding death panels would not die, even long after the 2010 Affordable Care Act (ACA) was passed by the US Congress and signed into law by Obama.[4]

Why would these rumors not go away? Why was it so hard to stamp out the myth of death panels once it was released into the world? In this chapter, I shift my focus from examining the patterns of why people accept or reject rumors to engaging the broad challenge of how to correct mistaken beliefs. How can we persuade people to reject rumors they consider true, or at least potentially true? Given the findings from the earlier chapters that conspiratorial dispositions and partisan motivations underlie rumor acceptance, how should we tailor our correction strategies to account for these factors and instead nudge people toward rejection?

In this chapter, I investigate these questions in the context of the rumors surrounding death panels. I begin by describing the psychological processes that make it particularly hard to refute rumors, with illustrations drawn from recent politics. Then, in a series of experiments, I study how ordinary citizens responded to actual rumors surrounding the health care reforms enacted by the US Congress in 2010. While rumors are difficult to squash, there are some strategies that may prove effective for countering rumors. I argue that refuting a rumor with statements from an unlikely source—a person who makes proclamations that run contrary to their personal and political interests—can increase the willingness of citizens to reject rumors regardless of their own political predilections.

This argument explicitly privileges the value of a costly signal—a message that is potentially damaging to its speaker—over authority granted through expertise or other means. Such an argument may seem counterintuitive. We might think that corrections from nonpartisan sources should be the most persuasive because they avoid perceptions of partisan bias. But the same conspiratorial dispositions that make people susceptible to rumors may also make them skeptical of such seemingly neutral authorities. As van der Linden and colleagues argue, "high levels of distrust in scientific, governmental, and journalistic authorities is a hallmark of 'the paranoid style of American politics.'"[5] In this case, the partisan motivations that lead people with conspiratorial dispositions to consider accepting a rumor may actually become an asset in persuading them to disavow that rumor. If sources who speak out against their own apparent interests can generate more credibility than seemingly neutral third parties, explicitly partisan sources denouncing rumors that benefit their party should be more effective than nonpartisan sources in persuading citizens to reject rumors. While such source credibility results are well known in the political persuasion literature, these insights have rarely been applied to the study of rumors. In the present context, pairing death panel rumors with statements from Republicans flatly debunking the rumor can lead citizens—Republicans and Democrats alike—to reject the rumor. Partisanship can thus function as a double-edged sword. Individuals with strong partisan identities, coupled with conspiratorial dispositions, may be especially susceptible to rumors and resistant to corrections. However, partisanship can also be leveraged to counter the spread of these rumors if corrections come from sources that are both overtly partisan and surprising.

Such corrections may not always sway those members of the public who instinctively accept rumors (the "believers" described in chapter 2), but they can also sometimes offer inroads to influencing those who remain unsure about these rumors' veracity (the "uncertain" group). As shown in chapter 3, there is a sizable group of individuals who are exposed to rumors but lack deeply entrenched opinions about whether these rumors are true or false. Whether these individuals are merely uninformed about and disengaged from politics, are skeptical about a rumor's evidentiary basis, or are genuinely unsure whether a rumor is true or false, well-tailored correction strategies can sometimes nudge this group of citizens toward rejection.

The results of my experiments are promising, but plenty of obstacles remain. Though source credibility can be an effective tool for debunking political rumors, rumors often persist even after concerted efforts at correction. Drawing upon psychological theories of "fluency"—a state of mind that characterizes the ease of information processing—I argue that rumors may acquire their power in part through familiarity. Specifically, I find that merely repeating a rumor can increase its strength: simply asking subjects to repeat a rumor to themselves—without any indication that it is true—makes respondents less likely to reject the rumor outright, even when repetition occurs as part of the debunking process. Moreover, evidence over time demonstrates that these effects persist even weeks after subjects read the initial story.[6] But the results may still be effective as part of a collective toolkit to fight misinformation and rumors.

How Do People Respond to Rumors?

Correcting rumors is no easy task, especially because those individuals who are most inclined to believe rumors may be the most resistant to correction by expert sources.[7] Beliefs about the trustworthiness of experts, such as medical professionals and scientists, have increasingly diverged along partisan lines. As the public response to the COVID-19 pandemic has made clear, science has become wrapped up in broader political debates.[8] As a result, we can no longer assume that expertise "speaks for itself" when it comes to correcting rumors.

However, this distrust long predates the pandemic—its roots go back decades. While it is possible that experts may have once been considered "neutral" referees, a large majority of citizens in both parties express skepticism that scientists are transparent about conflicts of interest, and the majority of conservatives believe scientists should focus on research rather than getting involved in policy debates.[9] This distrust of seemingly nonpartisan sources—particularly on the right—extends beyond science. In the context of health care, for example, a 2009 survey documented a 26 percentage point gap between Democrats and Republicans in their confidence that experts from the nonpartisan American Association of Retired Persons (AARP) could provide reliable recommendations about health care policy.[10] In short, nonpartisan sources may not be—and may never have been—the best source for debunking rumors across the board.

At the same time, partisan corrections are hardly guaranteed to be effective either. When evaluating new information, individuals pay attention not only to the *content* of this information but also to its *source*. That is, individuals are more likely to accept new information if it comes from a source they deem reliable. This idea of source credibility is well known in psychological research on persuasion but was not as well explored in the study of political rumors when I began my work.[11] Two key components of source credibility are (1) *expertise*, or the extent to which sources are able to give accurate information, and (2) *trustworthiness*, or the extent to which sources are willing to provide information that they assume to be correct.[12] Perceived trustworthiness plays an especially important role here.[13] When crafting rumor corrections, it is important to consider whether or not a given messenger is likely to be viewed as credible and, particularly, whether they are likely to be seen as a trustworthy source of the specific information they provide.

Some partisan sources may lack this credibility, especially if they are perceived to be pursuing their own partisan interests. Returning to the "death panel" example, President Obama sought to refute rumors about health care at a series of town hall meetings in New Hampshire and Colorado in August 2009, stating at one point "what you can't do—or you can, but you shouldn't do—is start saying things like, 'We want to set up death panels to pull the plug on grandma.' I mean, come on."[14] But his efforts did not shift the tides of public opinion. When we consider Obama's source credibility in this area, this result is not surprising. If citizens are skeptical of even ostensibly nonpartisan sources, then they are unlikely to find a president defending his own policy agenda much more convincing.

All told, attempts to debunk rumors often appeal to nonpartisan authorities as neutral referees of the truth. But in a time when people's dispositions and partisanship color how they perceive expert opinion, these seemingly neutral figures may speak with less credibility than is often assumed. Similarly, explicitly partisan sources may be similarly ineffective if they are perceived as untrustworthy or self-interested. In light of these concerns, what types of sources can maintain widespread credibility while avoiding partisan polarization?

POLITICAL RUMORS AND THE POWER OF PARTISANSHIP

To correct political rumors, a new approach seems necessary. Given what we know about growing skepticism of nonpartisan sources and the centrality of partisan motivations to the spread of rumors, I argue that we should leverage partisanship to make corrections more powerful. In particular, to correct rumors, we can rely on "unlikely" or "surprising" sources—overtly partisan agents who speak out against their own apparent political interests.

In the previous chapter, I presented evidence that belief in political rumors is a function of two factors: conspiratorial dispositions and partisan motivations. Though individual dispositions are difficult to change, we can design corrective strategies that target these partisan attachments. In this case, turning the power of partisanship on its head could be the key to developing effective corrective measures. As the Obama example above indicates, political leaders who speak out against rumors may not be able to meaningfully shift public opinion if their corrections are seen as self-interested or personally beneficial. More convincing, however, are partisan politicians who speak against their own apparent political interests. For these actors, corrections come with a risk of personal or professional consequences. If these sources stand to benefit from a rumor's continued spread and issue a correction anyway, this sends an especially strong signal about the rumor's veracity (or lack thereof). Thus, *who* corrects a rumor may be more important than *what* that individual says. Unlikely statements from prominent figures may make rumor rebuttals more credible.

This argument is consistent with the formal model proposed by Calvert.[15] Calvert concludes that "biased" advisors—those with strong priors toward a particular policy—are especially informative sources of information for decision makers.[16] If such an advisor rejects a policy that the decision maker presumed they would support, this unexpected advice could be "enough to reverse prior preferences."[17] It also aligns with a broader literature on costly signaling.[18] In particular, previous work finds that individuals place higher value on messages that are potentially damaging to a speaker's interests ("costly signals") than on messages that are unlikely to impose significant costs to the speaker ("cheap talk"). For example, members of the public may be more persuaded by politicians who speak out against their own party (or voice support for the opposing party) or by partisan media outlets that produce coverage that is at odds with their perceived ideological slant.[19] In the present context, a Republican who debunks a rumor about a

Democratic politician or policy could change the beliefs of *both* Democrats and Republicans (as well as Independents).

LIMITS TO CORRECTIONS

But finding credible sources for corrections may not be enough to extinguish the power of rumors. Psychologists have long recognized that retractions rarely eliminate the influence of misinformation on individuals' judgment and reasoning—a phenomenon known as the "continued influence effect."[20] This persistence of misinformation even after it has been corrected is troubling, as it suggests that even strong corrections may not be entirely able to eradicate belief in misinformation and rumors. More alarmingly, some scholars have suggested that the very act of trying to refute misinformation may, in fact, make things worse. In particular, some scholars argue that corrections may ironically strengthen individuals' belief in the original misinformation—what is known as a "backfire effect."

Previous research delineates two main categories of backfire effects: (1) worldview backfire effects and (2) familiarity backfire effects. First, worldview backfire effects occur when corrections that challenge people's worldviews entrench belief in misinformation.[21] In a series of highly influential experiments correcting false claims about topics such as the Iraq War and Obama's religion, Nyhan and Reifler found that when some subjects were shown corrections that contradicted their previous beliefs, they responded by becoming more, rather than less, supportive of the original misperceptions.[22] For example, conservatives who received information that Iraq did not possess weapons of mass destruction (WMD) were more likely to believe Iraq had those weapons than were conservatives who did not receive this correction.

These results are both disturbing and counterintuitive. If taken at face value, they suggest that attempts to correct the political misperceptions of ordinary citizens may be ill advised: corrections run the risk of bolstering inaccurate beliefs. Moreover, these findings contradict much of the received wisdom regarding how best to address rumors. In a comprehensive review of twenty-two different studies in both psychology and business, DiFonzo and Bordia find that the most frequent advice for reducing belief in a rumor is the use of rebuttals, the same strategy the Obama administration attempted in its 2009 town halls.[23] Similarly, in the most recent edition of *The Debunking Handbook*, over twenty misinformation scholars, across a wide range of disciplines, recommend providing clear and detailed corrections after individuals have been exposed to misinformation.[24]

However, more recent work has found that while worldview backfire effects may exist, they are extremely rare in practice.[25] In fact, the authors of the original Iraq WMD study have failed to detect worldview backfire effects in a number of follow-up studies.[26] Worldview backfire effects do not seem to be the default response to attitude-inconsistent corrections. Instead, people seem to update their beliefs to accommodate new information, even when this information runs counter to their political attitudes. This is not to say that worldview backfire effects never occur. In fact, later in this chapter, I replicate one of Nyhan and Reifler's original findings several years after their first study. But such effects are almost certainly the exception rather than the rule.

That said, other types of backfire effects may emerge even in the absence of strong prior attitudes. These effects, known as familiarity backfire effects, are said to occur because the act of debunking often involves repeating the original misinformation, making the misinformation feel more familiar and therefore more accurate. Familiarity backfire effects are typically attributed to the "processing fluency" of information. Fluency is "the subjective experience of ease or difficulty associated with completing a mental task."[27] Cognitive tasks can be described as ranging from effortless to effortful.[28] People have an internal sense of how hard they need to think to complete a task, and this awareness influences their everyday judgments and decisions. This phenomenon is directly relevant to the study of misinformation and its correction. Several psychologists have found that the ease with which a piece of information is processed affects individuals' judgments of its accuracy.[29]

When it comes to misinformation correction, the concept of fluency has primarily been studied in the context of repetition. For instance, numerous studies find that information that has been presented more frequently feels more familiar to citizens and, as a result, is more likely to be accepted as true, regardless of its content.[30] This is often described as an "illusory truth effect," wherein repeated statements are easier to process and therefore perceived to be more truthful, relative to statements seen for the first time.[31] The illusory truth effect goes beyond merely identifying or comprehending frequently presented information, a phenomenon that was first recognized in the 1980s.[32] Indeed, this effect is particularly powerful because of its robustness across situations, personality traits, and types of misinformation.[33] As a result, attempts to discredit falsehoods may fail because directly countering a rumor typically involves repeating that rumor. Merely mentioning a rumor could increase its fluency, thereby heightening its perceived accuracy.

Work by Skurnik, Yoon, and Schwarz highlights the potential perils of repeating misinformation in the context of corrections. These authors conducted an experiment in which some respondents were shown an informational flyer created by the Centers for Disease Control (CDC) to educate patients about the flu vaccine.[34] This flyer challenged "myths"—erroneous beliefs about the vaccine—with the proper "facts." As part of this experiment, a random half of subjects were immediately given a test that repeated the "facts and myths" information and were asked to mark which statements were true. The other half were given the test after a thirty-minute delay. Immediately after reading the flyer, participants were able to recall the information from the flyer almost perfectly—they misclassified "myths" as "facts" (and vice versa) at very low rates. However, after a half-hour had passed, subjects began to show a systematic error pattern. Consistent with a psychological state of increased fluency, these respondents were significantly more likely to misidentify the "myths" as "facts" than the reverse and were less likely to say they would get a flu shot (relative to participants who were asked their opinions immediately). In essence, the attempt to debunk myths about the flu shot instead had the effect of amplifying mistruths by subconsciously increasing the ease with which respondents processed those myths. Skurnik and colleagues interpret these results as evidence of familiarity backfire effects, wherein the repetition of myths enhanced factual misperceptions and reduced vaccination intentions.

Here too, however, subsequent evidence is ambiguous. A number of follow-up studies—including direct attempts to replicate Skurnik and colleagues' original findings—have failed to find significant evidence of familiarity backfire effects.[35] Furthermore, recent work finds that repeating rumors within the context of correction may facilitate improved belief updating.[36] All told, the current state of research is clear on the minimal prevalence of worldview backfire effects and ambiguous on the potential for familiarity backfire effects. Nevertheless, given the power of fluency and the illusory truth effect, it is important to consider the potential stickiness of misinformation, even in the absence of backfire effects.

CORRECTION DECAY

Even without a backfire effect, the effectiveness of even the most powerful corrections seems to fade over time.[37] Kuklinski and colleagues, for example, had some success in correcting false beliefs about welfare spending in the United States, but they also found that such learning is short-lived.[38] Recent research likewise finds that corrections have diminishing effects over time.[39] In chapter 6, I will present direct experimental evidence that individuals revert to baseline levels of belief in elite misinformation (spread by Donald Trump and Bernie Sanders) after periods as brief as a week.

Recent experience in the real world also demonstrates the short half-life of corrections. Consider the rumor that Obama was not born in the United States. In response to these false claims about his citizenship, Obama released his long-form birth certificate on April 27, 2011. Coincidentally, just before he did so, YouGov polled the American public from April 23 to April 26 to assess beliefs about Obama's citizenship. Once he released that long-form birth certificate, I convinced YouGov to conduct the poll again, with field dates from April 30 to May 3.

This dramatic (and well-covered) revelation seemed to finally turn the tide of the public's beliefs concerning Obama's citizenship. As table 4.1 demonstrates, the immediate effect of the announcement, just as the Obama administration hoped, was that more people rejected the rumor that he was not a citizen: after the release of the birth certificate, 67 percent of the public rejected the rumor, compared with only 55 percent a week earlier. This change was especially dramatic among Republicans. Prior to the release of Obama's birth certificate, only 30 percent of Republicans rejected the rumor about his citizenship. However, just a week later, after the birth certificate came out, nearly half of Republicans (47 percent) indicated that the rumor was untrue.[40] Moreover, this information seemed to have had a targeted impact. Belief in other misperceptions about the president—including false claims about his religion—remained essentially stable, indicating that the release of the birth certificate shaped beliefs only about Obama's citizenship.

At last, it seemed, the Obama administration had found a solution to its problem. But this moment was fleeting. One early clue was that the movement in beliefs was largely the result of fewer people saying they were not sure, as opposed to saying they did not accept the rumor. The pool of believers was largely unchanged. In light of this fact, to assess the lasting power of the release of Obama's birth certificate, I fielded a January 27–31, 2012, YouGov poll that asked again about Obama's birthplace. The results presented in figure 4.1 demonstrate that the power of Obama's birth certificate was indeed short-lived. Nine months later, rumor rejection rates fell back down to 59 percent—only 4 percentage points higher than before the birth certificate was released. Furthermore, by the time I next polled the public in July 2012, the positive impact of the long-form birth certificate on beliefs

TABLE 4.1. Change in Beliefs about President Obama over Time, April 2011

April 23—Before Release of Long-Form Birth Certificate, N = 1000

Please tell us whether you think the following statements about Barack Obama are true or false.

	True (%)	False (%)	Not Sure (%)
Barack Obama was born in the United States	**55**	**15**	**30**
Barack Obama is a Muslim	23	47	30
Barack Obama shares my values	33	43	24
Barack Obama is a Christian	44	24	32
Barack Obama is a strong leader	35	43	21
Barack Obama is a socialist	29	40	31

April 30—After Release of Long-Form Birth Certificate, N = 1000

Please tell us whether you think the following statements about Barack Obama are true or false.

	True (%)	False (%)	Not Sure (%)
Barack Obama was born in the United States	**67**	**13**	**20**
Barack Obama is a Muslim	22	48	30
Barack Obama shares my values	36	45	20
Barack Obama is a Christian	46	25	29
Barack Obama is a strong leader	39	44	17
Barack Obama is a socialist	32	40	28

Note: Percentages are rounded. For the Obama citizenship item, "False" and "Not Sure" responses are interpreted as a failure to reject the rumor while "True" responses are interpreted as a rejection of the rumor.

Source: YouGov, April 2011.

about Obama's citizenship had disappeared completely.[41] These results, also presented in figure 4.1, indicate that a little over a year later, the public was right back where it was before Obama released his long-form birth certificate. In April 2011, 55 percent of the public believed that Obama was born in the United States, and in July 2012, 55 percent of the public believed that he was born in the United States. Moreover, the share of people who thought Obama was not born in the United States was marginally *larger* in 2012, compared to 2011.

FIGURE 4.1. Change in Beliefs about President Obama over Time, 2011–2012

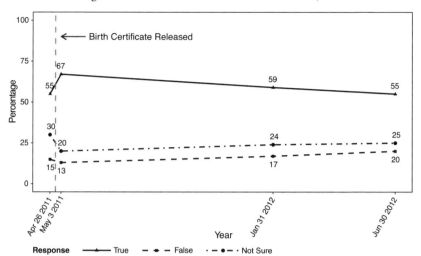

Note: This graph shows the percentage of the survey sample that accepted ("False"), rejected ("True"), and was unsure about the veracity of the birther rumor over time. The vertical line indicates the release date of Obama's long-form birth certificate on April 27, 2011. *Source*: YouGov, April 2011–June 2012.

This diminished effect of corrections over time is particularly problematic in light of the challenge that fluency poses. If one-off corrections will not durably counter a rumor, then repeated corrections may be necessary. Corrections may fade most quickly for rumors with the greatest fluency and widespread repetition, and constant rebuttals to offset this decaying effect may lack effectiveness.

THE ENDURING POWER OF RUMORS

The research discussed in the previous section underscores the foundation of the enduring power of political rumors. Political rumors are especially compelling because partisans are skeptical of nonpartisan sources and motivated to believe falsehoods about politicians and policies of the other party. Moreover, the strategy that is most often employed to counter rumors—directly confronting the rumor by repeating it, then debunking it—may serve to augment the processing fluency of the rumor, thereby decreasing the likelihood that citizens will reject that rumor out of hand and accelerating how quickly the effects of corrections decay.

To more effectively discredit these rumors, I emphasize how the credibility of the source of the correction can help moderate a rumor's spread. As argued earlier in this chapter, Republicans who debunk rumors about Democrats (and Democrats who debunk rumors about Republicans) may have greater standing than nonpartisan actors. These politicized voices may have the power to correct misinformed beliefs, helping to break the vicious cycle of rumors.

THE POWER OF UNLIKELY SOURCES

I begin by demonstrating the power of unlikely sources to correct misinformation through a replication of the aforementioned study on weapons of mass destruction (WMD) rumors by Nyhan and Reifler, albeit this time with a twist. As noted above, past work on correcting misinformation has historically focused on nonpartisan or independent sources. Nyhan and Reifler's study is a prominent example of this line of research, making the study an ideal candidate to explore the potential efficacy of unlikely partisan sources.[42]

In their original study, Nyhan and Reifler deliberately relied solely on nonpartisan cues.[43] In my replication, conducted in the spring of 2010, I sought to test whether partisan cues from surprising sources could increase the power of corrections in the context of the controversy surrounding WMD in Iraq. The original study had two conditions: (1) the WMD rumor alone and (2) the rumor with a correction from a nonpartisan source. This nonpartisan correction referenced the Duelfer Report, a report released by a US government-appointed special advisor to the Director of Central Intelligence on Iraq's weapons of mass destruction. In my replication study, I used these same treatments but added two additional conditions: (1) the rumor with both a correction from the nonpartisan CIA source and a correction from a Republican source (a quotation from then-senator Jeff Sessions confirming that "we found no weapons of mass destruction" in Iraq) and (2) a true control condition, where respondents were not presented with any information.[44] The correction from Sessions represents an unlikely source, given Republicans' incentives to maintain that the original premise for the invasion of Iraq was, in fact, sound. The true control condition allows us to measure the beliefs of individuals in the absence of any information, thereby providing a baseline to measure potential backfire effects. The dependent variable in this experiment was the same used by Nyhan and Reifler in the original experiment, a five-point Likert scale measuring agreement with the

FIGURE 4.2. Effect of Corrections on Belief in WMD Rumor, 2010

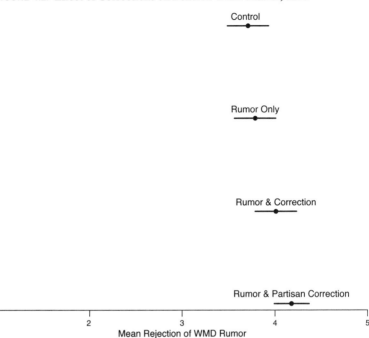

Note: The point estimates represent the mean belief in WMD for each condition. The lines represent the 95 percent confidence intervals. Higher scores indicate weaker belief in WMD rumor. *Source*: Amazon Mechanical Turk, 2010.

statement, "Immediately before the US invasion, Iraq had an active weapons of mass destruction program, the ability to produce these weapons, and large stockpiles of WMD, but Saddam Hussein was able to hide or destroy these weapons right before US forces arrived."

I find that unlikely sources can be effective in correcting factual misperceptions. The results in figure 4.2 are consistent with the original findings of Nyhan and Reifler: The nonpartisan correction reduces belief in the existence of WMD relative to the rumor-only condition—but only in a substantively small and statistically insignificant manner. However, the inclusion of the "unlikely source"—a Republican elite correcting a rumor that would otherwise benefit Republicans—significantly decreases belief in the WMD misperception relative to the rumor-only condition.

Moreover, the addition of the partisan correction also substantially attenuates the original backfire effect, which I replicated and present in figure 4.3.

FIGURE 4.3. Marginal Effect of Correction Partisanship on WMD Rumor Acceptance

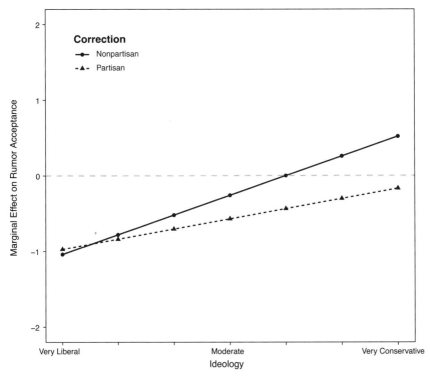

Note: The lines represent the marginal effects of correction partisanship on WMD rumor acceptance across various levels of ideology. The differences are not statistically significant, so I do not present confidence intervals for the predicted values. *Source*: Amazon Mechanical Turk, 2010.

Note that in this figure the direction of the outcome is reversed to match the original Nyhan and Reifler paper: higher scores reflect a larger marginal effect on support for the WMD misperception. Though the relatively small size of my study does not allow me to distinguish the size of these effects in a statistical sense, the direction of the substantive effect suggests that while the nonpartisan correction leads to a worldview backfire effect among the most conservative respondents, the partisan source diminishes this effect. At the very least, the correction from the unlikely source does not prompt conservatives to accept the rumor at higher levels than other conservatives who did not receive that correction. That is, my replication finds some support for the argument that unlikely-source corrections can successfully reduce factual misperceptions and suggests that such corrections guard against possible worldview backfire effects. More generally, corrections from unlikely sources were the most effective method for reducing misperceptions, a lesson I will next explore in the context of rumors concerning the ACA.

HEALTH CARE REFORM AND DEATH PANELS

To further test the potential effectiveness of unlikely sources, I investigated the rumors that circulated in 2009 and 2010 regarding the inclusion of death panels in the ACA. Recall that these rumors claimed that Obama's health care reform would allow government officials to decide whether individual citizens should receive health care based on a calculation of their level of productivity in society. One element of these rumors was the suggestion that elderly people would have to consult death panels to discuss end-of-life options like euthanasia. These rumors started with statements made by former New York lieutenant governor Betsy McCaughey but quickly spread to the conservative media.[45] A number of prominent Republican politicians added to the chorus, including Sarah Palin and Senator Charles Grassley, the ranking Republican member of the US Senate Finance Committee.[46]

These rumors were patently false and were publicly discredited in many forums. Yet they were widely known and accepted among the American public. A poll conducted by the Pew Center in August 2009 found that 86 percent of Americans had heard the rumor about the creation of death panels through the ACA. More troubling, 30 percent of the public thought the death panel rumor was true, with another 20 percent unsure of the veracity of the statement.[47] As described in chapter 2, this final class of respondents is also important for understanding the power of rumors. This 20 percent of the public represents the "uncertain" group—those who are unlikely to instinctively reject rumors, but they do not accept them out of hand. This malleability makes it possible to sway their opinion with corrections and is vital to impeding a rumor's spread. Persuading the uncertain group to reject rumors is important because any position short of rejection enhances a rumor's credibility.

The death panel rumor is a hard case for finding that corrections are effective, because the rumor persisted during the fielding of my experiment despite repeated attempts to debunk it. Consistent with other polling from the time, a July 2010 poll I conducted through YouGov found that 33 percent of the public thought the death panel rumor was true, with another 22 percent unsure. In a separate question, that same poll also found that 26 percent of the public thought that changes to the health care system would require elderly patients to meet with government officials to discuss end-of-life options, including euthanasia, while another 28 percent were unsure.[48] Moreover, among those who were incorrect, a large portion were also highly certain of their misinformed beliefs.[49]

The power of the death panel rumor extends beyond shaping the beliefs of the mass public—it also has serious policy consequences. In early 2011, the Obama administration announced that it would revise Medicare fee policies to remove funding for end-of-life counseling.[50] The vast reach of the death panel rumors hung heavily over this decision. Consequently, the spread of death panel rumors may have, at least indirectly, contributed to the end of an important Medicare service. Even after the Obama administration's revision, confusion about the provisions of the ACA did not go away. In 2015, a Vox/PerryUndem poll found that 26 percent of Republicans and 12 percent of Democrats still believed that the government was allowed to make decisions about patients' end-of-life care.[51] Indeed, more than ten years later, legal attacks on the ACA persist, and twelve states have yet to expand Medicaid.[52]

To preview the empirical results that follow, the studies confirm that unlikely sources are particularly effective for corrections. The highest rates of rumor rejection among respondents from both parties occurred when people received a correction from a Republican—a strategy that leverages both overt partisanship and surprise, given that the ACA rumors benefited Republican interests. These results suggest that the mechanism is not the result of simple elite cuing. The unlikely-source cue generated belief updating among *both* Democrats and Republicans, suggesting that the source's credibility came from speaking against its own interests, rather than just appealing to co-partisans. If these results were simply driven by partisans following their leaders, we would not expect to see changes among Democrats, who are unlikely to follow cues from Republican elites. Similar to the real-world findings regarding Obama's citizenship, corrections seemed to work largely by converting uncertain respondents.

But the findings also highlighted several limitations of corrections. As with the long-term dynamics of the release of Obama's birth certificate on the belief that he was a US citizen, the effects of my informational treatment were somewhat ephemeral; their impact faded after one week in the first study and after one month in the second. My second study, which incorporated a measure of rumor fluency, also found that repeated exposure to a rumor decreased rates of rumor rejection, even in the face of a strong correction. So, while using an unlikely source can be powerful for correcting misinformation, even the best strategies are not a "magic bullet" that can permanently eliminate misinformation.

EXPERIMENTAL DESIGN

In 2010, I conducted two studies to test the effects of different correction strategies on peoples' beliefs in rumors about the ACA. The studies varied the presentation of the rumor-related information across three dimensions: (1) the pairing of rumor and correction, (2) the partisanship of the correction source, and (3) the degree to which the respondent was induced to rehearse the rumor. These experiments also explored the effect of time on the influence of the treatments, recording responses not only immediately following the treatment but also at later points in time.

In both experiments, I was concerned with patterns of rumor *rejection*— the rate at which subjects definitively rejected false information. The psychological literature often takes the opposite approach, focusing on patterns of rumor acceptance.[53] I focus on rumor rejection because of the importance of the "not sure" response—a case I have made throughout this book. Any position short of outright rejecting a rumor—even an expression of uncertainty through a "don't know" or "not sure" response—is normatively undesirable because this expression of uncertainty allows believers to gain a stronger foothold in the mass public compared to the less prevalent disbelievers.

In some ways, I began these experiments with one hand tied behind my back. The experiments described in this paper are especially difficult tests of the power of rumors because they exploit real-world rumors rather than constructed rumors. Both experiments were conducted in the immediate wake of the passage of the ACA and used real-world quotes and facts drawn from the contentious debate surrounding the act. In doing so, I traded the ability to fully manipulate the information presented to respondents in order to maintain a realistic set of treatments. In addition, given that these experiments were conducted during an ongoing controversy, the effect sizes of my treatments will be smaller than if the information presented in the stories was completely novel to the subjects. Thus, the experimental effects that I find from exposure to my treatments are, by design, muted relative to a situation where I could control the full scope of the information presented.

ACA STUDY 1: SPRING 2010

In May 2010, two months after the passage of the ACA, I ran an experiment on an internet panel.[54] The primary purpose of this experiment was to examine the impact of the partisan identity of the provider of the rumor correction. I then used a delayed follow-up questionnaire to assess the role of repetition in enhancing the fluency of a rumor. Respondents were randomly assigned to one of four different experimental conditions in which they were shown news stories that I constructed about health care reform (along with a control condition, where respondents were not shown a story and were merely asked if they believed the rumor). The stories all dealt with the 2010 ACA but presented different details about the debate surrounding the plan (the full text of the treatments is in section "May 2010 Internet Panel Study Experimental Treatments" of the appendix).

In the first "rumor" condition, subjects were presented with the rumor in the form of quotations from opponents of the ACA, who warned of the possibility of death panels. In the second "rumor and nonpartisan correction" condition, respondents were presented with both the rumor information from the first condition and a nonpartisan correction of that rumor, in the form of a description of the end-of-life provisions of the ACA, as well as supporting quotes from the American Medical Association (AMA) and the American Association of Retired Persons (AARP). The third and fourth conditions introduced explicitly partisan information in addition to the nonpartisan correction. In the third "rumor and Republican correction" condition, the text from the "rumor and nonpartisan correction" condition text was reproduced, and a quote debunking the rumor from Senator John Isakson (who was a Republican who helped draft the end-of-life provisions and was identified as a Republican in the treatment) was added to the end of the story. In the fourth "rumor and Democratic correction" condition, the "rumor and nonpartisan correction" was also reproduced, and a separate quote containing a correction from Democratic Representative Earl Blumenauer was added to the end of the story.[55] The specific text of the quotes from Isakson and Blumenauer differed because they were drawn from real quotes, but the spirit of the corrections was the same. Moreover, an independent experiment conducted in November 2014 indicated that respondents perceived the two corrections as equally strong.[56] More generally, while the treatments differ in a number of ways, these differences were designed to mirror the political rhetoric surrounding the discussion of rumors concerning health care reform in the media.

Respondents were randomly assigned to one of five conditions (the four experimental treatments and the control). Respondents in the four experimental conditions first read the appropriate news article. All respondents were then asked a series of questions concerning the veracity of the death panel rumors and whether they support the health care plan. In the tables that follow, I present the results of the analysis of the euthanasia rumor item, which tapped most directly into the controversy surrounding the ACA provisions. It asked, "Do you think the changes to the health care system that have been enacted by Congress and the Obama administration require elderly patients to meet with government officials to discuss 'end of life' options including euthanasia?"[57] The results are very similar for the other rumor questions that ask about death panels. To minimize the number of tables in the body of the chapter, I do not include the analysis of this question below. However, in the interests of transparency, I present the full results in tables A11–16 in the appendix.[58]

In table 4.2, I present the answers to the euthanasia rumors question, broken down by experimental condition. I include a chi-square test of overall significance, which tests if there are any significant differences among any of the conditions. I also conducted a series of paired comparisons tests to assess significant differences between conditions. Because there are five conditions, there are a total of ten comparisons. I present full significance results for all the pairwise comparisons in tables A11 through A19 in the appendix but refer to these results in the text.

Several conclusions are readily apparent.[59] First, there is strong statistical evidence that the different presentations of the information affected rumor rejection levels. The correction conditions all seem to be effective, increasing rates of rumor rejection by 10 percentage points over the "rumor only" condition, largely by reducing the proportion of "not sure" responses.[60] As was the case with the Obama birthplace rumor discussed earlier in the chapter, the corrections seem to work by increasing rumor rejection rates through reducing the level of uncertainty surrounding the rumor—by moving members of the uncertain group to the believer group. That said, not all of the corrections are created equal. Republican correction—the unlikely source—is the most effective treatment in increasing rates of rumor rejection.

This result holds when we break up the sample into partisan groups.[61] Most importantly, the Republican correction is the most powerful treatment for *both* Republican and Democratic identifiers (see table A20 in the appendix for full results). That is, an unlikely source is the most powerful method for correction even among people who ideologically disagree with that source. Perhaps precisely because partisan motivations drive so much of the spread of misinformation, people listen carefully to sources speaking against their own interests even when they would normally discount information from them due to political differences. A simple elite cueing story alone cannot explain these results; after all, Democratic identifiers are more influenced by the Republican correction than by the Democratic correction.

TABLE 4.2. Effect of Treatments on Euthanasia Rumor Belief, May 2010

	Control (%)	Rumor Only (%)	Rumor + Nonpartisan Correction (%)	Rumor + Republican Correction (%)	Rumor + Democratic Correction (%)
Reject	57	46	60	69	60
Accept	12	17	14	15	17
Not Sure	31	36	26	16	24

Note: N = 876; $\chi^2(8) = 23.95$ Pr = 0.002.

Percentages are rounded. The rows present the percentage of respondents who reject, accept, or are unsure about each rumor. This is presented for each condition (represented by the column). Full pairwise tests of statistical significance are presented in Berinsky, "Rumors and Health Care Reform."

Source: Author's study, May 2010.

TABLE 4.3. Effect of Treatments on Health Care Policy Opinion, May 2010

	Control (%)	Rumor Only (%)	Rumor + Nonpartisan Correction (%)	Rumor + Republican Correction (%)	Rumor + Democratic Correction (%)
Support	51	42	46	48	37
Oppose	49	58	54	52	63

N = 876; $\chi^2(4) = 9.00$ Pr = 0.06.

Note: Percentages are rounded. The rows represent the percentage of respondents who support or oppose health care policy enacted by Obama. This is presented for each condition (represented by column). Full pairwise tests of statistical significance are presented in Berinsky, "Rumors and Health Care Reform." Support for health care policy was measured by a forced binary response item that asked the respondent whether he or she supported or opposed the "changes to the health care system that have been enacted by Congress and the Obama administration."

Source: Author's study, May 2010.

Thus, it is the informational content of the identity of the politician issuing the correction that matters. Turning partisanship on its head in service of correction, then, can help combat the spread of misinformation across citizens from all partisan stripes.

The benefits of corrections extend from rejection of the rumor to support for health care reform, as shown in table 4.3.[62] While the euthanasia rumor referred to in table 4.2 measures belief in the rumor, the policy item in table 4.3 measures whether the respondent supports the policies enacted by Obama's health care reforms. Though the effects are modest in size, both statistically and substantively, presenting the rumor by itself decreases support for the plan relative to the control condition (51 percent compared to 42 percent).[63] Presenting the rumor in combination with a nonpartisan correction or the Republican correction causes support to rebound, albeit modestly. However, neither of these correction conditions is statistically distinct from the "rumor only" condition. But interestingly, introducing the Democratic correction induces a backlash, reducing support for the plan to its lowest level across any condition.[64]

As table 4.4 shows, there is some evidence of a diminished effect over time. Based on the work described above, we might expect that fluency-based backfire effects would be most prominent after a delay. Specifically, respondents who were presented both the rumor and the correction should be less likely to reject the rumor outright than people who were given no information.

Here, I examine responses to the euthanasia rumor question for the subset of respondents who were interviewed in both waves. As expected, the respondents in the "rumor only" condition held steady in their beliefs. The effectiveness of the corrections faded across the board during the week between the survey waves, largely because the rates of "not sure" responses increased for respondents in those conditions.[65] Over time, the power of the corrections faded. The Republican correction remained the most effective treatment, but the rates of rumor rejection decreased by about 10 percentage points relative to the first wave. Furthermore, the rates of rumor rejection for both the "rumor + nonpartisan correction" and "rumor + Democratic correction" conditions were now lower than in the control condition (though this difference is not statistically significant). Thus, taking a longer time horizon into account, providing people with correct information in conjunction with a rumor may be no better than no information at all. These effects extend beyond rumor rejection to support for health care. Respondents who were exposed to the rumor, either alone or in combination with the nonpartisan correction, remained less supportive than people who received no information.[66]

ACA STUDY 2: FALL 2010

The first ACA study demonstrated that corrections from an unlikely source— Republicans debunking health care rumors—are the most effective way to counter rumors. But this study also suggests that the efficacy of corrections

TABLE 4.4. Effect of Treatments on Euthanasia Rumor Belief over Time, May 2010

Wave 1, May

	Control (%)	Rumor Only (%)	Rumor + Nonpartisan Correction (%)	Rumor + Republican Correction (%)	Rumor + Democratic Correction (%)
Reject	58	43	58	68	61
Accept	13	18	13	15	18
Not Sure	30	38	29	18	21

N = 696; $\chi^2(8) = 23.2$ Pr = 0.03.

Wave 2, May

	Control (%)	Rumor Only (%)	Rumor + Nonpartisan Correction (%)	Rumor + Republican Correction (%)	Rumor + Democratic Correction (%)
Reject	57	43	51	58	53
Accept	12	18	15	16	21
Not Sure	31	38	34	26	25

N = 696; $\chi^2(8) = 12.2$ Pr = 0.14.

Note: Percentages are rounded. The rows present the percentage of respondents who reject, accept, or are unsure about each rumor. This is presented for each condition (represented by the column). Full pairwise tests of statistical significance are presented in Berinsky, "Rumors and Health Care Reform."

Source: Author's study, May 2010.

diminished substantially over time. In order to build on this study and more directly test the fluency hypothesis, I fielded a second experiment as a module in late 2010.[67]

The subject of these experiments was again rumors concerning Obama's health plan. As in the first ACA study, I randomized the presentation of treatments that consisted of (constructed) news stories about health care reform. In this second study, I used a new design.[68] I had three different experimental conditions. The first was a "rumor" condition identical to the rumor condition in the May study. The second was a new "correction only" condition that did not mention the rumors concerning the death panel, but only described the actual provisions in the 2010 ACA.[69] I chose to hold the partisan content of the rumor correction at its most effective level, using the Republican correction in the form of the Isakson quote from the May study. The third, a "rumor + correction" condition, was identical to the "rumor + Republican correction" condition from the May study and presented both the rumor information from the first condition and the correction from the second condition.

Because of an error in fielding this study, there was no control group in this experiment. But based on the results of the first study, we have a good sense of the size of the effect of the treatments relative to the baseline.[70] I therefore compare the effects of the different conditions, relative to each other. This is an appropriate analytic strategy because the purpose of the experiment is to explore the effects of differences in the presentation of information, not the differences between the treatments and "no information."

In addition to the corrective strategy treatment, I designed a two-condition "rehearsal treatment" to directly test the expectations regarding fluency. Respondents who received the rumor information—either alone or in combination with the correction—were asked one of two types of recall questions after the story. The stated purpose of the task was to test what they could remember from the story, but the true purpose was to see whether rehearsing the rumors would increase the power of these rumors. Half of the respondents were assigned to an "irrelevant recall" condition, where they were asked a single recall question—a multiple choice question asking what office was held by Betsy McCaughey (who was quoted in the story)—while the other half were placed in a "long recall" condition and received two additional questions that asked them to identify the speaker of a particular quote that repeated the content of the rumor. Respondents were first asked to identify who said, "You have every right to fear. . . . [You] should not have a government-run plan to decide when to pull the plug on Grandma." Second, they were asked to identify who said that the health care reform bill requires "people in Medicare have a required counseling session that will tell them how to end their life sooner."

I was not interested in the answers they gave to these questions, per se. The simple task of answering the recall questions ensured that they would again read the incorrect information. This "rehearsal" of the rumor immediately following the presentation of the study should increase the fluency with which people process the information contained in the rumor.[71] Based on the psychological work on fluency, I expected this increased ease of processing rumor information to lower rumor rejection levels, regardless of whether the rumor was paired with a strong, partisan correction.

My respondents were interviewed first in October, and then again in November. The experiment was carried out in the October wave. I asked the

TABLE 4.5. Effect of Treatments on Euthanasia Rumor Belief, October 2010

	Control (%)	Correction Only (%)	Rumor + Correction (%)
Reject	48	54	60
Accept	29	23	20
Not Sure	23	23	20

N = 1000; $\chi^2(4)$ = 12.23 Pr = 0.02.

Note: Percentages are rounded. The rows present the percentage of respondents who reject, accept, or are unsure about each rumor. This is presented for each condition (represented by the column). Full pairwise tests of statistical significance are presented in Berinsky, "Rumors and Health Care Reform."

Source: CCES, October 2010.

rumor belief questions in both waves. I also asked about support for health care reform in the first wave.

The general pattern of the findings from the second study were in line with those from the first study. In table 4.5, I present the overall effects of the rumor information treatment on rumor rejection levels (setting aside the recall treatments for the moment). The correction conditions—whether in combination with the rumor or alone—led respondents to reject the euthanasia rumor at higher rates than in the "rumor only" condition, though only the "rumor + correction" condition is statistically distinct from the "rumor only" condition. Though in this study, unlike the first study or the Obama birth certificate example, the movement in beliefs was concentrated among the believers, rather than the uncertain. Thus, at least in the moment, the pairing of the rumor with the correction was a more effective strategy than simply presenting the correct information on its own (though the differences between these two conditions are not statistically significant). Again, the effect of the treatments extends from rejection of rumors to general support for health care reform.

The results of my first study suggest that the effectiveness of corrections wanes over time. Table 4.6 presents the distribution of responses for those individuals who completed both waves of the study.[72] This table demonstrates that, by the second wave, the gap between the "rumor only" and "rumor + correction" conditions diminished. As in the first study, the passage of time reduced the effect of the correction on rumor rejection rates.[73] It should be noted that this effect is not merely the result of the fading effectiveness of *any* information over time, since, one month later, the distribution of responses to the euthanasia question for respondents in the "rumor only"

TABLE 4.6. Effect of Treatments on Euthanasia Rumor Belief over Time, October–November 2010

	Wave 1, October		
	Rumor Only (%)	Correction Only (%)	Rumor + Correction (%)
Reject	48	55	63
Accept	27	24	19
Not Sure	25	21	18

N = 837; $\chi^2(4) = 14.22$ Pr = 0.01.

	Wave 2, November		
	Rumor Only (%)	Correction Only (%)	Rumor + Correction (%)
Reject	47	53	55
Accept	26	26	23
Not Sure	27	21	22

N = 834; $\chi^2(4) = 5.03$ Pr = 0.28.

Note: Percentages are rounded. The rows present the percentage of respondents who reject, accept, or are unsure about each rumor. This is presented for each condition (represented by the column). Full pairwise tests of statistical significance are presented in Berinsky, "Rumors and Health Care Reform."

Source: CCES, October/November 2010.

condition is unchanged. This differential pattern of information decay across conditions stands in contrast to the typical pattern of treatment decay found in similar studies.[74]

I next sought to see if the rehearsal treatment had the intended effect. The effect of rumor rehearsal on rejection of the euthanasia rumor is shown in table 4.7. The first two columns in the table pertain to the results among those respondents assigned to the "rumor only" story treatment. The first column presents the distribution of responses to the euthanasia question among subjects who were assigned to the "irrelevant recall" version of the rehearsal treatment. These respondents were only shown the McCaughey office identification question and therefore were exposed to the rumor only when reading the news story. The second column presents the distribution of the rumor question among those who were assigned to the "long recall" version of the rehearsal treatment. In addition to the McCaughey question, these respondents were given the two death panel quote-identification questions and therefore read two quotes that reiterated the rumor.

TABLE 4.7. Effect of Rumor Rehearsal on Euthanasia Rumor Belief, October 2010

	Rumor Only		Rumor + Correction	
	Irrelevant Recall (%)	Long Recall (%)	Irrelevant Recall (%)	Long Recall (%)
Reject	54	42	62	58
Accept	26	32	18	21
Not Sure	20	26	19	21

Rumor Only: N = 350; $\chi^2(2)$ = 5.49 Pr = 0.06; Rumor + Correction: N = 342 $\chi^2(2)$ = 0.67 Pr = 0.72

Note: Percentages are rounded. The rows present the percentage of respondents who reject, accept, or are unsure about each rumor. This is presented for each condition (represented by the column).

Source: CCES, October 2010.

My expectation was that respondents in this condition would be less likely to reject the rumor because they had rehearsed its content, thereby increasing its fluency. The next two columns of the table repeat this presentation for respondents in the "rumor + correction" condition. Since respondents in the "correction only" condition all received a single recall question unrelated to the rumor, the data from these respondents are omitted from the table.

Table 4.7 demonstrates that, as expected, simply rehearsing the rumor through answering the recall questions affected rates of rumor rejection. Additional exposure to a rumor, in the absence of any information about its veracity, was sufficient to decrease rumor rejection rates, even when the rumor was initially presented in combination with a powerful correction. Admittedly, this effect is not extremely large, but it was larger in the long versus irrelevant recall condition for both respondents in the "rumor only" and the "rumor + correction" condition.[75] Further, in line with the fluency hypothesis, table 4.7 shows increases in rumor acceptance as well as in uncertainty. Respondents did not simply become more uncertain, rather they were actually more ready to believe the rumor after repeated exposure.[76]

Because the rumor questions were asked in short succession to the treatment, it could be argued that these results are as much evidence of bringing rumors to the top of mind—or "priming"—as they are of fluency.[77] Specifically, the recall question might serve to "prime" respondents to consider the veracity of the rumor. Table 4.8 provides suggestive evidence that this rehearsal effect persists over time and is not merely the influence of

TABLE 4.8. Effect of Rumor Rehearsal on Euthanasia Rumor Belief over Time,
October–November 2010

	Wave 1, October			
	Rumor Only		Rumor + Correction	
	Irrelevant Recall (%)	Long Recall (%)	Irrelevant Recall (%)	Long Recall (%)
Reject	54	41	65	61
Accept	25	30	18	19
Not Sure	21	29	17	19

Rumor Only: N = 289; $\chi^2(2) = 4.82$ Pr = 0.09; Rumor + Correction: N = 285 $\chi^2(2) = 0.52$ Pr = 0.77

	Wave 2, November			
	Rumor Only		Rumor + Correction	
	Irrelevant Recall (%)	Long Recall (%)	Irrelevant Recall (%)	Long Recall (%)
Reject	52	41	59	50
Accept	25	28	22	24
Not Sure	23	31	19	25

Rumor Only: N = 289; $\chi^2(2) = 4.07$ Pr = 0.13; Rumor + Correction: N = 285 $\chi^2(2) = 2.45$ Pr = 0.29

Note: Percentages are rounded. The rows present the percentage of respondents who reject, accept, or are unsure about each rumor. This is presented for each condition (represented by the column). A parametric difference-in-differences test for change in the difference over time shows that the differences are stable; the results of the analysis are presented in Berinsky, "Rumors and Health Care Reform."

Source: CCES, October/November 2010.

ephemeral priming. This table presents the wave 1 and wave 2 results for those respondents interviewed in both waves of the study. The differences on the euthanasia question across recall conditions, which are substantively large (though, admittedly, not statistically significant), remain nearly identical a month later. This table also provides some suggestive evidence that, over time, the power of the correction diminishes. Though not statistically significant, the rumor rejection rates drop for respondents in the "rumor + correction" condition, especially for those in the "long recall" condition. The pattern of responses for those in the "rumor only" condition, however, remains stable. This is suggestive evidence that, merely increasing the fluency of a rumor increases its staying power. This result is potentially important because the "long recall" condition more accurately represents the intensity with which rumors are repeated and magnified in today's media environment.

Conclusion

By understanding how and why people come to reject false rumors, we can attempt to short-circuit these rumors' destructive influence. In three different studies using separate samples, I come to similar conclusions. The first, in the context of an examination of beliefs about the existence of weapons of mass destruction in Iraq, replicated an existing study and found that using an unlikely source increased the power of corrections and potentially mitigated backfire effects. In both the second and third studies, I demonstrated that this encouraging finding on the effectiveness of unlikely sources extended to other areas, notably in the context of health care policy. However, in the third study, I presented new evidence on an important limitation to corrections: repeated exposure to rumors may increase their fluency and therefore their acceptance. Though partisanship colors how citizens process information about public policy, my studies show that under the right circumstances— with the right arguments made by the right people—corrections can increase rumor rejection among citizens, regardless of their partisan predilections. In particular, corrections acquire increased credibility when politicians make statements that run counter to their personal and political interests.

These experiments present especially difficult tests for the power of corrections. In order to address most directly the question of how best to dislodge rumors, I used actual rumors that were circulating widely at the time of my studies. However, as a result, my treatments competed against the real-world rhetoric surrounding health reform in the political world. As I discuss below, media coverage of death panels oftentimes increased the rumor's fluency by repeating the rumor without an effective correction. That sustained media environment may therefore make it difficult for a single experimental correction to significantly increase rumor rejection rates. In addition, when constructing my treatments, I limited myself to actual statements made by politicians in the heat of the health care debate. Altogether, these factors curb the power of any experimental effects. My results emerge despite—and not because of—the political environment at the time.

As a result, though the substantive size of the effects in this chapter are admittedly modest, there are important lessons to take from these results. Both the real-world data from the case of Obama's contested birth certificate and the lab data from the first ACA experiment indicates that it may be extremely difficult to dislodge the beliefs of citizens who accept rumors. Even in the face of factual corrections, the size of the group of believers remained stable. But the data also show that the uncertain group can be swayed by corrective information. At the same time, the results from the second ACA experiment suggest that it is not impossible to move believers. Together these results suggest that, as counterintuitive as it may sound, policymakers and media actors should focus their efforts to influence the uncertain in addition to undertaking the difficult task of trying to convince the believers.

My findings also have important implications for developing strategies to debunk rumors. As I have repeatedly noted in this book, there is no single magic bullet that will stop the problem of misinformation. But the work presented in this chapter points to one strategy that has some promise. Just as important as how a rumor is debunked is who does the debunking. To correct rumors, we must account for the power of partisanship—and try to neutralize it. As noted above, politicians who attempt to counter rumors often appeal to nonpartisan authorities. For instance, to fight the death panel rumors, experts from the AMA and the AARP were called in to "speak the truth." But, ironically, in a polarized era, those nonpartisan authorities often *lack* authority because they are easily drowned out by more politicized voices. In the modern political environment, independent sources that are credible to both Democrats and Republicans are hard to find. Consider, for example, the AMA and the AARP: As mentioned above, a September 2009 NPR/KFF/ Harvard telephone survey assessed the level of confidence that the public had in various groups to "recommend the right thing for the country when it comes to health care."[78] The Democrats and Republicans surveyed indeed held similar views of the AMA. Among Democrats, 23 percent of respondents said they had a great deal of confidence in the AMA and 45 percent had a fair amount of confidence—not a ringing endorsement, but a reasonable level of trust. Republicans expressed similar levels of trust; 20 percent had a great deal of confidence and 45 percent had a fair amount of confidence. However, there were large partisan gaps in the assessment of the AARP. Among Democrats, 29 percent had a great deal of confidence and 40 percent had a fair amount of confidence. But among Republicans, only 16 percent had a great deal of confidence and 27 percent had a fair amount of confidence—overall, a 26 percentage point gap across the two categories.

That said, under the right circumstances, partisanship can be harnessed as a force for truth. In particular, politicized voices can help debunk false statements circulating in society. When I paired the "death panel" story with a quote debunking the rumor from a Republican who helped draft the end-of-life provisions, respondents—Republicans and Democrats alike—were far more likely to reject the euthanasia rumor. In the real world, these types of corrections from unlikely partisan sources exist, but they are admittedly rare. I performed a content analysis of all evening news stories broadcast from January 2009 to December 2012 that mentioned death panels on ABC, CBS, NBC, CNN, and FOX. While the rumor was presented without a correction only 7 percent of the time, corrections from unlikely sources were rare as well: only 10 percent of the stories paired the rumor with a correction from a Republican source.[79] Put simply, the media created an environment that fostered the continued spread of death panel rumors. Yet this does not have to be the case. There are usually partisans—like Senator Isakson on health care—who are motivated to speak the truth. Perhaps amplifying those voices could be effective. After all, though I find that the power of corrections fades and rumors regain their strength over time, both studies demonstrated that the Republican correction remained strong, even after weeks in the midst of a heated real-world debate about the future of health care reform.

Opportunities to debunk rumors through the use of surprising sources might be rare. There are good reasons that politicians might want to foster misinformation about the policies advanced by their opponents—a topic I explicitly turn to in the next chapter. As Hochschild and Einstein aptly note, "Politicians who misinform their hearers may be making the right strategic choice given their goals."[80] Counting on the goodwill of such politicians may be an overly optimistic strategy. However, corrections from unlikely partisan sources may still hold promise. Other scholars show in recent work that unlikely sources can meaningfully reduce misperceptions about voter fraud and climate change and are effective in campaign contexts.[81] Unlikely sources may also serve as credible correctors in nonpolitical settings.

On the other hand, it may be hard to find such silver linings to other troubling results regarding the effects of fluency. Fluency is a powerful force—one that may provide a mechanism for understanding how rumors take hold and persist. Simply asking subjects to repeat the rumor to themselves, without any indication that the rumor is true, increased their willingness to believe the existence of death panels, even weeks after they read the initial story. In the real world, rumors are repeated and cemented in the echo chamber of the internet.[82] This is true not just in the United States, but also in other countries.[83] Thus, the effects found here may play out on a larger scale in a variety of societies. But even given these findings, recent work suggests that backfire effects are not a universal phenomenon and may only appear under a limited set of conditions. As a result, while it remains important to identify the factors that heighten the risk of backlash against corrections, we can also rest easy knowing that such effects are almost certainly rare. Moreover, the power of fluency could be harnessed to increase the effectiveness of corrections. Just as rumors can multiply their power through repetition, perhaps corrections can as well.[84] Future work should explore such possibilities. Until we know how to correct false information, rumors and innuendo will remain powerful forces in politics around the globe, as we will see in the next chapter where I take a close look at the American experience in the time of Donald Trump.

5

Rumors and Misinformation in the Time of Trump

Since kicking off his first presidential campaign in 2015, Donald Trump has not stopped talking about voter fraud. Trump's win in the 2016 presidential election may have caught much of America by surprise, but for Trump, his Electoral College win was not enough. In the weeks after his undisputed victory, Trump repeatedly claimed—without any evidence—that he had soundly won the popular vote as well. For instance, in late November 2016, he tweeted, "I won the popular vote if you deduct the millions of people who voted illegally."[1] This dissemination of misinformation was nothing new for Trump. In fact, it began long before he ascended to the White House; his dogged attachment to the birther conspiracy about Barack Obama's place of birth began back in 2011.[2] It is perhaps not surprising, then, that Trump ended his presidency the same way he started it: by spreading rumors and misinformation. In the late days of the 2020 campaign, he railed against nonexistent voter fraud and insinuated that Joe Biden was controlled by people in "dark shadows."[3]

Biden's win in November did little to stop this rumormongering. Two days after the polls closed, Trump doubled down on his inaccurate claims and declared in a White House press conference, "If you count the legal votes, I easily win. If you count the illegal votes, they can try to steal the election from us."[4] Echoing the president's rhetoric, Trump supporters soon rallied a movement to "Stop the Steal," declaring that Trump had been cheated out of a deserved win. Over a month later, despite dozens of rejected court cases and no conclusive evidence of widespread fraud, Trump continued to spew false claims, tweeting, "Tremendous evidence pouring in on voter fraud. There has never been anything like this in our Country!"[5] His supporters continued to believe him. In mid-December, 38 percent of all registered voters—including 82 percent of Trump voters—believed that Biden was not the legitimate winner of the election, according to a CBS News poll. In the same poll, 49 percent of Trump voters said that if the Electoral College voted for Joe Biden, as expected, Trump should, "not concede, and do everything he can to try to remain for another term as president."[6]

Trump's baseless claims of voter fraud were not without consequences. On the contrary, his accusations of a stolen election turned violent on January 6, 2021, when members of the public attacked the United States Capitol for the first time in over two hundred years. On the day that Congress was set to certify the 2020 presidential election results, thousands of pro-Trump supporters descended upon Washington, DC, to decry the election as fraudulent. At a rally that morning, Trump repeated his unfounded claims that the election had been rigged against him and encouraged his supporters to march to the Capitol, telling them, "You'll never take back our country with weakness. You have to show strength, and you have to be strong."[7] His supporters took these words to heart. Soon after Trump finished his speech, a mob of protestors began to force their way into the Capitol building and quickly breached the perimeter. During the ensuing violence, four rioters and one Capitol Police officer died, and many more were injured.

While it may be difficult to directly attribute this violence to Trump's rhetoric, even after the situation began to escalate, Trump continued to stoke conspiracy theories about the election throughout the day on January 6. In the afternoon, through a video posted online, he claimed that "we had an election that was stolen from us" and "This was a fraudulent election." Later that evening, Trump again appeared to justify the rioters' attack on the Capitol as an impassioned response to voter fraud, tweeting, "These are the things and events that happen when a sacred landslide election victory is so unceremoniously viciously stripped away from great patriots who have been badly & unfairly treated for so long."[8] Trump's rhetoric had seemingly dangerous consequences. A YouGov poll conducted in the aftermath of the insurrection found that 21 percent of all voters supported the events at the Capitol—with substantially higher rates of approval (56%) among voters who believed that a substantial amount of voter fraud had taken place.[9] In this way, Trump's false claims of election maleficence not only clouded the final days of his presidency but also undermined the democratic process, with possible long-term consequences that are just beginning to be realized.

Though Trump's pervasive use of political misinformation—and its centrality to his political career—is unprecedented in some respects, it also represents the culmination of broader trends in American politics. As noted in chapter 2, there is a long history of leaders bending the truth in order to marshal political support.[10] But it is undeniable that Trump's rise to power brought something new to the political scene. Although previous presidents have stretched the truth and even lied at times, what sets Trump apart is the sheer volume of misinformation he spreads, the rate at which he repeats the same (debunked) rumors, and his fixation on claims that are deliberately deceptive, self-aggrandizing, and mean-spirited in nature.

Indeed, the number of false statements Trump has made in his brief political career is striking, to say the least. Throughout the 2016 Republican primary, PolitiFact, an independent fact-checking organization, awarded Trump a "pants on fire" rating—indicating a "statement that is not accurate and makes a ridiculous claim"—more frequently than all other candidates combined.[11] Likewise, during the general election, PolitiFact rated 70 percent of Trump's statements as at least partially false, compared with only 28 percent of Clinton's statements.[12] This penchant for spreading falsehoods extended into his presidency as well. Within his first ten months in office, reporters at the *New York Times* found that Trump made roughly six times as many false statements as Obama made during his entire presidency.[13] According to the *Washington Post*, by the summer of 2020 he had made over 20,000 false or misleading claims.[14]

In another departure from previous presidents, Trump also demonstrated a tendency to repeat many of the same rumors over and over again.[15] In the same analysis as above, the *Washington Post* identified approximately 500 cases in which Trump repeated variations on the same false claim at least three times. For example, on eighty-eight separate occasions, Trump made the incorrect statement that he had approved the largest tax cuts in history.[16] The frequency with which Trump repeated such false claims led the *Washington Post* to create a new category of fact-checking—the "Bottomless Pinocchio," awarded to politicians who "repeat a false claim so many times that they are, in effect, engaging in campaigns of disinformation"—a designation that Trump subsequently received a staggering fifty-six times.[17] In short, over the course of his presidency, Trump not only made a large volume of false claims but also continued to advance these false claims long after they had been resoundingly debunked.

While some of these claims (such as the scope of tax cuts) have clear political implications, many involve trivial details of little political import.[18] Moreover, regardless of its topic, a consistent theme across much of Trump's misinformation is its self-aggrandizing character.[19] For instance, in the beginning days of his presidency, Trump repeatedly boasted about the size of the crowds at his inauguration festivities.[20] However, many of his other false claims were much more inflammatory, such as his assertion that he witnessed thousands of Muslims celebrating after the destruction of the World Trade Center on September 11, 2001.[21]

Trump's use of information is therefore not entirely novel, but its sheer volume is impossible to ignore. Trump's fountain of misleading and inaccurate statements may cause some citizens—especially his loyal supporters—to believe and act upon unsubstantiated information.[22] This endorsement of misinformation has direct implications for political trust and the durability of democratic norms,[23] as evidenced by the account of the allegations of election fraud that opened this chapter.[24] Furthermore, the indirect effects of Trump's misinformation may extend beyond behaviors that are overtly political. For example, Trump frequently vacillated on the seriousness of the COVID-19 pandemic and at times advocated for behaviors—ranging from avoiding masks to injecting disinfectants to do-it-yourself vaccines—that were in direct opposition to public health guidance from officials within his own administration.[25]

This book reflects more than a decade of work on political rumors and misinformation, mostly predating Trump's rise to power. However, it is undeniable that Trump is at least partially responsible for the recent surge in scholarly work on political misinformation. Nevertheless, Trump is not the first, nor will he be the last, politician to spread rumors and stoke conspiracy theories. To the extent that elite misinformation continues to radiate through the public, following the analogy of the "pebble in the pond" described earlier in the book, we may see similar patterns of rumor belief even in a world where Trump's power and influence are greatly diminished.

In the rest of this chapter, I present the results from a series of complementary experiments that explore the consequences of elite endorsements of misinformation—with a particular emphasis on the influence of Donald Trump. The primary shift in focus in this chapter is therefore from the content of rumors to the source of such rumors.

In many ways, the findings of these experiments reinforce the lessons of earlier chapters. In particular, three consistent themes emerge across studies. First, citizens use the source of information as a heuristic for whether it is reliable or unreliable. Those individuals who support a politician are more likely to believe a claim if it is attributed to that politician, whereas those who oppose the politician may become more suspicious of its veracity. As was the case in the analyses presented in the previous chapter, a source's credibility matters. Second, though Democrats and Republicans may hold different beliefs prior to fact-checking, there are minimal partisan differences in how responsive people are to such corrections. That is, responses to corrections appear relatively symmetric across the aisle. Finally, fact-checking seems to temporarily improve the accuracy of individuals' factual beliefs, but it has little to no effect on their support for political leaders. Belief may be somewhat fungible, but support is not. At the same time, consistent with chapter 4, there are also limits to the effects of corrections; while people are generally receptive to fact-checks in the short-term, they quickly revert to their previous beliefs. The remainder of the chapter describes these studies in greater detail and concludes by discussing how these dynamics might operate in political contexts outside the United States.

Exploring Trump's Use of Misinformation

To better understand the effects of Trump's use of misinformation, I—in collaboration with Briony Swire-Thompson, Ullrich Ecker, and Stephan Lewandowsky—conducted a series of experiments assessing how elite misinformation (and fact-checks of such information) affects individuals' belief in particular claims, as well as their support for the candidates who made these claims. A summary of the four main experiments is presented in table 5.1.

The first experiment (Study 1) assessed the dual influence of source cues and fact-checking messages on individuals' factual beliefs and support for political candidates. This study predated the 2016 presidential primaries. We recruited US residents to participate in the study via Amazon Mechanical Turk in November 2015, when thirteen other candidates apart from Trump remained in contention for the Republican nomination. A summary of the experimental procedure is depicted in figure 5.1. Participants were shown eight statements that Trump actually made on the campaign trail. Half of the statements were false, and the other half were true. For example, one of the false statements was "There are 30–34 million illegal immigrants residing in the USA," while one of the true statements was "The US debt is $18 trillion."[26] When shown to participants, these statements were either explicitly credited to Trump or presented without attribution.[27] After viewing each

TABLE 5.1 Summary of Experimental Studies

	Timing	Sample Size	Survey Platform	Politician under Study
Study 1	Nov. 2015	1,776	Mechanical Turk	Donald Trump
Study 2	July 2016	960	Survey Sampling International (SSI)	Donald Trump
Study 3	June 2017	1,500	Mechanical Turk	Donald Trump, Bernie Sanders
Study 4	April–July 2017	370	University Classrooms, Online Polling Companies	Bill Shorten, Malcolm Turnbull

statement, participants rated their belief in each statement's accuracy, using a continuous eleven-point scale (0–10; rather than the discrete categories employed in the analysis in chapter 4). Following this step, they were told whether the statement they had viewed was true or false. The false statements were then corrected and the true statements were affirmed, with evidence provided from a nonpartisan source. (Throughout this chapter, I use the terms "fact-check" or "explanation" interchangeably to describe these messages).[28] Finally, after viewing all eight statements (and their associated explanations), participants re-rated both their belief in each statement's accuracy and their support for Donald Trump. Some participants provided these ratings immediately, whereas others did so after a one-week delay. This first study took place before the first primary, so the Republican presidential candidate was still unknown. We therefore separated Republicans who supported Trump from Republicans who did not support Trump.[29] We also made this distinction between subgroups of Republicans in the second and third experiments.

In the second experiment (Study 2), rather than varying the source of the *statements*, we tested whether the source of the *explanation* influenced how individuals responded to the fact-checking information. This experiment was conducted in July 2016. The Republican primaries were still ongoing at this time, and eleven candidates other than Trump remained viable options. As in Study 1, participants were presented with a series of true and false statements that Trump made on the campaign trail, before reading explanations of whether each statement was true or false. Unlike Study 1, these statements were always explicitly attributed to Trump. However, we

FIGURE 5.1.   Summary of Experimental Procedure

randomly varied whether the explanation referenced a nonpartisan, Democratic, or Republican source. Unlike the experiments presented in chapter 4, these explanations did not refer to specific political actors. Instead, we
used a more generic source cue. Specifically, we randomized the attribution
of the explanation to follow one of three forms: (1) "According to Democrats," (2) "According to Republicans," or (3) "According to a nonpartisan
fact-checking website." Participants rated their belief in each statement and
their support for Trump both before and immediately after reading these
explanations.

The final experiment (Study 3) was conducted in June 2017 and investigated whether there are partisan differences in how citizens respond to
fact-checks of prominent politicians. For this study, we used Bernie Sanders
as a left-wing comparison to Trump.[30] This experiment followed a similar
format as the previous studies. Participants were first shown a series of
accurate and inaccurate statements, made by either Trump or Sanders.
The statements by Trump were drawn from those we used in the previous experiments. For Sanders, we collected a new set of statements. For
example, one of the true Sanders items was "The United States spends
almost three times as much on healthcare per capita as the UK" and one
of the false statements was "ExxonMobil made $19 billion profit in 2009
but paid no taxes."[31] Participants were then informed whether each statement was true or false (using nonpartisan explanations of equal length).[32]
In addition to varying the *source* of the statements (Trump or Sanders),
we also manipulated the *ratio* of false to true statements, such that some
participants saw an equal number of true and false statements and others
saw a disproportionate amount of misinformation. Our goal in doing so
was to understand whether support for politicians decreases to a greater
extent when they are perceived as making substantially more false versus
true claims.[33] Finally, both before and after viewing these statements (and
their associated fact-checks), participants reported their belief in each
statement's accuracy, their perceptions of Trump's and Sanders's general
veracity, and their overall support for both politicians.

SOURCE CUES

These experiments provide insight into the importance of source credibility in shaping how people process political information. Specifically, these studies shed light on three important questions. First, are individuals more likely to believe both true and false statements when these statements are attributed to a prominent (but polarizing) politician they trust, such as Donald Trump? Second, does the efficacy of fact-checking depend on individuals' preexisting support for the fact-checked politician? And finally, does the source of the fact-check itself influence whether individuals update their beliefs in response to new information?

In regard to the first question, we expect individuals to use their prior political support as a heuristic of whether information is likely to be true or false. People tend to be more trusting of statements made by politicians they support and more incredulous of statements made by politicians they oppose. As noted in chapter 3, two key components of source credibility are expertise (the extent to which sources are able to give accurate information) and trustworthiness, (the extent to which sources are willing to provide information that they assume to be correct).[34] Individuals tend to evaluate sources as more credible if they share similar opinions.[35] As a result, it is reasonable to expect that individuals may appraise information differently based on whether it comes from a politician whom they support.

This is indeed what we find across our experiments. One consistent finding across studies is that participants' opinions of the politician making a given claim strongly influenced their assessment of whether this claim was true. For instance, in Study 1, if information was attributed to Trump, the subset of Republicans who supported Trump believed it more than if it was presented without attribution, whereas the opposite was true for Democrats. Figure 5.2 shows how participants' initial belief in each statement's veracity varied based on levels of Trump support, whether the statements were attributed to Trump, and whether the statements were true or false. For both misinformation and facts, attribution to Trump was associated with significantly less belief among Democrats and greater belief among Republicans who supported Trump. Among Republicans who did not support Trump—labeled "Republican nonsupporters"—source attribution reduced their belief in true statements but had no effect on their belief in misinformation. In other words, for this subset of participants, attributing information to Trump undermined its perceived credibility, even when

FIGURE 5.2. Effect of Source Cues on Pre-explanation Belief Score, November 2015

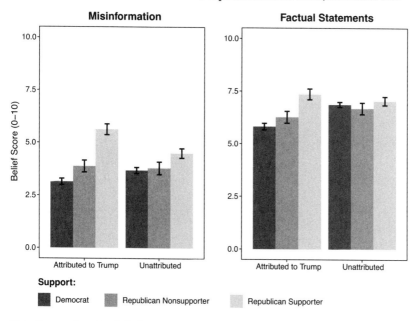

Note: Pre-explanation belief in statements attributed versus unattributed to Trump in Study 1, disaggregated by partisanship and prior support for Trump. Plots are displayed for false statements ("Misinformation," *left*) and true statements ("Factual Statements," *right*). The error bars denote 95 percent confidence intervals. Higher scores indicate stronger belief in the accuracy of the statement. *Source*: Amazon Mechanical Turk, November 2015.

it was actually true. Our statistical analysis suggests that these effects are extremely unlikely to be due to chance.

Figure 5.3 shows that these findings from Study 1 replicate in the second experiment as well. As a reminder, in this second study, all claims were explicitly attributed to Trump. Before reading the fact-checking messages, participants' belief in each statement differed based on their prior support for Trump. Republican supporters believed both true and false statements far more than Republican nonsupporters and Democrats, and Republican nonsupporters believed the information more than Democrats. Though not shown here, in Study 3, similar patterns were evident for both Trump and Sanders. In sum, citizens consistently use partisan cues to evaluate whether the information they encounter is likely to be true. The greater their degree of support for a given politician, the more accepting they are of this politician's statements.

FIGURE 5.3. Pre-explanation Belief Score by Political Support, July 2016

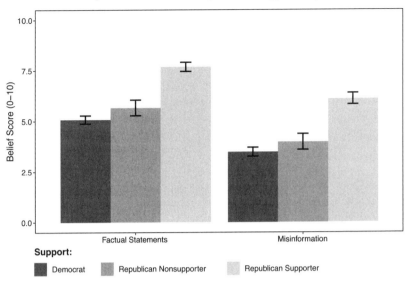

Note: Pre-explanation belief in statements attributed to Donald Trump in Study 2, disaggregated by partisanship and prior support for Trump. Plots are displayed for true statements ("Factual Statements," *left*) and false statements ("Misinformation," *right*). The error bars denote 95 percent confidence intervals. Higher scores indicate stronger belief in the accuracy of the statement. *Source*: Survey Sampling International, July 2016.

The preceding results suggest that individuals' baseline beliefs are conditioned in part on their political allegiances. How effective, though, are fact-checking messages in improving the accuracy of these beliefs? How much does the source of a fact-check matter? Are individuals more receptive to corrections from sources they already trust, such as co-partisan politicians? Or, as was the case in the experiments presented in chapter 4, are corrections from surprising sources—Republicans correcting statements made by Trump—more impactful?

When individuals are told that information they previously thought to be true is false, they may not necessarily update their beliefs accordingly. Instead, the extent to which people actually change their beliefs post-correction may depend on motivated cognition. Specifically, as discussed in chapter 4, individuals may be more likely to resist fact-checks and cling to the original misinformation when the fact-checks run counter to their preexisting beliefs or worldviews. For example, if a Democratic politician's statement is deemed false, Democrats may be more reluctant to accept this correction, relative to their Republican counterparts.

As described in chapter 4, when it comes to correcting misinformation, trustworthiness may be more important than expertise in instilling source credibility.[36] The most effective way to reduce political misperceptions might therefore be to have fact-checks come from sources that individuals trust, such as a member of the political party with which they identify. However, as demonstrated in the same chapter, source credibility extends beyond shared partisan identity. For example, a Republican correcting a fellow Republican could be even more convincing than a source that is expected to be more critical (such as a Democrat).[37] Thus, a Democrat's belief in misinformation originating from a Republican source, such as Trump, may be more strongly mitigated by a correction that comes from a Republican, rather than Democratic, source.

How effective, then, were different sources at improving belief accuracy? By and large, we found that fact-checking messages improved the accuracy of individuals' factual beliefs. In Study 1, there was a large, bipartisan shift in individuals' beliefs in response to nonpartisan explanations. While initial belief in Trump's false statements was higher for Trump supporters, even these supporters were willing and able to adjust their views in response to fact-checking.

However, consistent with the findings in chapter 4, these effects degraded over time for everyone. After a one-week delay, participants in the first experiment partially "re-believed" the misinformation and partially forgot the facts. Thus, even if individuals update their beliefs temporarily, fact-checks seemingly have a short half-life. As a result, once inaccurate information enters the public sphere, it may be difficult to permanently correct. The full trajectory of belief change over time in Study 1 is shown in figure 5.4. The left side of this figure plots belief ratings among participants who were shown statements attributed to Trump, whereas the right side shows belief ratings for participants who were shown these same statements without attribution. Immediately after reading the fact-checks, both Democrats and Republicans displayed a substantial amount of belief change, as evidenced by their stronger belief in true statements and weaker belief in false statements. However, these gains generally diminished over the course of one week for both misinformation and facts.[38]

SOURCE OF FACT-CHECKING

In Study 1, the source of the corrections was uniformly nonpartisan. However, as noted above, it could be the case that explicitly partisan sources—including both co-partisan politicians and so-called surprising sources—may likewise be effective cue-givers. In Study 2, we thus varied the identity of

FIGURE 5.4. Effect of Fact-Check and Timing on Belief Score, November 2015

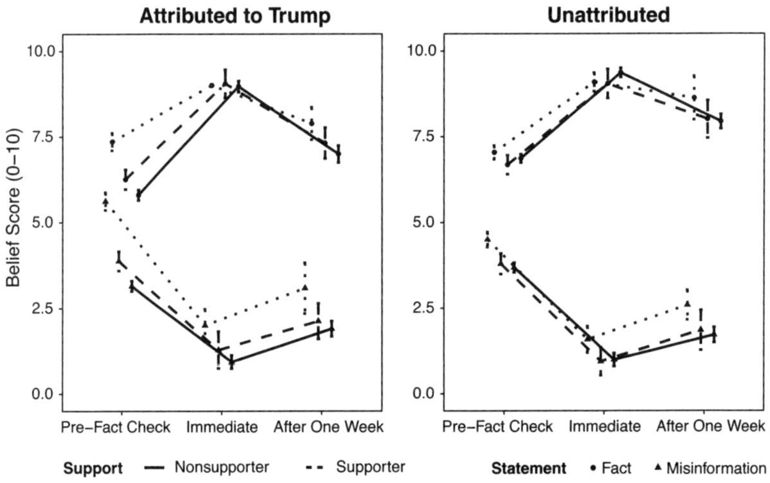

Note: Belief in misinformation and facts in Study 1, disaggregated by partisanship and prior support for Trump. Post-explanation belief score was measured either immediately or after a one-week delay. Plots are displayed for statements that are attributed to Trump (*left*) and statements that are not attributed to Trump (*right*). The error bars denote 95 percent confidence intervals. Higher scores indicate stronger belief in the accuracy of the statement. *Source*: Amazon Mechanical Turk, November 2015.

the fact-checking source (Democratic, Republican, or nonpartisan). To preview our results, we find little evidence that the source of the fact-checking message influenced whether participants updated their factual beliefs. This finding marks a notable departure from chapter 4, which found that corrections from a surprising source (a partisan source correcting other in-party members) were most effective in reducing misperceptions about health care policy. Although at odds with my prior studies concerning the death panel rumors, these results are heartening, in that they suggest that elite misinformation can be corrected even when leaders are unwilling to speak out against their fellow partisans.

Figure 5.5 presents the change in participants' factual beliefs after receiving the fact-checking messages. Immediately post-exposure, both Democrats and Republicans showed a substantial amount of belief change, in the expected direction. That is, their belief in misinformation diminished, and their belief in facts increased. Despite baseline differences in individuals' belief in statements made by Trump, individuals of all partisan stripes seemed amenable to belief change in response to fact-checking information.

FIGURE 5.5. Effect of Fact-Check on Belief Score by Correction Source, July 2016

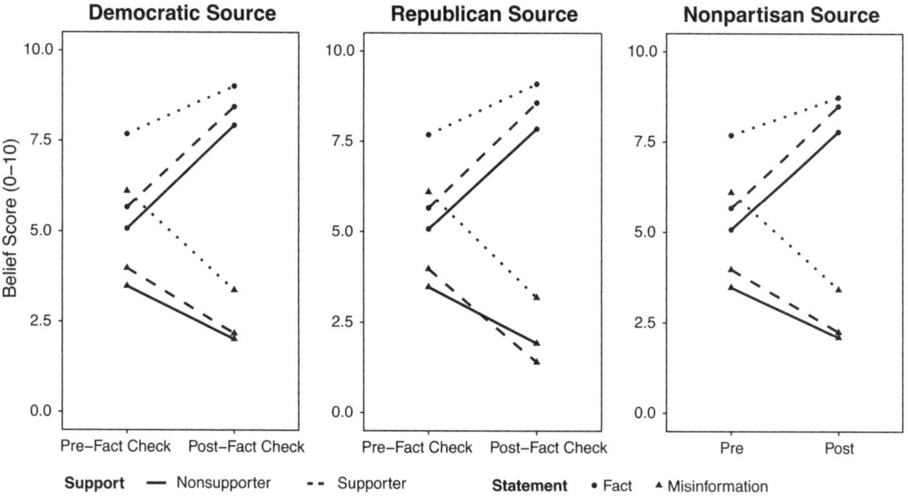

Note: Belief in statements attributed to Trump in Study 2 over time, disaggregated by partisanship and prior support for Trump. The results are displayed across experimental conditions that vary in correction source. The error bars denote 95 percent confidence intervals. Higher scores indicate stronger belief in the accuracy of the statement. *Source*: Survey Sampling International, July 2016.

PARTISAN SYMMETRIES

The previous two studies deal exclusively with statements made by Trump. How symmetrical, though, are these findings across the political spectrum? This question speaks to an ongoing debate over whether liberals and conservatives exhibit cognitive differences that might make the latter group especially susceptible to misinformation. Much of this work begins with the observation that in the United States, misinformation seems to be more prevalent in right-wing circles.[39] The primary explanation for this empirical regularity focuses on individual differences in the personalities of liberals and conservatives. John Jost and his various coauthors have been the preeminent advocates for this line of thinking, which generally builds on principles of system justification theory. System justification theory holds that certain personality traits and cognitive styles predispose individuals to defend the existing social, economic, and political order.[40]

Expanding on this general insight, these scholars argue that these same personality traits and cognitive styles have consequences for the political ideology individuals are likely to adopt.[41] Specifically, individuals with certain personality traits—for instance, those who are less open to new experiences but are conscientious—are motivated to reduce uncertainty and oppose change. These tendencies enhance the attractiveness of a conservative ideology because such an ideology, according to Jost and his colleagues, is centered on resistance to change and acceptance of inequality. Thus, the personality traits that undergird individuals' attempts to manage fear and uncertainty make certain tenets of conservatism especially attractive.[42]

These same personality traits that are correlated with conservatism might also increase one's susceptibility to political misinformation. For example, conservatism is associated with lower reflectiveness, tolerance of ambiguity, and open-mindedness, greater reliance on intuitive (type 1) information processing, and stronger resistance to information that challenges one's worldview.[43] Moreover, conservatives are more likely than liberals to distrust government officials and hold a paranoid ideation, both of which can feed conspiratorial thinking.[44] Taken together, these findings suggest that the same personality traits that lead individuals to embrace a conservative ideology may also predispose them to believe and share misinformation. For scholars who adopt this view, such as Jost and colleagues, partisan and ideological differences in belief in and responses to political misinformation reflect stable, dispositional differences in the composition of the two major political parties in the United States.[45] Conservatives may be less likely than their liberal counterparts to reject rumors about their political rivals because the same personality traits that attract them to conservative ideals also increase their likelihood of engaging in motivated processing of political (mis)information.

However, this literature is not without critics. An opposing strand of research holds that individuals of all political orientations are motivated to discount information that runs counter to their political attitudes and accept information that confirms these attitudes.[46] Along these lines, a number of studies have found evidence of motivated reasoning across the political spectrum—not just on the right. For example, Washburn and Skitka find that both liberals and conservatives were less likely to correctly interpret scientific results when these results conflicted with their prior attitudes.[47] Similarly, Claassen and Ensley find no difference in how Republicans and Democrats reacted to allegations of political malfeasance, such as using dirty campaign tricks.[48] Specifically, they find that both Democrats and Republicans were much more concerned about alleged misconduct when a politician was affiliated with the opposing party than they were about a member of their own party. It is therefore possible that the cognitive pro-

FIGURE 5.6. Effect of Fact-Check on Belief Score by Elite Endorsement, June 2017

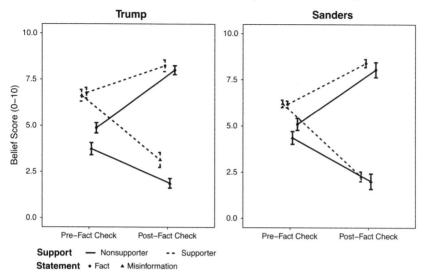

Note: Belief in statements attributed to either Trump or Sanders in Study 3 over time, disaggregated by prior support for Trump and Sanders. The error bars denote 95 percent confidence intervals. Higher scores indicate stronger belief in the accuracy of the statement. *Source*: Amazon Mechanical Turk, June 2017.

cesses guiding political preferences and support are similar across partisan and ideological strata.

Supporting this view, the data from our third experiment point to symmetrical behavior across the political divide. As shown in figure 5.6, all groups were generally responsive to fact-checking messages.[49] Consider first the Trump results in the left panel of the figure. Before viewing the fact-checks, Trump supporters were much more likely to believe his statements than nonsupporters, regardless of whether these statements were true or false. After viewing these fact-checks, however, these differences largely dissipated— particularly when it came to true statements. In addition, though Trump's supporters continued to report significantly stronger beliefs in his false statements, relative to nonsupporters, their overall levels of belief dropped substantially post-correction, compared to their pre-correction baseline.

As shown in the right panel of figure 5.6, a similar pattern emerged for Sanders as well. For participants presented with statements from Sanders, supporters initially reported substantially more belief in both true and false statements, compared with nonsupporters, and were worse at discerning truth from fiction. However, after the provision of fact-checking messages, supporters and nonsupporters exhibited similar levels of belief in both types of statements.[50] This result, it should be noted, differs from the Trump condition, where supporters and nonsupporters maintained some degree of disagreement regarding the misinformation items post-correction. It may be that Trump supporters are so saturated by corrections of his false statements in the media that some have become inured to such corrections.[51]

Finally, it should be noted that we found no evidence of backfire effects in any of our three studies, a result consistent with recent work on this question.[52] That is, in none of our studies did we find any evidence that exposure to fact-checking led to *stronger* belief in misinformation, even when the original misinformation aligned with individuals' partisan identities and previous political allegiances. Instead, fact-checks were similarly effective for both supporters and nonsupporters (and both Democrats and Republicans), increasing belief in true statements and decreasing belief in false statements.

POLITICAL SUPPORT

Across three separate studies, spanning several years and multiple prominent politicians, participants on both sides of the political spectrum updated their beliefs when presented with factual evidence. These results are encouraging, insofar as they suggest that facts still have a place in political discourse. But the good news seems to stop there. In all of our experiments, we found a very small correlation between belief change and levels of political support. That is, updated factual beliefs did not translate into updated support for political candidates. In short, learning that a prominent leader has made false claims seems to have minimal impact on subsequent levels of support. As shown in figure 5.7, in Study 1, correcting Trump's false statements decreased belief in those statements but had no meaningful impact on participants' feelings toward Trump or their likelihood of voting for him. This was true both immediately post-correction and one week later.[53]

This disconnect between factual beliefs and political support was not unique to Trump. As figure 5.8 demonstrates, in Study 3 we found limited evidence that exposure to fact-checking messages diminished support for Sanders either. However, interestingly, we did observe some differences based on the ratio of true versus false statements. When participants were shown an even number of true versus false statements, we saw a similar pattern as in Studies 1 and 2: participants reported virtually identical support pre- and post-correction. On the other hand, when participants were

FIGURE 5.7. Effect of Fact-Check and Timing on Support for Trump, November 2015

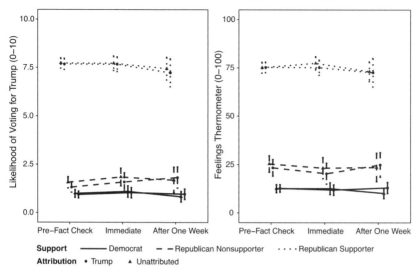

Note: Support for Trump in Study 1 over time, disaggregated by prior support for Trump and source attribution. Post-explanation belief score was measured either immediately or after a one-week delay. Higher feelings-thermometer scores indicate warmer/more positive feelings toward Trump. *Source*: Amazon Mechanical Turk, November 2015.

shown a disproportionate number of false statements, they were slightly less supportive of the politician to whom these statements were attributed, suggesting that politicians who establish a reputation for dishonesty may incur at least some electoral costs. This result is particularly interesting given that fact-checking sites consistently acknowledge that Trump makes far more false statements than other politicians, including Sanders.

However, on the whole, it appears that politicians who disseminate misinformation face few political ramifications. Why might political support be largely impervious to fact-checking? Several dynamics could be at play. First, this disconnect could reflect the fact that attitudes and behavioral intentions may be more consequential, and therefore more difficult to change, than specific factual beliefs. Even if supporters and nonsupporters have strong feelings toward Trump, those core attitudes need not constrain their views on the particular issues discussed in the presented statements, such as the total cost of the Iraq War or the exact levels of voter turnout in the 2016 election. Thus, people may be able to update their factual beliefs without having to modify their overarching attitudes and political support.

FIGURE 5.8. Ratio of True to False Statements on Support for Trump and Sanders, June 2017

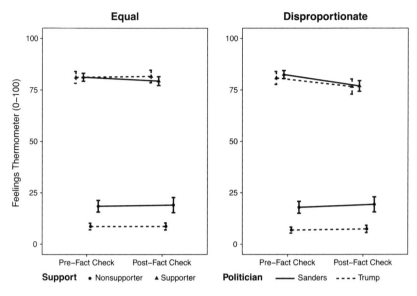

Note: Changes in political support in Study 3 based on the ratio of true to false statements made by Trump or Sanders. In the "Equal" condition (*left*), participants were shown four true and four false statements. In the "Disproportionate" condition (*right*), participants were shown only one true statement but again saw four false statements. Results are disaggregated by prior political support and source of information. The error bars denote 95 percent confidence intervals. Higher feelings-thermometer scores indicate warmer feelings toward the politician. *Source*: Amazon Mechanical Turk, June 2017.

Another possibility is that voters simply do not care if politicians lie. Events that influence trust, such as political scandals, often affect people's voting preferences.[54] However, politicians' reputations are surprisingly resilient: more than half of US incumbents implicated in scandals are subsequently reelected.[55] Along these lines, recent work argues that "lying demagogues" can maintain authentic appeal among certain groups not in spite of but rather *because* of their lying.[56] Specifically, politicians who make blatantly false claims can distance themselves from the mainstream political establishment by flouting recognized norms of truth telling. In doing so, they may be able to enhance their perceived authenticity among supporters who feel alienated by this establishment. However, people might also rationalize their preferred candidates' false statements as unintentional errors, rather than deliberate attempts to deceive. Perhaps being perceived as inaccurate is less costly than being perceived as dishonest or immoral.

Alternatively, it could be the case that the scale of misinformation matters, such that large effects are only seen after reaching some (unknown) tipping point. In Studies 1 and 2, participants were shown as many accurate as inaccurate statements–an approach that perhaps obfuscated the rate at which Trump actually spread misinformation. In other words, we might have presented a version of Trump that was overly truthful. Had they been shown a more accurate picture of Trump's fact-checking record—the one that led the *Washington Post* to create a new "bottomless Pinocchio" category— supporters might have been more likely to change their attitudes.

Would our results have differed, then, if participants had learned that a politician they favored tends to tell mostly lies? As shown in Study 3, the answer is yes, but not by much. When we varied the ratio of true ver- sus false statements, we found that higher rates of misinformation were met with a harsher rebuke, but the effects remained small. These results are consistent with previous research suggesting that negative information about a preferred candidate might not decrease favorability ratings unless the amount of negative information reaches a sufficient magnitude.[57] In this way, individuals' voting preferences and political support may only shift when politicians have been implicated in the spread of large quantities of misinformation. This dynamic likely operates primarily among supporters versus nonsupporters. Nonsupporters of both Trump and Sanders did not reduce their favorability for either politician, regardless of the ratio of mis- information displayed, largely because their attitudes were already at a floor. The potential for negative information to shift attitudes seems therefore to be conditional on prior levels of support.

That disproportionate presentations of misinformation did (slightly) impact feelings toward both candidates is positive for society, as reminders of the fact that reputational risks incentivize politicians to be more truth- ful.[58] However, the small size of this effect must make us question verac- ity's place in contemporary US democracy. If people have already decided they support a politician, fact-checking may do little to disabuse them of this notion. People may not do a good job of keeping a running tally of inaccuracies versus truthful statements. Alternatively, they may do a poor job of integrating new information—in this case, fact-checks—into their overall assessments. Regardless of the mechanism, the result is the same: fact-checking seems unable to effectively hold politicians accountable for spreading misinformation.

More broadly, the lack of reputational consequences is just one of sev- eral limitations to corrections. Study 1 also suggested, for example, that the effects of fact-checking are ephemeral at best.[59] Even if people are able to change their beliefs immediately post-correction, such belief change may be fleeting. Further, an individual's previous worldview and political preference may influence the durability of corrections, leading to patterns of "motivated forgetting."[60] For example, if a Democratic politician is fact-checked, Democrats who support this politician may initially update their factual beliefs but conveniently forget the correction at an accelerated pace, thus eventually reverting to their preexisting beliefs.

Misinformation beyond the American Political Context

Though this book largely focuses on the American political context, misinformation is not simply an American problem. To situate our experimental results in a comparative context, my co-authors and I fielded a final study in Australia that employed a similar empirical framework as our previous experiments (Study 4). As in Study 3, our design enabled us to contrast the effects of misinformation from two contemporary politicians—one on the right, one on the left—who were otherwise comparable across other dimensions.

Between April and July of 2017, we recruited an Australian sample consisting of 370 participants from the University of Western Australia and online polling companies. In place of Trump and Sanders, we used statements from the Australian leaders of the left-wing Labor Party (Bill Shorten) and right-wing Liberal Party (Malcolm Turnbull).[61] As context, Turnbull and Shorten were particularly well-suited for comparison, as they were similarly unpopular with Australian voters at the time of the study and, despite their ideological differences, were perceived as similar, occasionally even being referred to in the Australian media as "terrible twins."[62] As with our earlier experiments, we used real statements from these politicians. For example, one of the true statements was about the youth unemployment rate in Australia, and one of the false claims was about average commute times. As in Study 3, we varied the ratio of true to false statements for each politician, in order to assess whether the effects of fact-checking on political support differ based on the perceived frequency with which each politician makes false claims.

Following our previous studies, we hypothesized that fact-checks would decrease support for these politicians—but only when the number of false statements far outstripped the number of true statements.[63] Overall, we largely replicated our findings in the US context. However, we found that corrections had much larger—and more negative—effect on support for Australian versus American candidates.[64] One limitation, though, was that this study did not assess whether changes in factual beliefs and political support persisted over time, raising the possibility that these larger effects may have been fleeting, as they were in Study 1.

Similar to the previous findings, the fact-checking messages were again effective in changing peoples' factual beliefs, regardless of their political ideology. By and large, participants did not reject the fact-checks, even if the original statements came from politicians they supported. In fact, the corrections decreased belief in false claims to a *greater* extent if the false statements came from a favored politician. It is important to note that the types of statements presented were potentially less likely to challenge individuals' core values and therefore were less likely to provoke motivated reasoning. Nevertheless, the fact that participants across multiple countries were open to changing their beliefs in response to corrections bodes well for combatting misinformation worldwide.

The most significant difference between the American and Australian studies, however, was in their response to differing rates of misinformation. Within the Australian sample, we found—consistent with the American sample—that participants did not shift their feelings toward either politician when presented with an even number of true and false claims. However, when participants were shown substantially more false than true statements, we observed a much larger reduction in political support in the Australian context. That is, Australians responded strongly and harshly to high rates of misinformation, whereas American voters hardly shifted their support. These results suggest that cultural context may shape people's expectations of politicians and their responses to political deception.

Although we cannot be certain of the origins of these cross-national differences, several factors may be at work. First, politicians may only suffer political consequences for spreading misinformation when participants expect politicians to be truthful. There is good reason to believe that such expectations may be more prevalent in the Australian context. The Organization for Economic Cooperation and Development (OECD) in 2017 reported that citizens' confidence and trust in the national government was 45 percent in Australia but only 30 percent in the United States.[65] If Australians are more trusting of government officials, they may be more punitive toward politicians who spread falsehoods. Second, preferential voting has pushed Australian politics toward the center, whereas in the United States the two major parties advocate for fundamentally different policy agendas.[66]

United States citizens may therefore be more likely to maintain support for politicians who engage in wrongdoing, as the policy differences across parties are comparatively stark (and their dislike toward those on the opposite side of the political spectrum is notably greater).[67] The electoral costs of misinformation may therefore be more severe when citizens feel they have viable alternatives. Finally, one major difference between the American and Australian political systems is that voting is compulsory in the latter country.[68] As a result, Australian citizens may express dissatisfaction with politicians by downgrading their support, as simply not voting is not an option. Nevertheless, despite these important contextual differences, it does not seem to be the case that Trump is unique—but rather that Americans may generally react differently to misinformation than individuals in other countries.[69]

Conclusion

Although elite misinformation has long been a feature of American political life, Donald Trump has taken the dissemination of such information to new heights. Whether espousing conspiracy theories about his predecessor's place of birth or casting doubt on election results, Trump repeatedly and persistently pushed the boundaries of acceptable behavior for national leaders—and did so with seemingly few consequences for his own political fortunes. The experiments presented in this chapter provide some insight into this phenomenon. Both the supporters and opponents of Trump shared one important characteristic: people were more likely to believe statements made by politicians they supported and less likely to believe statements by politicians they opposed—regardless of whether these statements were true or false. Further, while efforts to correct elite misinformation effectively reduced political misperceptions, they seemed to have little impact on support for politicians who make false claims.

These findings are especially concerning for democracy, because they do not appear unique to Donald Trump. Instead, Study 3 shows that both left- and right-wing individuals seem equally susceptible to misinformation, albeit similarly responsive to fact-checking messages. Though Trump's presidency has ended (for now), the existence of relatively weak association between factual beliefs and political evaluations implies that politicians who disseminate misinformation will continue to emerge and are likely to find success when they do. Although our third experiment—and our Australian replication—suggests some limits to the amount of misinformation politicians can spread without compromising their reputations, it is clear that the use of misinformation is not inherently disqualifying for either Democrats or Republicans. However, the lack of partisan asymmetries within a controlled survey environment does not mean that misinformation is comparable across Democratic and Republican circles in the real world. In the next chapter, I explore the consequences of differences in the structure of partisan information environments for individuals' endorsement of misinformation and responses to corrections.

6

The Role of Political Elites

The previous chapters have shown that in many ways, Democrats and Republicans demonstrate strikingly similar patterns of behavior when it comes to misinformation. The observational data in chapter 3 showed that both Democrats and Republicans in the mass public are more likely to believe rumors when such rumors target the opposing party. Moreover, the experimental data in chapters 4 and 5 demonstrated that members of both parties are willing to update their beliefs when presented with corrections—including of rumors concerning the existence of WMD in Iraq, rumors about provisions in the ACA mandating death panels, and misinformation spread by elites. But there are also important differences across party lines. Republicans seem more willing to accept rumors about Democrats than the reverse. Is this difference a result of inherent differences between liberal and conservative ways of thinking, or is it a symptom of something different?

To better understand this asymmetry, I move my attention to the producers of misinformation, turning somewhat from the discussion of the mass public—the believers, the disbelievers, and the uncertain. I draw on longstanding theories of public opinion formation to argue that disparities in rumor rejection between Democrats and Republicans may arise from the top-down way that many citizens come to understand the political world. I posit that asymmetry in the patterns of rumor rejection at the mass level at least partially stems from differences in how Republican and Democratic elites discuss and respond to political rumors.[1] This position is consistent with general theories about the structure of mass opinion in American politics but stands in contrast to several existing explanations in political science and psychology, which attribute variation in the volume and type of misperceptions held by Democrats and Republicans to individual-level differences in genetic, personality, and cognitive characteristics. These explanations focus on the demand-side aspects of misinformation and frame individual responses to rumors as a bottom-up process. As chapter 3 made clear, these factors are undoubtedly important, but we also need to pay attention to the structure of the larger information environment. Specifically, if we focus only on the behavior of consumers of misinformation, we will miss important features of the production side of political misinformation—in particular, the manner in which elites talk about rumors.

Republican politicians interact with rumors differently than their Democratic colleagues do. These discrepancies in elite engagement with the information environment are in turn reflected in mass opinion. Notably, I find that the amount of attention elites have devoted to political rumors and the force with which those rumors are corrected varies substantially across the two major parties. Republican leaders generally seem to spread rumors at a higher rate than Democratic leaders, and when they speak out against rumors, they tend to issue softer corrections that fall short of rejecting the rumors outright. These differences in the flow of discourse among groups of elites spill over to mass opinion.

There are important normative stakes in figuring out whether differences across party lines stem more from consumers in the mass public or producers among the political elite. Of course, both top-down and bottom-up processes almost certainly play a role in the spread of misinformation. But their relative balance matters greatly for diagnosing the causes and consequences of misinformation in the current political environment. If differences in rumor acceptance are primarily a function of personality traits or cognitive processes, democratic disorder can be traced directly back to the preferences of citizens. But if rumormongering among the mass public is largely a product of elite behavior, then the dysfunction runs from the top down. As I have argued elsewhere, members of the mass public are only as competent and wise as their leaders give them the resources to be.[2] Given the distractions of their day-to-day lives, most citizens are only tangentially engaged with the world of politics and therefore delegate the time-consuming task of collecting and evaluating information about complex political events to politicians and other political elites with whom they identify.[3] If those trusted sources introduce rumors into the information ecosystem, then the public is far more likely to accept them. In turn, this suggests that combatting the spread of rumors depends on the restraint of the same partisan political actors who politically benefit from their perpetuation—a tall order to be sure.[4] As my analyses of the ACA experiment in chapter 4 demonstrate, sources speaking out against their partisan interests are the most effective in combatting rumors. But if elites are part of the problem, then we cannot necessarily rely on such corrections to emerge organically, particularly among members of the Republican Party. To the extent that there is an imbalance in the willingness of politicians across the two parties to spread and amplify political rumors, this imbalance will be reflected in the public's embrace of these rumors.

The Conditional Effects of Political Information

To begin this discussion, I return to the observational data on patterns of rumor acceptance and rejection discussed earlier in the book. In chapter 3, I explored how personal disposition and partisan motivation interact to foster acceptance of political rumors. But these two variables are not the only correlates of support for political rumors. Building on my earlier work, I demonstrate here that levels of political information are also an important component of individuals' belief in political rumors.

At the close of chapter 3, I showed that higher levels of political information—measured as the number of correct answers to factual questions about politics—are associated with higher rumor rejection rates, regardless of the partisan content of the rumors.[5] Consider the July 2010 study that was the primary focus of that chapter: figure 6.1 presents the relationship between information and rumor rejection levels, aggregating across all seven rumors measured in this study—those that target Democrats, those that target Republicans, and the nonpartisan Roswell rumor.[6] In the aggregate, those respondents who are more politically engaged are more likely to reject rumors of *all* partisan stripes. This relationship holds for rumors about both Democrats and Republicans, though the slope on the Democratic rumor line is, admittedly, not particularly steep (see figure 6.2). In short, respondents with higher observed levels of political information are more likely to reject rumors—regardless of their target.

This analysis could be taken as evidence that political information is a universal salve that can cure the ills of political misinformation. Indeed, many of the proposed solutions to the problem of misinformation—particularly in political science—have assumed that the proper remedy to a lack of information is to provide citizens with *more* information. This work is based on a long intellectual tradition tracing back to the early days of behavioral

FIGURE 6.1. Relationship between Political Information and Rumor Rejection,
July 2010

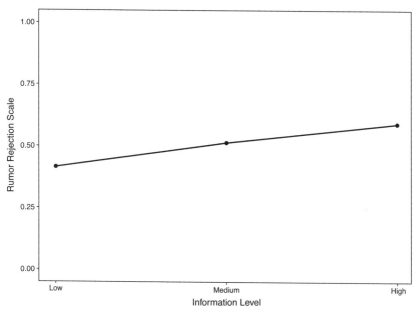

Note: The plot shows the average rumor rejection score across levels of political
information, aggregating across seven rumor items (refer to table 1.1). Higher scores
indicate weaker belief in the veracity of the statements. *Source*: YouGov, July 2010.

survey research. A large and enduring body of scholarly work documents
widespread gaps in political knowledge among the American public.[7]

But is more information really the cure?[8] The analysis and discussion in
the previous chapters should make the reader skeptical that this observed
relationship between political information and rumor rejection could be easily translated into a policy recommendation. In particular, the ACA experiments demonstrated that providing people with correct information does
not, in all cases, improve rates of rumor rejection, especially in the long run.

Furthermore, any remaining hope that information in and of itself could
serve as a remedy for misinformation may be dashed after examining the
relationship between political information and rumor rejection more closely.
As chapter 3 demonstrated in detail, partisanship profoundly shapes the way
that citizens process political rumors. What happens when we introduce
that factor into our analysis? Accounting for the partisanship of the respondents complicates the relationship between information and rumor belief in

FIGURE 6.2. Relationship between Political Information and Rumor Rejection by
Rumor Target, July 2010

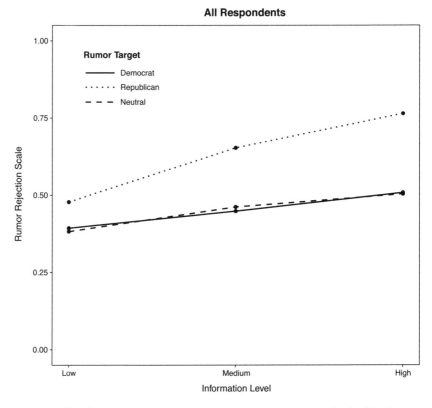

All Respondents

Note: The plot shows the average rumor rejection score across levels of political
information for Democrat-based, Republican-based, and neutral rumors (refer to
table 1.1 for a complete list of rumor items). Higher scores indicate weaker belief in
the veracity of the statements. *Source*: YouGov, July 2010.

important ways. In particular, I find that the relationship between political
information and rumor rejection is heavily conditioned by respondents'
partisan predilections.

Returning to the analysis of the 2010 data, figure 6.3 replicates the analysis of figure 6.2, but does so separately for self-identified Democrats and
Republicans.[9] As figure 6.3 shows, Democrats follow the pattern observed
to this point: regardless of the target of the rumor, respondents with higher
levels of information are more likely to reject rumors about both Democrats and Republicans. Although Democrats are more likely to reject rumors
about fellow Democrats than they are rumors about Republicans, the rates
of rumor rejection generally increase with levels of political information

FIGURE 6.3. Relationship between Political Information and Rumor Rejection by Rumor Target and Respondent Partisanship, July 2010

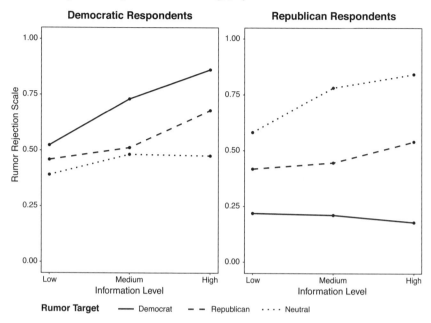

Note: The plots show the average rumor rejection score across levels of political information for Democrat-based, Republican-based, and neutral rumors (refer to table 1.1 for a complete list of rumor items). Separate plots show this relationship among Democratic respondents (*left*) and Republican respondents (*right*). Higher scores indicate weaker belief in the veracity of the statements. *Source*: YouGov, July 2010.

across all types of rumors. However, among Republicans, the patterns are very different. Whereas high-information Republicans are more likely than low-information Republicans to reject rumors about Republicans, high-information Republicans are—if anything—*less* likely than low-information Republicans to reject rumors about Democrats. That is, Republicans who are better informed about and more engaged with politics are more likely to endorse negative rumors about Democrats.

This asymmetry cannot be explained away by the particulars of this one data-collection effort. In an aggregate analysis summarized in figure 6.4, I cast a much broader net across a wide range of surveys (summarized in table 3.1), encompassing many different years and rumors.[10] The partisan differences in the relationship between political information and rumor rejection shown in figure 6.3 are found here as well. When it comes to politically neutral rumors, such as rumors about UFO sightings, Democratic

FIGURE 6.4. Relationship between Political Information and Rumor Rejection by Rumor Target and Respondent Partisanship, Aggregate Analysis

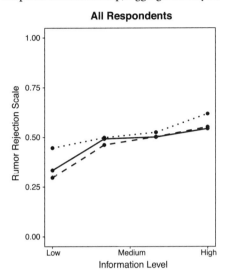

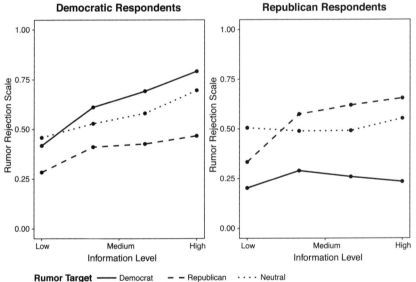

Note: The plots show the average rumor rejection score across levels of political information for Democrat-based, Republican-based, and neutral rumors (refer to table 1.1 for a complete list of rumor items). Separate plots show this relationship among all respondents (*top*), Democratic respondents (*bottom left*), and Republican respondents (*bottom right*). Higher scores indicate weaker belief in the veracity of the statements. There are four categories of information in this graph, compared with the three-category measure employed in the July 2010 study, because the larger size of the pooled sample allows use of a finer-grained measure.
Source: Aggregation of Surveys (summarized in table 1.1)

and Republican partisans behave nearly identically: as information levels increase, so too do rates of rumor rejection. A similar pattern characterizes Democrats' response to partisan rumors—increased levels of political information are associated with increased rates of rumor rejection, regardless of the target of the rumor. For Republicans, though, increased levels of information are associated with increased rumor rejection rates only for rumors about Republicans. For rumors that target Democrats, the relationship between political information and rumor rejection is essentially flat. These patterns of rumor belief again underscore the broader point from chapter 3: when it comes to political rumors, where you stand depends in large part on where you sit. At least for Republican respondents, partisanship provides a strong barrier to rejecting rumors—even among those Republicans who are highly engaged with the political world.

Other work has likewise highlighted the role of partisanship and ideology in conditioning the relationship between political knowledge and belief in rumors and conspiracy theories. Using some of the same data—including the ANES questions that Eric Oliver and I helped design (see chapter 3 for discussion)—Miller and colleagues also find that higher levels of political knowledge increase the likelihood that conservative respondents endorse conspiracy theories targeting the ideological Left, but the same relationship does not hold for liberal respondents.[11] Polling data from Fairleigh Dickinson University in 2012 also evinced these same partisan asymmetries: Democrats were more likely to reject conspiracy theories when they knew more about current events, whereas high-information Republicans became less likely to reject them.[12]

These patterns extend beyond conspiracy theories to other types of political rumors. For instance, Nyhan found in two separate surveys from 1993 and 2009 that Republicans who self-identified as knowing more about health care reform proposals from the Clinton and Obama administrations were the least likely to reject false rumors about those plans.[13] Similarly, Nyhan, Reifler, and Ubel found that Republicans were more resistant to corrections about rumors about health care reform when they demonstrated higher levels of political knowledge.[14] Finally, in a study of rumors that Obama manipulated official Bureau of Labor Statistics unemployment numbers before the 2012 election, Nyhan found that Republican "respondents with high political knowledge are paradoxically less likely to believe the unemployment statistics are accurate than those with low or medium political knowledge" and are "more likely to believe the statistics are being manipulated."[15] For Democrats, on the other hand, greater knowledge correlates with higher rates of rumor rejection. All in all, there is substantial evidence—accumulated from numerous studies tracking a diverse range of rumors and conspiracy theories—that political information is associated with opposing patterns of rumor belief for Democrats and Republicans.

However, though my results are consistent with the work of these scholars, their analyses raise more questions than they answer. The observational data discussed thus far provide evidence of some intriguing relationships, but they cannot tell us *why* Democrats and Republicans exhibit such divergent patterns of rumor rejection across levels of political information. Are Republicans more innately prone to false beliefs than Democrats? Such stark differences between the two groups would be somewhat puzzling given the symmetries found in the Sander and Trump experiment presented in the last chapter. Or is there something in the current information environment that feeds this asymmetry? In other words, does the fault lie with the people or with the politicians? In the rest of this chapter, I will bring to bear additional observational and experimental evidence in an attempt to answer this question.

Why the Divide? The Potential Role of Personality

Why might Republicans and Democrats in the mass public react in different ways to political rumors? As discussed in depth in the previous chapter, some scholars argue that the difference has something to do with the way in which members of the two parties process political information. To briefly recap that discussion here, these scholars argue that conservatives fundamentally differ from liberals in their personality traits and cognitive styles.[16] As a result of these personality differences, conservatives in the mass public may be more likely than liberals to engage in motivated processing of political (mis)information and therefore more likely to endorse rumors about their political rivals. Along these lines, Miller and colleagues posit that belief in conspiracy theories serves both an ideological and psychological function.[17] In particular, similar to my argument in chapter 2, they assert that belief in conspiracy theories is highest when individuals possess three traits: a *conspiratorial mindset* that engenders lower levels of trust, a commitment to a particular *ideological worldview*, and the *political sophistication* necessary to make connections between conspiracy theories and this worldview. They find, consistent with the results above and my earlier analysis, that this last dimension—political knowledge—operates differently for conservatives and liberals: Whereas conservatives exhibited higher levels of conspiracy endorsement as political knowledge increased, these same patterns were not visible for liberals. Over the last thirty years, partisanship and ideology have become increasingly intertwined in the United States.[18] Perhaps, then, Republicans may exhibit stronger belief in attitude-consistent rumors, compared with Democrats, because conservatives are more prone to motivated reasoning than are liberals.

However, other researchers make the case that motivated reasoning occurs among citizens *across* the political spectrum—not just those on the political right.[19] Frimer, Skitka, and Motyl, for example, find that both conservatives and liberals are willing to forgo cash payments to avoid hearing opposing views on the same-sex marriage debate.[20] Similarly, Guay and Johnston use an experiment to test whether "need for certainty"–a core personality trait associated with conservatism—increases politically motivated reasoning.[21] They find that, though political conservatives do report a higher need for certainty, this desire for certainty does not increase the likelihood of engaging in politically motivated reasoning. Instead, they find more symmetry than asymmetry between conservatives and liberals in the extent to which they engage in politically motivated reasoning. Taken together, these works cast doubt on the extent to which personality and cognitive traits underlie partisan differences in belief in political rumors—much less explain why the observed information gradient is as large as it is.

Elite Discourse and the Supply Side of Misinformation

These previous approaches to conceptualizing rumor belief focus on the individual-level characteristics that make rumors particularly appealing to certain audiences. However, understanding the flow of rumors through society also requires an examination of the supply of information available to consumers. In chapter 2, I introduced the metaphor of the pebble in the pond. When considering the spread of any rumor throughout society, I argued that we can identify the creators, believers, disbelievers, and uncertain groups of individuals. The latter three groups are primarily situated in the mass public and have been the primary focus of the empirical results presented thus far. But it is also important to consider the kinds of messages sent by the creators and hard-core believers at the elite level. The balance of these elite signals, and the way in which they shape the larger information environment, can greatly influence the structure of mass opinion.

As V. O. Key aptly noted, "the voice of the people is but an echo. The output of an echo chamber bears an inevitable and invariable relation to the input [of political leaders]."[22] Similarly, in other work, I have likened elite discourse to radar: elites send "signals" about how events in the political world relate to their constituents' interests, and citizens with similar political predispositions echo back public opinion that is consistent with those signals.[23] That is, elite discourse helps members of the public connect a political rumor to their underlying predispositions and values, which they might not otherwise see as salient to their interests. Within this framework, we might understand the asymmetry between Republicans and Democrats by considering how political elites talk about rumors—which outlooks are sent into the mass public and "echoed back," to use Key's language. The more attention an individual pays to the political world (as indexed by their level of political information) the more likely they are to receive these signals—and the more likely they are to echo back the gist of those rumors. This argument differs from previous individual-level approaches to characterizing rumor belief, in that it focuses less on the relative tendencies of individuals in the mass public to engage in motivated reasoning and instead emphasizes the top-down role of elites in providing cues to individuals about which rumors to believe and which to reject.

As I will demonstrate in the next section, there are two primary ways in which elite discourse on rumors differs between Democrats and Republicans. The first is the *volume* of rhetoric—how much Democratic and Republican elites actually talk about rumors. The second is the *tone* of corrections issued. Broadly speaking, corrections can range from firm corrections that definitively rebuke the rumor (e.g., "this is completely false") to soft corrections that equivocate and hedge (e.g., "I don't believe this, but people are entitled to their own opinion"). The later type of correction is often akin to what Muirhead and Rosenblum term "support without responsibility."[24] Although some recent studies find limited evidence that the tone of corrections shapes their effectiveness, these studies have largely focused on corrections issued by other social media users.[25] I depart from this approach by examining the frequency and content of corrections issued by party elites and other prominent political figures.

The extant literature on communication identifies several sources of uncertainty that might affect the perceived credibility of information communicated to the public by such elites, such as adding caveats or by emphasizing the limitations of the information at hand.[26] For instance, highlighting the uncertainties of scientific knowledge may alter public perceptions of scientists' competence, compromising the perceived credibility of information.[27] Similarly, drawing attention to elite disagreement on an issue may also decrease confidence in presented claims.[28] In the remainder of this chapter,

I consider how such variation in elite discourse around misinformation might shape the beliefs of the mass public.

Both the volume and tone of elite discourse could influence mass beliefs via the mechanisms already explored in this book. First, if multiple elites within a given party call attention to a particular rumor, this repeated activation of the rumor might enhance its credibility. Indeed, as chapter 4 discussed, repeated exposure to rumors increases their plausibility simply because the content feels more intuitively familiar. Moreover, even if political elites do not endorse rumors outright, their failure to decisively reject these rumors might facilitate their continued spread, as chapter 3 highlighted when discussing the significance of "don't know" responses to questions about rumor beliefs. Collectively, a high volume of rumors and weak corrections can thus instill strong rumor beliefs among a broad swath of the mass public. Low volume and strong corrections, by contrast, may expose fewer people to rumors and make them more likely to reject these rumors out of hand. If different groups of elites—Democrats and Republicans—talk about these rumors in different ways, we would expect to see the resulting echoes through divergence in mass opinion along partisan lines.

To understand the consequences of these differences between the parties, it is first important to establish that differences in the volume of rumors and the tone of corrections across parties actually exist. To this end, I collected and analyzed two sets of observational data to help establish the nature of the (mis)information landscape. This analysis strongly suggests that the patterns of discourse across party lines have been highly imbalanced in the last several years, with Republican leaders more likely than Democratic leaders to both spread misinformation and issue weak corrections. However, these results do not necessarily imply a causal relationship between elite rhetoric and mass opinion toward rumors. I therefore next turn to a series of experiments designed to test this relationship more systematically. This controlled environment makes it possible to identify the potential effects of this rhetoric more precisely than with observational data alone. However, the results of these experiments are notably mixed. Consistent with previous work, I do not find evidence that the tone of corrections meaningfully alters rumor beliefs.[29] That said, my experimental results nonetheless replicate some of the observational results that both Democrats and Republicans are more likely to believe rumors about politicians from the opposing party, suggesting that patterns of elite conflict can spill over into the mass public.

The Information Ecosystem

To understand and quantify the balance of elite discourse, we need to systematically examine that discourse. One way to measure the volume of elite misinformation might be to look at fact-checking websites. Indeed, a number of existing works examine the relative quantity of fact-checks across the two political parties as a means of estimating partisan asymmetries in the spread of misinformation.[30] However, fact-checking sites may not provide an objective measure of partisans' propensity to disseminate rumors and conspiracy theories. In particular, the focus of these fact-checks may not reflect the balance of misinformation in the larger environment. Fact-checking organizations cannot check every story, so they must pick and choose which stories to investigate.[31] For example, during former president Donald Trump's time in office, fact-checkers focused their resources on correcting the unprecedented volume of misinformation he spread, which may have hampered their ability to track and rebut false claims made by other political figures. Moreover, empirically, there is little overlap in the particular statements checked across different fact-checking organizations, suggesting potential selection bias in the topics—and politicians—they choose to fact-check.[32] Consequently, instead of focusing on fact-checks of individual claims, another possibility is to identify outlets that systematically spread misinformation and track how often political elites share content from those sources.

In line with this alternative approach, I examined the extent to which political elites shared links to misinformation on Twitter. While Twitter itself may not be representative of the larger information ecosystem, as a public space Twitter is an extremely useful platform for tracking the spread of misinformation by political elites. Members of Congress primarily use it to advertise their political positions and disperse political information.[33] Moreover, one in four voters use the platform; political accounts are among the most followed on Twitter; and 70 percent of Twitter users get political news through the site, which they trust more than information received through other social media channels.[34] Perhaps most importantly, Twitter plays a large role in setting the overall media agenda: it is one of the most-used websites by journalists for their job.[35]

To characterize the flow of information on Twitter, I employed data collected by the Lazer Lab consisting of tweets by individual members of Congress from the beginning of 2019 through November 2020. These data recorded the frequency with which members of Congress shared content from disreputable outlets.[36] Following Grinberg and colleagues, I distinguish between different types of untrustworthy news sources.[37] For presentational purposes, however, I focus on a measure that indicates whether the online news-rating tool NewsGuard classified a given source as generally failing "to meet basic standards of credibility and transparency."[38] Because this classification applies to the *domain* rather than to the particular story or content shared, in the analysis that follows I implicitly assume that any link to one of these disreputable outlets is a link to a piece of misinformation. In addition, because I measure spreading misinformation simply based on the presence of a link to a domain classified as untrustworthy, and do not consider the valence of the language that accompanies the link, I also assume that any link shared is an endorsement of that piece of misinformation rather than a refutation—an assumption that is supported by previous academic work in this area.[39] But, it should be noted, to the extent that elites are resharing links to refute them, such a process might overstate my estimates. In this sense, the test here should be seen as a conservative test of my theory. In addition, the results shown below are robust to the use of the alternative measures of low-credibility sites that Grinberg and colleagues employ; regardless of which measure I use, I find that Republicans in Congress share far more links to untrustworthy websites than do Democrats.[40]

Figure 6.5 shows the rate of tweets shared by Republicans and Democrats that contained a link to an outlet classified by NewsGuard as "fake news," normalized by the total tweet activity for each party.[41] The disparity is striking. Though the rates of sharing are admittedly small for this type of content, Republicans share links to untrustworthy sites far more frequently than do Democrats. This pattern persists if I limit the analysis to just those "super spreader" representatives who rank among the top five percent of members of Congress sharing misinformation on Twitter.[42]

Moreover, the partisan gap is also evident if we focus on the *number* of members of Congress who spread misinformation, rather than the total rate of misinformation spread. Figure 6.6 shows the percentage of Democratic and Republican political leaders with Twitter handles who shared *at least one* link to a site that publishes misinformation, as identified by News-Guard. While over 60 percent of Republican leaders with Twitter handles shared at least one link to an untrustworthy news site on Twitter, just under 40 percent of Democratic leaders did so. As noted above, the fact that misinformation is coded at the domain level may inflate these estimates.

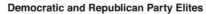

FIGURE 6.5. Rate of Sharing Links to Fake News Outlets on Twitter

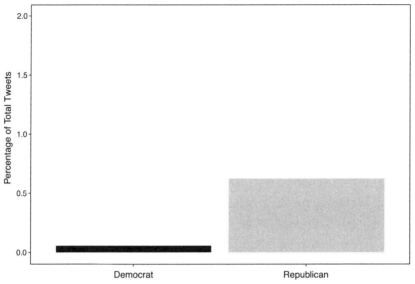

Note: The graph shows the percentage of total tweets shared by Democratic and Republican party elites that contained a link to a fake news outlet. *Source*: Lazer Lab, 2019–2020.

FIGURE 6.6. Percentage that Shared at Least One Link to a Fake News Outlet on Twitter

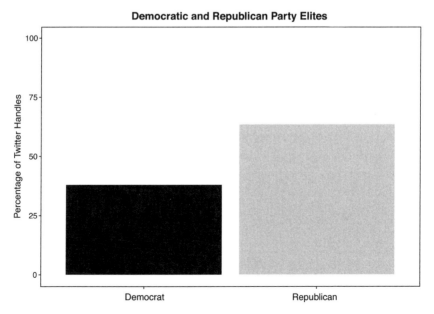

Note: The graph shows the percentage of Democratic and Republican party elites with Twitter handles who shared at least one link to a fake news outlet. *Source*: Lazer Lab, 2019–2020.

Further, as also noted above, some of these links may be shared along with a warning or rebuttal, rather than as an endorsement. Regardless, engaging with and sharing content from a source that regularly disseminates misinformation could plausibly be seen as an endorsement of its credibility. This over-20 percentage point difference between Democratic and Republican political leaders offers suggestive evidence that Republican and Democratic politicians present systematically different pictures of the political environment to their followers. The resulting message here is clear: Though some Democrats publicize information from fake news outlets, Republican elites do so far more often.[43]

THE TONE OF CORRECTIONS

Measuring the tone of corrections also requires the collection of new data. To this end, I collected statements from elites concerning specific rumors that were reported in major media outlets. In particular, I used LexisNexis to search print and television stories about several of the political rumors discussed in earlier chapters. I began by collecting articles that referenced the following three rumors: "birther" rumors that Obama was not born in the United States, rumors that Obama is a Muslim, and claims of voter fraud in Ohio in the 2004 presidential election.[44] I selected these rumors because they span the political spectrum and were all widely circulated (and therefore received ample media coverage). However, while we tried to search as comprehensively as possible *within* each rumor by employing a variety of search terms, it is important to note that these are not intended to be a representative sample of all political rumors.

From the stories identified via the search terms, I extracted statements from elites—including politicians, officials, journalists, and other public figures—that addressed the rumor, and I identified the party membership of each elite. In some cases, the statement was a direct quote, and in others, the text was a paraphrase of a statement.[45] I then tasked a team of researchers with coding whether the statement was a "definitive correction" that is clear and does not contain statements that may weaken or undercut the correction, or a "soft correction" that refutes the rumor but also contains language that undermines the initial correction or fosters ambiguity as to whether or not the rumor is true.[46] However, in this initial attempt, I struggled to achieve acceptable levels of agreement among the coders. The lines between definitive and soft corrections were simply not clear enough that these coders always agreed which was which.[47]

FIGURE 6.7. Crowdsourced Strength of Rumor Corrections by Partisanship of Corrector

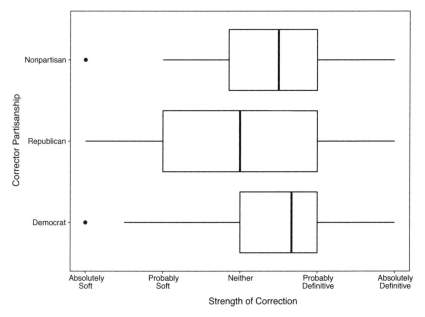

Note: The plot shows the relationship between corrector partisanship and the crowdsourced strength of the correction. I measured the strength of the correction using a five-point scale ranging from "Absolutely Soft" to "Absolutely Definitive." *Source*: Independent rating collected via workers on Amazon Mechanical Turk.

Rather than abandoning this venture, I shifted my strategy to a crowd-sourced measure. I recruited a number of individuals to rate the tone of the collected corrections on a five-point scale ranging from "absolutely defini-tive" to "absolutely soft," with each individual rater coding multiple state-ments.[48] I then estimated the mean strength of the correction by combining data from each individual respondent's assessment of its strength.

Figure 6.7 presents the distribution of the resulting estimates of correc-tion strength, broken down by the partisan identity of the individual who issued the statement. Fifty-three of the statements rated came from Republi-cans, while thirty-one came from Democrats. Where the corrector was non-partisan, or the partisan identity of the corrector was unclear, we labeled them "nonpartisan."[49] This figure makes clear that Republican leaders generally pro-vide weaker corrections than Democratic leaders when they do offer such cor-rections. These results again support the claim that the rhetoric of Republican elites differs in both tone and substance from their Democratic counterparts.

EXPERIMENTAL EVIDENCE

The observational evidence above supports the argument that elite discussion of political rumors varies along party lines. Republican elites seem to spread rumors at a higher volume and to correct them with a softer tone—or they do not correct them at all. Given theoretic expectations, we would expect these signals from Republican elites to be echoed by Republican members of the mass public—especially those individuals who are aware of and pay close attention to elite rhetoric. But this evidence is merely consistent with such a story, not dispositive. To identify this relationship more clearly, I turn to experimental evidence that manipulates the specific nature of elite discourse to evaluate its effects on mass opinion.

Before doing so, however, it is helpful to revisit the results of experiments presented in chapters 4 and 5, which also shed light on these theoretic claims. In these previous studies, I found only limited evidence that Democrats and Republicans process political rumors in innately different ways. Instead, both sets of studies underscore the key role of elites in shaping mass belief in political rumors among both Democrats and Republicans. For instance, in chapter 4, I found that the mere act of repeating a rumor can make it more difficult to correct. As a result, if Republican leaders are more likely to repeatedly disseminate rumors, as we saw in the previous section, then we would expect Republicans in the mass public to be more likely to endorse these rumors. Consequently, the partisan differences in sharing of misinformation on Twitter shown earlier may contribute to more persistent rumor belief among Republicans.

Furthermore, the studies in chapter 5 suggest that partisan asymmetries in rumor belief are not likely to originate in personality or dispositional differences between conservatives and liberals. In these studies, I find that both Democratic and Republican respondents used elite cues as a heuristic for judging the accuracy of political claims, rating statements as more likely to be true (or false) when they came from a politician they supported (or opposed). Moreover, respondents across the aisle updated their factual beliefs after receiving corrections of misinformation—regardless of whether the original misinformation was attributed to a politician they supported or opposed.[50] Taken together, these results suggest that an imbalance in exposure to elite discourse has important ramifications for the types of beliefs that citizens adopt.

Whereas these previous experiments used actual rumors from the political world, this chapter presents the results of two studies that used *hypothetical* rumors in an effort to exert greater control over the information presented to respondents. Using real versus constructed rumors imposes a trade-off between providing naturalistic treatments and controlling for background influences. The former enhances the external validity of the findings, but it increases the possibility that people's responses are shaped by their preexisting awareness of and exposure to information about particular rumors. Using hypothetical rumors allows me to circumvent these concerns about prior familiarity, thus enabling me to better assess the specific theoretical claims made in this chapter about the influence of elite discourse on belief in political rumors.

The goal of both experiments was to test whether the *identity* of the corrector—a Democratic or Republican elite—and the *tone* of the correction—definitive versus soft-interact to affect rates of rumor rejection for both Democratic and Republican respondents. This design essentially holds information about the rumor itself constant but experimentally manipulates three variables: (1) the partisanship of the rumor's target, (2) the partisan identity of the individual correcting the rumor, and (3) the tone of this correction. With this design, I can explore whether elite signals have the same effect among both Democrats and Republicans. If citizens from both parties respond in the same way to elite rhetoric, it should give us greater confidence that elite rhetoric is an influential mechanism in the real world.

The first hypothetical rumor concerned campaign finance. Following Thorson, I chose campaign finance as the subject because it was a story that could plausibly taint both Democratic and Republican politicians.[51] Specifically, the story presented respondents with allegations that a candidate in a congressional election in Indiana had improperly accepted money from foreign donors. Unlike the rumors about the ACA examined in the last chapter, this design has the advantage of testing a single rumor that could plausibly implicate both parties. This makes it possible to explore if the partisan asymmetries in rumor acceptance seen in the real world are mirrored in a controlled experimental setting—that is, whether Republicans are more likely to accept rumors about Democrats than the reverse.[52] As noted above, the study's design varied three main dimensions. First, I manipulated the *partisan identity of the rumor's target*. In other words, I varied whether the politician accused of campaign finance violations was a Democrat or Republican. Second, I varied whether the *source of the correction* was attributed either to a Democrat, a Republican, or a spokesperson for a nonpartisan group. Finally, I varied the *strength of the correction* to be either definitive or soft.[53]

This experiment turned out to be a mixed bag of sorts.[54] Most notably, I did not observe a significant difference in rates of rumor rejection based on whether the source issued a definitive or soft correction. More puzzlingly, though, I failed to replicate consistent findings from past experiments on political rumors. For example, I find no difference in rumor beliefs based on whether the correction came from within or outside the respondent's political party, although I did find that citizens were more willing to accept the rumor if it was about members of the opposing party.[56] This suggests that the problem might have been with the materials used in the experiment, rather than the theoretical mechanism it was designed to test. One possibility is that the rumor itself was too pallid. When comparing claims about campaign finance violations to the types of eye-catching rumors that actually circulate in the political world, the campaign finance rumor may simply not have been colorful enough to elicit much of a reaction. Likewise, the rumor in question focused on the potentially illegal actions of a single individual—a far cry from some of the more wide-ranging conspiracies afoot in real-world elite discourse.

To address these concerns, I fielded a second experiment with a more dramatic (albeit again constructed) rumor: that the government was planning to resurrect controversial mind-control experiments.[57] Specifically, the vignette suggested that the government had revived CIA experiments from the 1950s and '60s related to mind-control techniques. Although the rumors of this program's revival were purely fictional, the previous CIA experiments actually took place; in the original MKUltra project, the CIA used dangerous drugs on "unwitting test subjects, like drug-addicted prisoners, marginalized sex workers and terminal cancer patients."[58] Unlike rumors about campaign finance irregularities, then, these mind-control rumors were more evocative of other types of high-stakes conspiracies requiring coordinated action by government actors. Replicating the design of the campaign finance reform experiment, I varied the target of the rumor, as well as the strength and partisan source of the correction. To make the rumor applicable to either party, the Republican condition attributed the resurrection of the program to the Trump administration, whereas the Democratic condition claimed the experiments were restarted toward the end of the Obama administration. The soft correction included phrases such as "it all seems a little odd to me," compared to the definitive correction's rebuke that "there is absolutely no truth to this claim," and attributed the rumor's origin to bored conspiracy theorists.[59]

As with the campaign finance experiment, respondents in this study do not seem to respond differently to definitive and soft corrections (fig. 6.8).

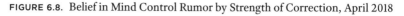

FIGURE 6.8. Belief in Mind Control Rumor by Strength of Correction, April 2018

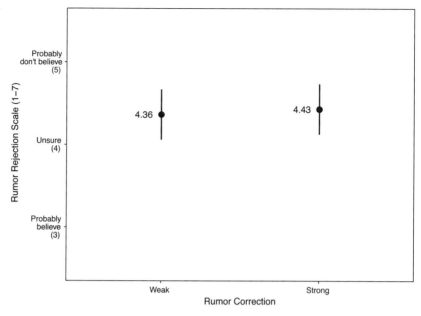

Note: The point estimates represent the mean rumor rejection score for weak and strong corrections. The lines represent the 95 percent confidence intervals. *Source*: Survey Sampling International, April 2018.

The rumor rejection scale on the y-axis is a continuous measure constructed from questions asking respondents whether they believe the government is involved in a secret mind-control program, and whether they felt strongly or not about their belief. A person who scores seven on the scale is someone who strongly disbelieved the mind control story, a four is someone who was not sure—even when pressed to choose—and a one is someone who strongly believed the story. There is, however, one wrinkle to the story. Figure 6.9 highlights modest differences in rumor correction rates when we compare rumors corrected by an "unlikely" source (someone from a different party) to rumors corrected by a "likely" source. I partially replicate the previous finding that corrections from "unlikely" sources are more powerful when a rumor pertains to a copartisan. Here, it is people from the opposite party that represent such an unlikely source. In sum, the mind-control experiment provides additional evidence that partisan symmetries exist in rumor beliefs, but it falls short of empirically confirming the theoretical intuition that the way elites talk about rumors is an important factor in shaping those beliefs.[60]

FIGURE 6.9. Belief in Mind Control Rumor by Rumor Target and Corrector, April 2018

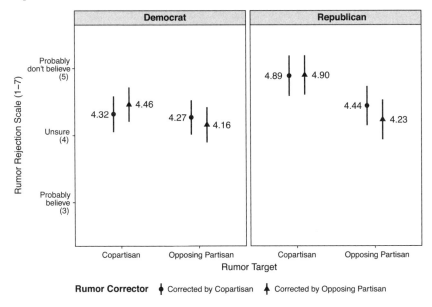

Note: The point estimates represent the mean rumor rejection score for rumors that target politicians of the same party as the respondent ("Copartisan" rumor target) and politicians of the opposite party as the respondent ("Opposing Partisan" rumor target). These results are disaggregated by the partisanship of the person who issued the correction (copartisan = same party as the respondent; opposing partisan = opposite party as the respondent). Results are shown for respondents who identify as Democrats (*left panel*) and respondents who identify as Republican (*right panel*). The lines represent the 95 percent confidence intervals. *Source*: Survey Sampling International, April 2018.

Conclusion

Elites play a fundamental role in mass politics, and this is no less true in the realm of political rumors than it is in the realm of mainstream issues. I focus on the producers of information and the structure of the information environment. Differences in the mass public reflect differences in how political elites communicate, both in terms of the volume of misinformation they share and in the tone that they take when correcting rumors. My research shows how political elites may perpetuate political rumors by differentiating the way Republicans and Democrats spread rumors through the volume of rhetoric and tone of corrections issued. Overall, I found that Republican elites are more likely than Democratic elites to spread misinformation and to issue weaker corrections to political falsehoods when they do discuss the veracity of such claims. Because Republican politicians are the ones who are more likely to add fuel to the fire, it also implies that followers of the Republican Party are more likely to be exposed to political rumors and therefore are more susceptible to them.

However, the impact of such differences in the world of politics remains unclear. I conducted two experiments to test whether differences in the tone of the correction have an impact on rumor rejection rates. While the experimental results do not provide definitive support for these claims, they confirm that unlikely sources make a difference when correcting misinformation. Further research is necessary to clarify the mechanisms behind these dynamics, but there is strong evidence that there are partisan differences in the structure of the information environment. Thus one conclusion is clear: attributing the problem to members of the mass public overlooks the important role that elites play in eroding the information ecosystem. Political elites may not necessarily create rumors, but they can certainly exacerbate the problem by magnifying the work of the creators.

7

Conclusion

In an 1822 letter to W. T. Barry, James Madison wrote, "A popular Government, without popular information, or the means of acquiring it, is but a Prologue to a Farce or a Tragedy; or, perhaps both."[1] Whether we, as a country, are in the midst of a farce or a tragedy is an open question, but one thing is certain: our society is in trouble.

Throughout the summer of 2022, with the midterm elections in sight, many public figures were still litigating the outcome of the long-settled 2020 presidential election in the court of public opinion. In June Peter Navarro, the former White House trade adviser under President Trump, refused to comply with a subpoena from the Select House Committee to Investigate the January 6th Attack on the United States Capitol regarding his involvement in a plan intended to delay certification of the Electoral College votes and send them back to state legislatures. This plan followed on the heels of a thirty-page report Navarro released in the month before the insurrection on purported election fraud with three chapters: "The Immaculate Deception," "The Art of the Steal," and "Yes, President Trump Won."[2]

Such sentiments were common among Republican elites. Indeed, a belief that the 2020 election was stolen was widespread among the leading Republican candidates for office in the November election. Kay Ivey, the governor of Alabama, ran a reelection ad in April 2022 claiming, "The fake news, big tech, and blue-state liberals stole the 2020 election from President Trump."[3] Of the 159 election deniers whom Trump endorsed for office in the 2022 election cycle, over 80 percent won their Republican primary contest.[4]

Furthermore, the *Washington Post* found that among the six battleground states that decided the 2020 vote—Arizona, Georgia, Michigan, Nevada, Pennsylvania, and Wisconsin—candidates who refused to accept the legitimacy of the presidential election claimed almost two-thirds of the GOP nominations for state and federal offices having authority over conducting and certifying elections.[5]

Specific allegations of malfeasance surrounding the election were numerous. Activists in North Carolina and Ohio claimed that voting machines were connected to the internet and hacked. An associate of MyPillow executive Mike Lindell, the prominent Trump ally who spent millions of dollars promoting allegations that the 2020 election was stolen, claimed to have discovered secret algorithms used to rig the election.[6] And a since-deleted tweet that went viral claimed that over 14,000 dead people voted in Wayne County, Michigan, a county that Joe Biden carried with 68 percent of the vote.[7]

Individually, such rumors might gain only limited traction. But, collectively, this tsunami of rumors and misinformation can snowball and compound doubt among large swaths of the mass public. As the evidence presented in this book has shown, the total impact of a political rumor can be greater than the sum of its individual parts. Looking at recent public opinion polls, this does indeed seem to be the case: uncertainty and skepticism are pervasive. A June 2022 YouGov poll found that 36 percent of all citizens thought voter fraud was "widespread" in the 2020 election, and a further 17 percent were unsure. Moreover, among Republican identifiers, a 65 percent supermajority of Republican identifiers believed voter fraud was widespread during the 2020 election, and another 11 percent were unsure.[8] The rumors and innuendo that have persisted in the wake of the 2020 election certainly have undermined public confidence in our democratic system.

This current state of affairs should come as little surprise. After all, Madison warned of the dangers that might arise when the public could not come to a shared understanding of political reality. What this means for the future of this country remains to be seen. But we are at a difficult moment, and there are no easy paths forward.

Summary

I began this book by exploring the meaning and consequences of political rumors and misinformation in the United States. In chapter 2, I conceptualized political rumors and provided a brief overview of the role rumors have historically played in American politics. While such rumors are by no means a new phenomenon, there has been a resurgence recently in scholarly and public interest in misinformation and conspiracy theories. Moreover, the rise of the internet, and social media in particular, has offered rumor producers new platforms with which to spread false information and allowed them to reach audiences that would not ordinarily see or seek out this content. Rumors have therefore become ubiquitous in modern society, as visible to the wider public today as they have ever been, if not more so.

I then explicitly considered the relationship between political rumors and their audience. Rumors, broadly speaking, are a form of misinformation that arises not only from a deficiency of facts but also from the presence of unsubstantiated information. In addition, rumors are characterized by their social transmission, both on and offline. Specifically, I analogized the movement of rumors through society as akin to tossing a pebble in the pond, with rumors' potency decreasing in strength as they ripple outward from their original source. I argued that rumor transmission begins with a core group, known as the creators, who manufacture and disseminate a particular rumor—the actors who drop the pebble in the water. People in the next group, the believers, absorb the strongest ripples and accept the rumor as truth. Disbelievers, on the other hand, lie far from the center, where the ripples are weakest, and reject the rumor as false. In between the believers and the disbelievers lie the uncertain. Members of this group fail to completely reject or accept the rumor. While this final group is a collection of heterogeneous individuals— disengaged citizens who are detached from politics, skeptical individuals who question official information, and the truly unsure—together they form a politically consequential group of citizens who inadvertently lend credibility to rumors by failing to repudiate them. Anyone who does not fully reject a rumor contributes to its validity and reinforces the overall doubt and skepticism surrounding political facts.

In the final portion of chapter 2, I explored how the current media environment facilitates the spread of political rumors. Historically, rumors spread primarily via word of mouth. But with the rise of mass media, the internet, and social media, there are many more paths by which rumors can travel. As a result, rumors can quickly spread beyond their creators and core group of believers to individuals who might not encounter or seek out the information on their own. They may therefore permeate a broader swath of the public as people are incidentally exposed to mistruths on their social media feeds and other internet platforms. This type of exposure can be particularly consequential because it can increase familiarity with unsubstantiated beliefs, thereby moving individuals from the outer ring of disbelief to the ring of uncertainty. Repeated and persistent encounters with misinformation might not just increase rates of rumor acceptance but could also lead people to become uncertain, thereby bolstering the credibility of rumors.

In chapter 3, I moved to the empirical study of political rumors using a variety of experiments and survey data I collected over ten years. In a series of surveys, I measured belief in various rumors that cover a broad range of political topics, from claims about President Obama's citizenship to conspiracies concerning illegal immigrants voting in presidential elections. In general, I found that many people are not prepared to outright reject rumors, and that the group of believers and the uncertain comprise a critical mass of the citizenry—over half the public in many cases. Moreover, the believers are sincere in their beliefs, and these beliefs are relatively stable over time.

I next explored the factors that shape patterns of rumor belief in the mass public. Overall, I argue that there are certain kinds of people who are generally more likely to embrace rumors than others. Specifically, the key to understanding who fails to reject political rumors is to examine the interaction of personality and political predispositions. On one hand, I find there is an underlying tendency that leads individuals to embrace rumors regardless of their content. However, I also find that politics plays a critical role in shaping belief. Individuals process rumor information through a partisan lens; Democrats are drawn to rumors that impugn Republican policies and politicians and vice versa. It is the combination of these two factors—conspiratorial dispositions and partisan motivations—that explains acceptance of conspiracy belief. Rumors find the greatest support among citizens who are both conspiratorially inclined and deeply partisan.

In chapter 4, I moved from examining the content and correlates of rumor beliefs to exploring strategies to correct them. While there is no "silver bullet" solution to rectify the problem of misinformation, this does not mean that we should give up all hope—the search for the perfect need not come at the expense of implementing the good. I outline one possible solution for increasing the proportion of the public who actively reject rumors. While the content of a corrective message is important, so too is the identity of the person delivering that correction. In particular, I found that corrections delivered by "surprising sources" are most effective in correcting misinformation. These surprising sources can be partisan agents who speak out against their own apparent political interests. A politician correcting the rumors that would benefit them is a costly signal. In my experiments, my unlikely source was a Republican politician who corrected the death panel rumor—a rumor that implicates the Democratic Party. I find this type of correction to be the most powerful treatment for *both* Republican and Democratic identifiers. Thus, turning partisanship on its head in the form of a surprising correction can help combat the spread of deleterious political misperceptions across citizens from both sides of the partisan aisle.

While my findings point to the potential effectiveness of surprising corrections, however, they also identify a number of limitations. First, as further work in chapter 5 showed, the use of surprising sources to deliver corrections does not ensure success in all cases. But even when these corrections increase rates of rumor rejection, their traction can be limited. Prior research suggests that corrections have a diminishing effect over time. Confirming earlier research, I find that the effects of even the strongest corrections—surprising sources from Republicans debunking health care rumors—fade over the course of a week. More troublingly, I find evidence that the strength of a rumor can be increased through repetition. Specifically, asking respondents to rehearse the content of a rumor increases its familiarity and thereby reinforces belief in the rumor. Respondents did not simply become more uncertain of the rumor's veracity, but they were actually more likely to believe the rumor after repeated exposure. Thus, it may be easier to make a rumor stronger than it is to make that rumor go away. This result is especially powerful given that, precisely because of their social nature, rumors are typically repeated and commented on in the current political discourse.

Later in chapter 5, I more explicitly considered the relationship between political rhetoric and mass rumor belief. I presented the findings of a series of four experiments conducted between 2015 and 2018 that test the effect of elite endorsements of misinformation, with a particular emphasis on Donald Trump. While elites have long employed misinformation for personal and political gain, Trump's penchant for spreading falsehoods has heightened interest in the consequences of political misperceptions since he first announced his candidacy in late 2015.

Four notable findings emerge from these experiments. First—and perhaps not surprisingly—I found that citizens use their prior political support as a heuristic for whether information is likely to be true or false. For instance, if information was attributed to Trump, Republican supporters of Trump believed it more than if it was presented without attribution, whereas the opposite was true for Democrats. Second, there appears to be only a slight asymmetry across individuals who identify with different ideologies in their resistance to correction. While I found some evidence that corrections are less effective among Trump supporters than Sanders supporters, these differences are not large. Individuals of all ideological stripes are generally responsive to fact-checking messages. Contrary to the claims of some scholars, there is minimal evidence that conservatives are less responsive to rumor corrections compared to liberals. Third, as noted above, I also find some qualification of my conclusions in chapter 4 of the importance of "surprising sources." In chapter 4 I found that the source of the fact-checking message influenced whether the respondents updated or "corrected" their beliefs. In the context of the experiments presented in chapter 5, I did not find evidence of such dynamics, suggesting that no correction strategy can serve as a universal salve. Future research should explore the limitations of unlikely sources and the context under which they are most successful. Finally, the results of the studies conducted by my co-authors and myself have important implications concerning the use of misinformation as a political strategy. Individuals who updated their factual beliefs did not, on average, lower their support for political candidates. The Australian experiment underscores that this distinction between belief and support is not necessarily a universal phenomenon. But, in the United States at least, spreading misinformation may carry few costs for the perpetrator because elites do not appear to be substantially penalized by voters for participating in campaigns riddled with misinformation.

In chapter 6, I conclude my analysis by moving from an exclusive focus on the *consumers* of rumors and misinformation to an examination of the *producers* and *purveyors* of such falsehoods. In previous chapters, I have shown that partisan attachments play a critical role in how individuals process rumors and their correction. In other words, I argue that the composition of the pool of believers depends heavily on one's partisan attachments. But in the final section of my book, I argue that these partisan differences are at least partially attributable to top-down processes at the elite level—namely, differences in the composition of the pool of creators.

Revisiting the analyses I originally presented in chapter 3, I began with observational data on the patterns of rumor belief in the public. In general, I find that increased attention to politics—as indexed by levels of factual political information—is associated with a greater propensity to reject rumors. But this is not the case across the political spectrum. For Democratic identifiers, increased levels of political information are associated with increased rates of rumor rejection, regardless of the partisan target of the rumor. For Republican identifiers, however, increased levels of political information are associated with *decreased* rates of rumor rejection when the target of the rumor is Democrat. That is, Republicans who are more knowledgeable about politics are *less* likely than Republicans with lower levels of knowledge to reject rumors that maligned Democratic actors. Thus, while there are partisan differences in the rates of rumor rejection across all levels of political information, the difference in rates of rumor rejection between Democratic- and Republican-targeted rumors increases as attention to politics increases—and this difference is much greater for Republican respondents than for Democratic respondents.

The remaining portion of chapter 6 focused on addressing *why* Democrats and Republicans exhibit such divergent patterns of rumor rejection across levels of political information. To explore the role of political elites in shaping these differences, I examined two types of data—one a set of political tweets and the other a set of press coverage of political rumors—to help establish a more nuanced picture of the (mis)information landscape. The analysis strongly suggests that patterns of elite discourse diverge sharply along party lines. Most notably, at the time of the study, Republican leaders were much more likely to spread misinformation and issue weak corrections, compared with their Democratic counterparts.

However, these descriptive studies only allow us to explore the correspondence between elite discourse and mass opinion. To address questions of causality, I also conducted two survey experiments that varied the partisan identity of elites who correct misinformation and the tone of their correction. Interestingly, I do not find that the tone of the correction—whether it was definitive or soft—influences individuals' rejection of rumors. That said, my results nonetheless replicate prior findings that both Democrats and Republicans are more likely to believe rumors about politicians from the opposition party, suggesting that patterns of elite conflict can indeed spill over into the mass public.

In any case, the absence of evidence of a direct causal link between elite rhetoric and mass opinion is not evidence of the link's absence. Over seventy-five years of public opinion research have demonstrated the centrality of opinion leaders in shaping the beliefs of the mass public. Given these dynamics, it is impossible to understand the current landscape of political misinformation without understanding the role of elites in propagating this misinformation. To this end, I find striking differences in rumor dissemination and correction across parties. Although future research is needed to better understand the relationship between the supply and demand side of political rumors, these initial results suggest that attempts to curb the spread of misinformation must start at the top. As I have written elsewhere, in a democratic society, citizens are only as good as their leaders. In this time of pervasive rumors and misinformation, our leaders are clearly failing us.

Where Do We Go from Here?

This book is not without hope, but it does not tell a happy story. I started my research over a decade ago, asking why it was that ordinary citizens consistently cling to fanciful stories about political figures and events. I wanted both to understand political behavior and to craft the tools that could help disrupt the vicious cycles of suspicion and mistrust created by political rumors and misinformation. I have made far more progress on the former goal than on the latter. That is unsatisfying but not surprising, given the state of the United States and other countries around the world.

Rumors and misinformation are here to stay. They have been here for a long time and they are not going away anytime soon. So what should we do? One thing is readily apparent: There will not be any simple solutions to the problems posed by rumors and misinformation; there is no magic formula or code to break. Instead, we must struggle as best we can with the messy problems that lie at the intersection of individual cognition and social relations.[9]

That said, just because the problem is difficult does not mean that we should give up. Instead, we should think holistically and broadly about the problem. No one is going to find a simple cure-all solution to eradicate belief in misinformation and rumors. No one scholar or team of scholars is going to save us. What we need is an all-encompassing strategy that attempts to counter misinformation and rumor in many different ways at many different points in the process of their spread—a Swiss cheese model of rumor mitigation. This means correcting misinformation and limiting its dissemination. That is, we need to target both the suppliers of misinformation and the consumers of misinformation through a variety of strategies.

To begin, limiting the dissemination of rumors is crucial because of how individuals process information. As I have discussed, the repetition of a rumor can breed familiarity. Familiarity, in turn, can breed fluency—an easier recall of misinformation. And fluency can eventually lead to acceptance. To break this cycle, we need to account for the behavior of suppliers of information—the statements of politicians and other political elites. In a society in which most citizens most of the time do *not* pay close attention to politics, the nature and tone of what politicians *do* successfully communicate to the public critically shapes how people think about mainstream political issues. There may be a fine line between exaggeration and truth when it comes to political rhetoric, but the line between supported claims and misinformation is much starker. When politicians veer toward the misinformation side of the line, their actions and words can have effects that reverberate through society. Any solution to the problem of rumor and misinformation would ideally involve holding responsible political elites more accountable for their behavior.

But, in practice, such change will be extraordinarily difficult. Political actors do not necessarily have incentives to behave in such a manner—and, in fact, may profit from the spread of rumors. As leaders have long known, while political misinformation and rumors may adversely affect the health of society as a whole, individual bad actors can derive immense political benefit from dissembling and confusion. As my analysis in chapter 5 demonstrates, in the contemporary United States these same politicians do not lose political support even when their supporters learn they are not telling the truth. The suppliers have little intrinsic incentive to change their behavior, so we should not assume they will. Thus, while reducing the dissemination of rumors and misinformation by political elites could, in theory, be an effective solution to the problem, in practice we must recognize that the spread of false rhetoric from politically prominent figures will likely continue.

Given the current environment and an ongoing supply of rumors and misinformation, it is important to think about how best to minimize the impact of debased elite discourse at the level of the individual. Such work begins with a question of which kinds of people we should try to target our efforts toward. When I began this work, I thought the answer was clear: we should focus on trying to convert those individuals who willingly accept political rumors—the believers, to use the parlance of this book. Over time, I have come to realize that this group should not be the only object of influence. We must also target uncertain citizens, who neither accept nor reject rumors. These individuals are important because the failure to reject a rumor—even as the result of disengagement or skepticism—can help that rumor spread. That is, we must attempt to deal with the broader circles of belief described in my analogy of the pebble in the pond.

One way to contain rumors is to reduce the likelihood that the uncertain group will be incidentally exposed to these rumors. Several scholars have demonstrated that exposure to information through social media platforms and in-person interactions can serve to inform—and misinform—the citizens who do not pay close attention to politics. Insulating these uncertain individuals from the believers—the purveyors of misinformation and rumors—might therefore be an effective strategy. In essence, we should limit the spread of rumors and misinformation to the small group of individuals who are most conspiratorially inclined. Although the existence of these pockets of conspiratorial actors can be dangerous in and of itself—as the events of January 6, 2021, suggest—we must recognize that these groups also pose an indirect threat, in that they can increase the power of their radical beliefs by fostering uncertainty within the broader mass public. The dynamics of social media make it difficult to ensure that information stays within the echo chambers, enabling radicalized pockets to convey misinformation more widely. Walling off these pockets from the rest of the information ecosystem may ease the problem. In extreme cases, social media companies could remove potentially incendiary and harmful content, such as when Facebook removed content that contained the phrase "stop the steal" in January 2021.[10] But companies are reticent to take action against content unless that content has a high likelihood of leading to offline harms, because those companies are rightfully reluctant to limit speech in general. The indirect harms arising from incidental exposure, while dangerous, may not meet such standards. However, other softer-touch actions could be effective. For example, the use of "closed groups" on Facebook—which allows any user to join a group but presents the content of that group's page only to those users who are members of that group—or decreased visibility of conspiratorial content by social media companies can reduce incidental exposure to the broader community.

My argument here differs from traditional academic thinking. Richard Hofstadter wrote about the paranoid mindset affecting only the margins of society. But given the potential for information to spread through modern media, the paranoid worldview of the few could have an outsize effect on the many. Thus, it is critical to cordon off hubs of misinformation, even if doing so might foster increased radicalization within those hubs.

There is even more that can be done to mitigate the consequences of political rumors and misinformation. We can also try to correct misinformation after people have been exposed to it. That is not easy, as this book and other research have shown. But some strategies can help. I have advanced one technique: focusing on the messenger delivering the correction as much as the message itself. This is not to minimize the importance of determining the "truth"; the hard work of determining the base of knowledge that rests on supported facts is a critical task that should be undertaken by subject field experts. But making such judgment is not in itself enough to diminish the influence and impact of rumors in society. The truth is not self-correcting.

We need to draw upon lessons from political science and psychology and ensure that we have the best sources delivering those messages.

Contrary to popular belief, nonpartisan and other objective sources, such as fact-checking organizations, are not always the most effective messenger to deliver corrections. In at least some circumstances, trusted sources, including partisan leaders who speak out against their apparent interests, may be able to reach and persuade an even broader audience. Leveraging these trusted sources can be especially valuable because, under some conditions, a properly delivered message can persuade not just the uncertain but even some believers who would otherwise cling to their unsubstantiated beliefs. To be clear, my recommendation to use "surprising sources" to debunk rumors and misinformation is not a foolproof plan. The use of such sources was effective in correcting the death panel rumors in my experiments in 2010 and 2011. And, as noted in chapter 4, other scholars have demonstrated the effectiveness of using such sources to correct rumors and misinformation about other issues, including the environment and allegations of voter fraud. But delivering corrections through individuals who speak against their apparent interests does not always work—as my own research in chapter 5 demonstrates. A strategy that works in one place at one moment in time might not work at other times and in other contexts. The problems of rumors are fluid, and our efforts to find solutions must not stop just because one strategy worked in one case.

It is therefore critical to draw from a wide-ranging menu of potential methods of correcting misinformation. For example, Bode and Vraga recommend promoting links to "related" stories as a way to correct misinformation in particular posts.[11] Others focus less on *where* to place corrections and instead ask *how* best to scale up the fact-checking process—for instance, by leveraging the "wisdom of the crowd."[12] Still others have looked beyond individual corrections and instead suggest more generalized approaches to combatting misinformation, including providing individuals with digital literacy tips or devising educational programs designed to familiarize people with common misinformation techniques.[13] These are but a few examples of potential interventions, and as our understanding of the psychology underlying the process of correcting misinformation continues to evolve, new and different solutions may emerge. For instance, as discussed in chapter 4, some of the early work on the psychology of countering misinformation indicated that some corrections could induce an ideological backfire effect. That is, the act of correcting misinformation might, in fact, strengthen individuals' belief in the original misinformation. This finding led to the wide adoption of strategies that included not repeating misinformation under any circumstances, and especially when correcting that misinformation.[14] However, as also noted in chapter 4, more recent work suggests that repeating rumors within the context of a correction may actually help people correctly update their beliefs. We must therefore adjust our correction strategies in line with current scientific knowledge. All told, cleaning up the mess of misinformation after it has been released is hard, but the task is still worth pursuing.

Furthermore, correcting specific rumors and pieces of misinformation post-exposure is but one strategy that can be employed to combat misinformation. Significant progress has been made in advancing techniques that can enable citizens to better defend against misinformation and rumor before initial exposure. These techniques include *inoculation*, or teaching people to recognize techniques commonly employed by purveyors of misinformation; inducing *lateral reading*, skills that encourage individuals to verify what they are reading as they are reading it; and providing *media literacy tips* for engaging with digital content.[15] That said, a word of caution is in order. While these techniques hold great promise, we must also be wary of the unintended consequences of interventions that are based on fostering critical thinking skills. Many of these interventions to fight rumors and misinformation are predicated on encouraging skepticism of particular pieces—and particular types—of political content. For example, Guess and his colleagues advocate using tips such as "Be skeptical of headlines," "Investigate the source," and "Check the evidence." Surely this is wise and reasonable advice. But we also need to be careful about going too far. The best way to ensure that people do not accept particular pieces of misinformation is to have them be skeptical of *all* information. But such a mindset can be destructive in a democratic society. Being skeptical of all things leads to trusting nothing, which is precisely why the existence of a substantially sized group of individuals who are uncertain of the veracity of rumors and misinformation is so dangerous. There is a fine line between productive skepticism and rejection of authority. Staying on the right side of that line is the difficult goal of democracy. In defending against misinformation, we must ensure that we do not destroy trust in *every* part of the information ecosystem.

In addition, we should take a broad approach to using individual-level interventions to improve the quality of the larger information environment. One way to do this is to target not just false beliefs, but also the sharing of those false beliefs on social media. People's decisions to share content, in part, determines what their friends and contacts see on social media. This in turn determines what information diffuses throughout society. Exposure to these kinds of rumors and misinformation can be dangerous when individuals who would not ordinarily seek out such information are incidentally exposed to it. One way to curtail the sharing of undesirable misinformation is through preemptive strategies that urge individuals to be more discerning in the content they share online. One example of this is known as an "accuracy nudge," a subtle cue designed to shift people's attention toward accuracy, with the goal of reminding them to share only content they perceive to be accurate.[16] Given the ways by which individual-level decisions can shape the aggregate information ecosystem, we should do what we can to elevate the quality of content that is shared.

All of these interventions—from unlikely source corrections to the accuracy nudges—individually have small effects on the willingness of ordinary people to believe and share rumors and misinformation. But collectively, a large tool kit of interventions may have a substantial effect on rates of rumor rejection among the mass public. Different strategies to stop the spread of misinformation have different advantages and disadvantages, and those techniques are more or less effective in different contexts. By combining a number of strategies, we can create a more effective collective response. Moreover, this collective effort does not need to stop here. Individual interventions may work better in concert with each other—one strategy might not simply fill in the holes left by other approaches but may reinforce and strengthen those interventions by contributing to the design of a culture of truth. Put simply, the whole could be greater than the sum of its parts.

At the same time, we must view the battle against misinformation as a constant fight and continue to experiment to hone our techniques. As the political world evolves and the context of the information landscape changes, we should rigorously evaluate—and reevaluate—response strategies. We must not only develop new techniques, but also ensure that the interventions we have used before continue to be effective.

Back to Elites

To balance this somewhat hopeful note, let me sound a note of caution by returning to a point I made earlier: the battle to curb the spread of rumors and misinformation should begin with elites and the ways in which they talk about politics. There remains a fundamental problem with the modern political system—one not so easily glossed over. The elephant in the room (so to speak) concerns the partisan asymmetry in the prevalence of discussion of rumors and misinformation among political leaders as discussed in chapter 6. At the present moment, rumors are far more prevalent on the right than on the left. We need to recognize and acknowledge this fact, as difficult as it may be to point to the faults of one party over the other. To do so is not to say that Republican politicians are evil or that Republican identifiers in the mass electorate are inherently more susceptible to and interested in political rumors. After all, the research in this book (alongside the research of other scholars) demonstrates that, given the same information environment, rumors can infect the political thinking of citizens on both sides of the aisle. But, as this research also demonstrates, identifiers of both parties are not situated in similar information environments. Elites from each party diverge in the way they talk about and engage with political rumors. And, as a result, ordinary citizens live in different informational worlds.

The analysis presented in chapter 6 is consistent with John Zaller's model of top-down model of opinion leadership, as presented in his 1992 book, *The Nature and Origins of Mass Opinion*. Ordinary citizens follow the cues provided by the political leaders they chose to listen to, and they do so to a greater extent when they pay more attention to politics. But further insight into the dynamics of mass politics comes from Zaller's reworking of the notion of top-down politics, as revised in his 2013 article, "What Nature and Origins Leaves Out." According to Zaller, ordinary citizens are especially likely to follow the party line on issues and matters they do not have strong feelings about. As he argues, "once voters come, for whatever particular reason, to identify with a party, they must decide what they think of the rest of its agenda. . . . [W]e should not expect narrowly motivated partisans to maintain disagreement with their chosen party on the bulk of its agenda. Once they identify with a party, . . . they will accept cues favoring the party's broad agenda."[17] Such agendas could include even fanciful beliefs or misleading claims. As Zaller aptly notes, people come to identify with a party by various paths, but having adopted that identity, they are likely to follow the party line on a bundle of issues, regardless of their personal connection to those issues.

In the situation of political rumors, it is almost certainly the case that few individuals would place their belief in such misinformation as the reason to choose one party over the other. But given the bundling of positions within a party agenda, the acceptance of—or at least the failure to reject—rumors could occur as a natural consequence of adopting their chosen party identity, thereby embracing that party's agenda. In other words, citizens could fail to reject rumors because, either explicitly or implicitly, their partisan leaders do not ask them to. Rumor acceptance (or at least nonrejection) follows the peripheral path described by Zaller. People—at least those inclined to some level of conspiratorial thinking—adopt their views on political rumors as part of a larger package of beliefs comprising the party agenda. Once people adopt a given partisan identity, they shift their auxiliary beliefs to align with the party line. As such, partisans might not support a party *because* of rumors but may believe rumors because of their party support. Such beliefs may be acquired via a peripheral path, but the public's stated acceptance of rumors can disrupt communication from citizens to elites in important ways.

Consider the following scenario. Some political leaders take positions where they embrace—or at least only ambiguously denounce—rumors about their opponents to appeal to what they think their core party activists want to hear. But the activists are not the only recipients of such signals because such positions are transmitted through the broader media. Leaders indoctrinate their broader base by exposing their supporters to such rhetoric as part of the party agenda. In essence, party leaders drop a pebble in the pond of the information ecosystem, and ripples of this rumor spread into a broader circle of their supporters. Republican politicians might not speak strongly against rumors because they are afraid of the possible electoral consequences of taking such a stand—perhaps drawing a challenger in the primary from the right. The case of Liz Cheney, the Wyoming congresswoman who lost her leadership position and then the Republican primary for her district in July 2022 after speaking out against Trump's unfounded accusations of voting fraud in the 2020 election, provides one such cautionary tale for ambitious politicians. But such rhetoric can create beliefs among those citizens only tangentially engaged with the political world. Thus, the unintended consequences of appealing to the actual or latent opinions of the party core lead to a wide dissemination of rumors in the mass public, thereby setting in motion a vicious circle. Republican politicians have played a role in opening a Pandora's box of rumors, misinformation, and distrust. And, in time, perhaps Democratic politicians will do the same in an effort to gain political advantage. The consequences of such actions for the American political system are potentially disastrous. Politicians therefore need to take responsibility for closing that box.

Here is the tricky part. Cass Sunstein asks a central question concerning solutions to the problem of misinformation: should a solution "be addressed to the suppliers of conspiracy theories, with the goal of persuading them, or should it be addressed to the mass audience, with the goal of inoculating people against pernicious theories?"[18] Clearly, we should do both. But how can we, when it is the politicians who are the problem? Sunstein asks his question in the context of providing advice in formulating a government response to campaigns of misinformation. What do we do when the conspiracies are supplied by political leaders, some of whom are in direct control of the government? Given the top-down dynamics of public opinion and political cognition, we are in a very tight spot.

Sunstein's advice puts a great deal of responsibility in the hands of political leaders. But it may be the only way forward. In a world in which most of the people most of the time do not pay attention to politics, the actions and words of political elites—the politicians who *do* pay attention to politics—are the key to shaping how citizens think about and respond to political events. Researchers can and should develop tools that help citizens to engage rumors and misinformation and help separate the wheat from the chaff of information. But in the end, such tools may be of little use when the information environment is weaponized by political leaders to blunt their impact.

But lest I end this book on a defeatist note, I want to emphasize that there still may be hope. Lots of people are deeply invested in countering rumors and misinformation. Their efforts should be brought together. We need to have scholars, social media executives, media organizations, and politicians work together in a collaborative way, rather than a competitive one. While we must encourage politicians to speak the truth, we must also encourage the news media to deliver proper corrections and to speak out against false information. We must encourage voters to hold politicians who campaign on a web of lies electorally accountable. We must encourage everyday citizens to be discerning, but not overly skeptical, consumers of information.

Finding such solutions to the problem of rumors and misinformation will not be easy, but we have to give it a try. Several pieces of the puzzle may already be falling into place. The outputs of individual research teams may be small effects and inconsistent findings. But there are a growing number of scholars across a variety of disciplines working hard to diagnose and solve the problems caused by the spread of political rumors and misinformation. We should adjust the standards by which we assess the success of interventions. It may not be possible to "solve" the problem of rumors and misinformation, but small steps toward alleviating the problem should be seen as a win. In addition, we need to fight rumors and misinformation on a broader battlefield. We should target our efforts at the believers—individuals who willingly accept political rumors. But we must also target the uncertain citizens who lie in that dangerous space between acceptance and rejection. Progress may be slow, but with an expanded view of the nature of the problem, it can be steady as well. Deployed in combination, different strategies targeted at different groups of individuals may lead to collective solutions that bring society to a better place.

NOTES

Chapter 1. Introduction

1. "Joint Statement from Elections Infrastructure Government Coordinating Council & the Election Infrastructure Sector Coordinating Executive Committees," Cyber Security and Infrastructure Security Agency CISA, November 12, 2020, https://www.cisa.gov/news/2020/11/12/joint-statement-elections-infrastructure-government-coordinating-council-election.

2. See, for example, Danforth et al., "Lost, Not Stolen."

3. Rick Klein, Alisa Wiersema, and Quinn Scanlan, "Trump Renews Threats to GOP over Election Lies: The Note," ABC News, October 14, 2021, https://abcnews.go.com/Politics/trump-renews-threats-gop-election-lies-note/story?id=80567206.

4. Rosalind S. Helderman, Isaac Arnsdorf, and Josh Dawsey, "Doug Mastriano's Pa. Victory Could Give 2020 Denier Oversight of Election," *Washington Post*, May 18, 2022, https://www.washingtonpost.com/politics/2022/05/18/doug-mastrianos-pa-victory-could-give-2020-denier-oversight-2024/.

5. Kira Lerner, "Kari Lake Is One of 4 'Big Lie' Swing State GOP Guv Candidates. They Could Upend the 2024 Presidential Election," *AZ Mirror*, August 25, 2022, https://www.azmirror.com/2022/08/25/kari-lake-is-one-of-4-big-lie-swing-state-gop-guv-candidates-they-could-upend-the-2024-presidential-election/.

6. "Replacing the Refs," States United Democracy Center, September 14, 2022, https://statesuniteddemocracy.org/resources/replacingtherefs/.

7. Olmsted, *Real Enemies*.

8. Dowd, *Groundless*.

9. Weeks and Garrett, "Electoral Consequences," 402.

10. While rumors have received more popular attention in recent years, as I discuss in chapter 2, their actual prevalence is not necessarily greater now than in the past.

11. David W. Moore, "Three in Four Americans Believe in Paranormal," *Gallup*, June 16, 2005, https://news.gallup.com/poll/16915/three-four-americans-believe-paranormal.aspx.

12. See, for example, Jonah Goldberg's writings on birthers and truthers: "This Is . . . ," July 2, 2005, http://www.nationalreview.com/articles/228219/ring-truth-ers/jonah-goldberg and http://www.nationalreview.com/corner/199430/birthers-v-truthers-again/jonah-goldberg.

13. See, for example, David A. Graham, "America the Ignorant: Silly Things We Believe about Witches, Obama, and More," *Newsweek*, August 24, 2010.

14. After initially answering the question, respondents were also asked how strongly they held these views. The initial branch of the question and the follow-up probes were used to create seven-point scales used for analysis later in this book.

15. Two of the Democrat-targeted rumor items were very similar questions about the provisions of the 2010 Affordable Care Act. I employed these two items because the survey results reported here were included as a control group in a larger experimental design investigating

the effectiveness of various corrections to health care misinformation (reported in chapter 4). However, it should be noted that all of the results I report here and in chapter 3 are virtually the same if I include only one of the two health care items in the rumor scales instead of both items.

16. Allcott and Gentzkow, "Social Media and Fake News."

17. Garrett and Bond, "Conservatives' Susceptibility."

18. Here I am making a descriptive point, not a normative statement. When I present the findings in table 1.1 to audiences of highly educated academics and professionals, there is always someone who asks, "Why is that statement on there? That isn't misinformation! That isn't a rumor—it's true!" If readers have the same reaction, I have made my point; belief in wild notions is widespread throughout the public.

19. Brendan Nyhan, "Pundits Blame the Victims on Obama Muslim Myth," August 24, 2010, https://www.brendan-nyhan.com/blog/2010/08/pundits-blame-the-victims-on-obama-muslim -myth-.html.

20. Sunstein, "The Daily We," 25.

21. Jana Winter, "Exclusive: FBI document warns conspiracy theories are a new domestic terrorism threat," *Yahoo! News*, August 1, 2019, https://news.yahoo.com/fbi-documents-conspiracy -theories-terrorism-160000507.html.

22. For a review, see Crocco et al, "Analysis of Cases." It should be noted that while this research points to grave political consequences, their effects remain mostly in the realm of theory. Many authors motivate their analyses by pointing out its capacity to harm yet refrain from actually quantifying those consequences. One notable exception to this trend is in the realm of health, where several scholars have examined the effect that misinformation can have on health outcomes, such as vaccine compliance. Betsch, "Innovations in Communication," uses a survey experiment to illustrate that participants who are exposed to information critical of vaccines believe that vaccines pose a higher risk than those who were not exposed five months later. Vinck et al. exhibit a similar dynamic in their survey in the Democratic Republic of Congo, demonstrating that those who believed particular rumors about Ebola were much less likely to express willingness to accept the Ebola vaccine ("Institutional Trust"). This work extends to other health precautionary measures (see Brainard, Hunter, and Hall, "Agent-Based Model," and Brainard and Hunter, "Misinformation," for two examples). Relying on a variety of methods, from agent-based modeling to survey experiments, these authors explicitly consider the effect, albeit the short-term effect, of misinformation rather than just study its prevalence or identify the antecedents of citizens' belief in such claims.

23. Kuklinski et al., "Misinformation," 790–816.

24. Kuklinski et al., "Misinformation," 790–816; Gilens, "Political Ignorance"; and Pasek, Sood, and Krosnick, "Misinformed about the Affordable Care Act?" 660–673.

25. McKay and Tenove, "Disinformation as a Threat."

26. Rosenblum and Muirhead, *A Lot of People Are Saying.*

27. Rosenblum and Muirhead, *A Lot of People Are Saying*, 3–4.

28. Hochschild and Einstein, *Do Facts Matter?* 66.

29. Nyhan, "Why the 'Death Panel' Myth Wouldn't Die."

30. Nyhan, Reifler, Edelman, et al., "Effects of Semantics"; Nyhan and Reifler, "When Corrections Fail," 303–330.

31. Berinsky, "Assuming the Costs of War"; Berinsky, *In Time of War*; Hopkins, Sides and Citrin, "Muted Consequences."

32. For a review of the work circa 2019 see Wittenberg and Berinsky, "Misinformation and Its Correction."

33. Wood and Porter, "Elusive Backfire Effect," 135–163.

34. Ross and Anderson, "Shortcomings"; Schul and Burnstein, "When Discounting Fails."

35. Thorson, "Belief Echoes."

36. Berinsky, *In Time of War.*

Chapter 2. Rumors in the Political World

1. See, for example, Roose, "What Is QAnon?"; Forrest, "What Is QAnon?"; TMZ, "Donald Trump"; and TMZ, "Ex-QAnon-er."

2. See Pew Research Center, "Political Divides, Conspiracy Theories and Divergent News Sources Heading into 2020 Election," September 16, 2020, https://www.pewresearch.org /journalism/2020/09/16/political-divides-conspiracy-theories-and-divergent-news-sources -heading-into-2020-election/.

3. Catherine Lucey, "Trump Praises QAnon Followers as 'People That Love Our Country,'" *Wall Street Journal*, August 19, 2020, https://www.wsj.com/articles/trump-praises-qanon -followers-as-people-that-love-our-country-11597883634.

4. Green, though, has expressed some public distancing from QAnon since the 2020 election. See Bess Levin, "Marjorie Taylor Green: I Only Believe Some of What QAnon Says about Dems Being Satanic Pedophile Cannibals, Okay?" *Vanity Fair*, February 4, 2021, https://www.vanityfair .com/news/2021/02/marjorie-taylor-greene-fake-mea-culpa.

5. Olmsted, *Real Enemies.*

6. Dowd, *Groundless.*

7. Uscinski, *Conspiracy Theories*, 285; Cheathem, "Conspiracy Theories."

8. Donovan, "How Idle Is Idle Talk?"

9. Allport and Postman, "Psychology of Rumor"; Allport and Lepkin, "Wartime Rumors." Allport and Postman, "Psychology of Rumor," likewise explore how rumors spread and evolve over time. They describe various rumors that arose during World War II and note that the rumors became sharper and more easily conveyed as they proliferated through the public. These historical findings guide my larger study of rumors but are not directly relevant to the present project, which concerns the structure of rumors currently in circulation and strategies to debunk those rumors.

10. Bysow, "Gerüchte."

11. Stanton, "You're Living in the Golden Age."

12. Lazer et al., "Science of Fake News"; Tandoc, Lim, and Ling, "Defining 'Fake News.'"

13. Graves, *Deciding What's True*; Thorson, West, and Mendes, "Measuring Physiological Influence"; Amazeen, "Making a Difference."

14. Uscinski and Parent, *American Conspiracy Theories*. Neither is the current day the first time that leading voices have declared a new age of conspiratorial thinking. As Uscinski points out in *Conspiracy Theories*, claims that we are living in a "new age" of conspiracies are a common refrain. In 1994, the *Washington Post* said that Bill Clinton's presidency "marked the dawn of a new age of conspiracy theories" almost twenty years after the *Los Angeles Times* wrote in 1977 that the United States had "become as conspiracy prone . . . as the Pan-Slav nationalists in the 1880s Balkans," and thirty years after the *New York Times* declared 1964 the year of conspiracy theories, given their popularity among the mass public.

15. Olmsted, *Real Enemies.*

16. Ellis and Fine, *Global Grapevine,* 4.

17. DiFonzo and Bordia, "Rumor, Gossip and Urban Legends," 13.

18. Sunstein, *Going to Extremes*, 6.

19. Weeks and Garrett, "Electoral Consequences," 402.

20. Ellis and Fine, *Global Grapevine;* Allport and Postman, "Psychology of Rumor."

21. Flynn, Nyhan, and Reifler, "Nature and Origins."

22. Hochschild and Einstein, *Do Facts Matter?*

23. Hofstadter, *Paranoid Style*, 37.

24. Keeley, "Of Conspiracy Theories," 116.

25. Kay, "Among the Truthers"; Clarke, "Conspiracy Theories"; and Keeley, "Of Conspiracy Theories."

26. Ellis and Fine, *Global Grapevine*, 53.

27. Weeks and Garrett, "Electoral Consequences," 402.

28. Sunstein and Vermeule, "Conspiracy Theories," 207.

29. Keeley, "Of Conspiracy Theories."

30. Allport and Postman, "Psychology of Rumor," ix; Rosnow, "Communications as Cultural Science," 27.

31. Uscinski and Parent, *American Conspiracy Theories*.

32. Specifically, such institutions, according to Uscinski and Parent, are ones in which "knowledge claims are the result of a socially distributed network of inquirers trained in assessing knowledge claims, with methods and results made public and available for security" (*American Conspiracy Theories*, 33; following Levy, "Radically Socialized Knowledge").

33. In a related vein, writing about political misinformation more generally, Hochschild and Einstein define "facts" as "a state of affairs that given a suitable mobilization of evidence can be said to exist" (*Do Facts Matter?* 35). For these authors, such mobilization is represented by "nearly unanimous agreement among experts who have relatively little ideological or partisan motivation" (36).

34. Sunstein, *On Rumors*.

35. This widespread social transmission is often tied to rumors' affective content. In their review of the literature of rumor psychology, DiFonzo and Bordia identify five factors related to rumor transmission: uncertainty, importance, lack of control, anxiety, and belief ("Rumor, Gossip"). In addition, in their study of urban legends—a related conceptual category—Heath, Bell, and Sternberg found that subjects were more likely to pass along stories that scored high in disgust ("Emotional Selection"). For instance, people were more likely to repeat a story about a man drinking a soda with pieces of dead rat inside than an identical story in which the man discovered the rat before he drank the soda.

36. It is important to note that figure 2.1 considers belief in particular pieces of misinformation on a rumor-by-rumor basis. As we will see in the next chapter, there are some factors that increase the probability that certain people accept rumors across the board. But just because people accept one rumor does not mean that they will necessarily accept another. Rumors are not monolithic.

37. Other scholars have proposed similar typologies for delineating the actors involved in the diffusion of rumors and other forms of misinformation. For example, Zehmakan and Galam distinguish between "Seeds," who start and believe a rumor; "Agnostics," who reject rumors and conspiracy theories; and "Others," who may either believe or disbelieve a rumor on the basis of the information to which they have been exposed ("Fake News"). Similarly, Tambuscio and Ruffo, in their study of urban legends, forward a model in which individuals are either "Believers," who support the hoax, "Fact-Checkers," who actively debunk the hoax, or the "Susceptible," who can either believe or reject the hoax ("Fact-Checking Strategies").

38. Sunstein, *On Rumors*; Goertzel, "Conspiracy Theory."

39. More recently, other scholars have likewise attributed the production of so-called "fake news" to a similar profit motive (Braun and Eklund, "Fake News"; Tucker et al., "Social Media"; Tynan, "How Facebook Powers Money Machines").

40. After all, just because a group is small does not mean that it is unimportant. These creators can serve as opinion leaders for a politically significant portion of the population, even if that population itself does not engage in the production of rumors. Consider, for instance, the case of the John Birch Society in the early 1960s. The John Birch Society was a right-wing political group,

founded by Robert Welch in the 1950s, that achieved political prominence. But the group was very small in number. The incidence of John Birch members in the general population ensured that only one or two such members would be captured by a random sample survey, as indeed was the case in the 1964 American National Election Study (see Converse, "Changing Conceptions," for a discussion). But the John Birch Society provided a voice for a particular set of beliefs and helped shape the social and political environment at the time.

41. Other works have characterized believers using different terminology, such as the "misinformed" (Kuklinski et al., "Misinformation") or "actively misinformed" (Hochschild and Einstein, *Do Facts Matter?*), for those individuals who hold inaccurate or unsubstantiated beliefs with a high degree of confidence (see also Graham, "Misinformation Inoculation"; Li and Wagner, "Value of Not Knowing"; Pasek, Sood, and Krosnick, "Misinformed").

42. Goertzel, following Seth Kalichman, argues that these people—those individuals who have a psychological propensity to believe in conspiracies and engage in conspiratorial thinking—comprise the second tier of the "Conspiracy Theory Pyramid Scheme." In his view, these people are fed information by the top-tier intellectuals—"writers and intellectuals who publish books and articles and give speeches that reinforce and legitimate conspiracy theories" ("Conspiracy Theory," 226).

43. Although see, for instance, Li and Wagner, "Value of Not Knowing."

44. See, for example, Morgan Halvorsen, "Not Every QAnon Believer's an Antisemite. But There's a Lot of Overlap between Its Adherents and Belief in a Century-Old Antisemitic Hoax," Morning Consult, June 28, 2021, https://morningconsult.com/2021/06/28/qanon-antisemitism-right-wing-authoritarianism-polling/.

45. Berinsky, *Silent Voices*, 26.

46. Li and Wagner, "Value of Not Knowing." See also Luskin and Bullock, "'Don't Know'"

47. Morales, "Obama's Birth Certificate." Similarly, a *New York Times* article from late 2016 concerning birthers reports as the central quantity of interest the percentage of people who reject the rumor and say that Obama was born in the United States (Dropp and Nyhan, "It Lives").

48. Allport and Postman, "Psychology of Rumor."

49. Faye, "Governing the Grapevine"; Library of Congress, "World War II."

50. Olmsted, *Real Enemies*, 7.

51. For reviews, see Persily et al., "Misinformation"; Tucker et al., "Social Media."

52. Olmsted, *Real Enemies*, 7.

53. Zhuravskaya, Petrova, and Enikolopov, "Political Effects."

54. In addition, once a rumor is out in the world, it may gain a permanence that was missing in earlier times. As Sunstein argues, "In the era of the Internet it has become easy to spread false or misleading rumors about almost anyone. . . . Material on the Internet has considerable longevity. For all practical purposes, it may even be permanent" (4).

55. Phadke, Samory, and Mitra, "What Makes People Join."

56. Uscinski and Parent, *American Conspiracy Theories*.

57. For summaries, see Roose, "What Is QAnon"; Ohlheiser, "You'll Never Guess."

58. Journalists themselves have voiced concerns about the potential for mainstream media coverage to create new waves of belief in rumors and conspiracy theories. For instance, in a discussion about how best to report on QAnon, CNN's Donie O'Sullivan notes, "Where is the tipping point of yes, there is something happening on the internet, and yes, some people are engaging, but by us covering it, are we unintentionally giving it more oxygen?" Fu, "Embedded."

59. Lazarsfeld, Berelson, and Gaudet, *People's Choice*.

60. Annie Jacobsen, "The United States of Conspiracy: Why, More and More, Americans Cling to Crazy Theories," *New York Daily News*, January 10, 2019, https://www.nydailynews.com/opinion/united-states-conspiracy-americans-cling-crazy-theories-article-1.949689.

61. Morello, "Conspiracy Theories."

62. Roose, "Why Conspiracy Theories"; Adrienne LaFrance, "Going Online in the Age of Conspiracy Theories," *Atlantic*, October 21, 2015, https://www.theatlantic.com/technology/archive/2015/10/going-online-in-the-age-of-conspiracy-theories/411544/; Merlan, *Republic of Lies*.

63. Sunstein, "The Daily We"; Negroponte, "Digital Revolution"; Sunstein, *Going to Extremes*; and Pariser, *Filter Bubble*.

64. Prior, *Post-Broadcast Democracy*.

65. Cinelli et al., "Echo Chamber Effect"; Sasahara et al., "Social Influence"; Tokita, Guess, and Tarnita, "Polarized Information Ecosystems."

66. Choi et al., "Rumor Propagation."

67. Vicario et al., "Spreading of Misinformation."

68. Eady et al., "How Many People"; Arguedas et al., "Echo Chambers."

69. Guess et al., "Avoiding the Echo Chamber," 5.

70. Nguyen, "As Trump's Problems Mount"; Guess et al., "Avoiding the Echo Chamber."

71. See Bakshy, Messing, and Adamic, "Exposure"; Barberá et al., "Tweeting from Left to Right"; Gentzkow and Shapiro, "Ideological Separation"; Flaxman, Goel, and Rao, "Filter Bubbles"; Nelson and Webster, "Myth of Partisan"; Fletcher, Robertson, and Nielsen, "How Many People."

72. Guess et al., "Avoiding the Echo Chamber," 9.

73. Scharkow et al., "How Social Network Sites": Stier et al., "Post Post-Broadcast Democracy?"

74. Jürgens and Stark, "Mapping Exposure Diversity."

75. Guess et al., "Less than You Think"; Guess, "(Almost) Everything in Moderation"; Boutyline and Willer, "Social Structure."

76. Anspach and Carlson, "What to Believe?"; Druckman, Levendusky, and McClain, "No Need to Watch"; Levendusky, "Why Do Partisan Media."

77. Tsfati et al., "Causes and Consequences"; Vargo et al., "A Systems Perspective."

78. Kim, Chen, and Gil De Zúñiga, "Stumbling upon News"; Weeks, Ardèvol, and Gil de Zúñiga, "Online Influence?"; Weeks et al., "Incidental Exposure."

79. Lee and Kim, "Incidental Exposure to News."

80. Weeks, Lane, and Hahn, "Online Incidental Exposure."

81. This inadvertent exposure may also motivate political action. Indeed, there is suggestive evidence that incidental exposure to political news is especially correlated with higher levels of participation among individuals with lower interest in politics (Vaccari et al., "Political Expression").

82. Settle, *Frenemies*.

83. Settle, *Frenemies*, 14.

84. Settle, *Frenemies*, 15.

85. Settle, *Frenemies*, 44.

86. See "News Use across Social Media Platforms in 2020," Pew Research Center, January 12, 2021, https://www.pewresearch.org/journalism/2021/01/12/news-use-across-social-media-platforms-in-2020/.

87. Mitchell et al., "Americans Who Mainly Get Their News."

Chapter 3. The Roots of Rumor Belief

1. Or perhaps they do a little of both.

2. Ben Smith, "Belief and Dislike," Politico, August 30, 2010, https://www.politico.com/blogs/ben-smith/2010/08/belief-and-dislike-028889.

3. Gerber and Huber, "Partisanship"; Bullock et al., "Partisan Bias."

4. It could also be that people answer rumor questions in the affirmative because they want to affect the news by creating "interesting" stories. However, this kind of behavior seems less plausible and is less discussed by political commentators.

5. Berinsky, *Silent Voices*. It could, of course, be the case that people deceive even themselves and agree with a statement so as to further solidify their personal preferences on a matter. Such behavior is akin to the process of self-deception (Paulhus, "Measurement and Control"). But from a practical standpoint, when respondents report their constructed beliefs accurately and do not engage in willful deception in their relationship with the survey interviewer, those responses should not be considered expressive responses.

6. Paulhus, "Measurement and Control"; Berinsky, *Silent Voices*.

7. Berinsky, "Rumors and Health Care Reform."

8. Berinsky, *Silent Voices*.

9. All of the experiments yield point estimates that are small in magnitude and statistically indistinguishable from zero. These null results are therefore not simply the artifact of under-powered experiments. The small point estimates provide consistent evidence of the absence of expressive responding.

10. Peterson and Iyengar, "Partisan Gaps."

11. Graham makes the case that some individuals who state incorrect factual beliefs are, in fact, uncertain about their beliefs ("Measuring Misperceptions?"). Such adherence to incorrect factual statements might be better seen as "miseducated guesses." From this perspective, some individuals who express adherence to misperceptions might be expressing sentiments that arise from confusion and differential knowledge rather than firm belief. From my perspective, the relevance of this argument is tempered in my work because, as I discussed in the previous chapter, I am adopting a normative standard by which the failure to reject rumors (rather than the acceptance of rumors) is undesirable. Thus, even if some of the expressed false beliefs of individuals, in fact, represent uncertainty on their part, the mere failure to reject a rumor statement is problematic.

12. The ANES questions were included on the 2012 post-election survey (conducted from November 2012 to January 2013). These items were modified from a battery of questions proposed by Eric Oliver and me. The questions follow a different response format than those used on the YouGov surveys. The topic and spirit of these items, however, are very similar to the questions I included on my own surveys and have the advantage of being asked during the 2012 election campaign. In particular, four rumor-based questions were asked. Two of these rumors implicated Obama: the question of his birthplace and the existence of death panels in the Obama-led health care reform. The other two incriminated the Right, insinuating that the federal government was involved in 9/11 and in the flooding of New Orleans after Hurricane Katrina. The ANES also asked a fifth question relating to the policies of the Obama administration: "Do the policies of the Obama administration favor whites over blacks, favor blacks over whites, or do they treat both groups the same?" This question seems different in kind from the rumor questions I generated (and different from the other ANES questions as well). I therefore set it aside for the purposes of this analysis. The 2012 ANES consisted of two separate data collection efforts: a traditional face-to-face sample and an internet sample, collected by GfK/Knowledge Networks. In table 3.1, I present only the face-to-face results because only these interviews allowed the respondents to volunteer a "don't know" response, which better captures the different circles of belief, in line with the question response format of my survey. Admittedly, the internet survey better mirrors the mode employed in the YouGov surveys, but the lack of an explicit "don't know" response on the ANES internet survey questions makes direct comparison with the results of my survey difficult. I should note that in the multivariate analyses that follow later in the chapter, I make use of the full sample.

13. I chose these particular questions because they had all been asked by other survey organizations.

14. This group of rumors is obviously not balanced, in large part because it was extremely difficult to find rumors that were endorsed by the political Left. In the analysis of the July 2010 data that follows, I check the robustness of the results by including only a subset of two of the Democratic-based rumors in place of the four-item scale. The results do not change appreciably, indicating that any difference in the Republican-based and Democratic-based analysis is not a function of the unequal number of items in the scales. I also asked whether respondents thought that vaccines were safe as a general measure of inclination for conspiratorial thinking. I found that those respondents who were suspicious of vaccines were more likely to accept rumors about *both* Democrats and Republicans.

15. The appendix contains a full list of survey items. In the last quarter of 2010, I conducted a survey as part of a module on the 2010 Cooperative Congressional Election Study (CCES). I asked many of the same rumor questions as on the July 2010 survey but modified some of the items—for instance, referring to the Bush administration in the question about 9/11—and added rumor items related to immigration (Ellis and Fine, *Global Grapevine*). These items are listed in table 3.3. I again asked a set of these items in a May 2011 survey (table A1) as well as in the 2014 CCES survey (table A3). Table 3.4 lists the questions I asked in my December 2017 survey. Some of these items replicate questions asked in earlier surveys. However, I also dropped some questions that had faded into obscurity—the question regarding John Kerry's medals most notably—and added some questions to reflect rumors that had emerged in the wake of the 2016 presidential election. In a similar vein, my surveys in 2019 included additional topical rumor questions (see table 3.5 and A4).

16. It should be noted that the November 2014 survey included only the first branch of the question. Because of resource constraints, I did not include the follow-up questions.

17. The results of these surveys can be found in figures A1–4 in the appendix.

18. Berinsky, *Silent Voices*.

19. I also attempted to perform an unsupervised content analysis of the responses to the open-ended probes. Unfortunately, the text data in these answers did not provide a sufficient base for meaningful analysis.

20. To return to the argument by Graham regarding self-awareness of misperceptions described in a previous footnote, even if someone is taking a "miseducated" guess as opposed to expressing a deeply held belief, they are still not rejecting the rumor. Thus, by considering rumor rejection as the normatively desirable state, Graham's argument would only serve to shift the balance of the composition of the normatively undesirable group and would not change the implications of the argument made throughout this book about the consequences of failure to reject rumors by members of the mass public.

21. I also asked two questions relating to health care rumors in both waves. Since these questions served as dependent variables for the ACA rumor experimental study discussed in chapter 4, I did not expect them to exhibit the same levels of stability as the questions that were unrelated to the experimental treatment.

22. These tables were generated using the weights provided by YouGov. The results show even greater stability if I use the unweighted data.

23. Converse, "Nature of Belief Systems"; Ansolabehere, Rodden, and Snyder, "Strength of Issues"; and Gerber et al., "Assessing the Stability."

24. To use the example from earlier, people who tend toward a conspiratorial orientation would accept both the "birther" and "truther" conspiracies. However, since the birther rumor targets a Democratic politician and the truther rumor targets a Republican politician, we would expect, on average, significant differences in the partisan composition of truthers and birthers.

25. Kay, "Among the Truthers," 12.

26. Thompson, *Counterknowledge*.

27. Allport and Postman, "Psychology of Rumor," 181.

28. Goertzel, "Belief in Conspiracy Theories."

29. Douglas, Sutton, and Cichocka, "Psychology of Conspiracy," 541.

30. Bruder et al., "Measuring Individual Differences." See also Abalakina-Paap et al., "Beliefs in Conspiracies"; Darwin, Neave, and Holmes, "Belief in Conspiracy."

31. Lewandowsky, Oberauer, and Gignac, "NASA Faked the Moon Landing." Interestingly, Wood, Douglas, and Sutton et al. found that even mutually incompatible conspiracy theories are positively correlated in endorsement: the more people believed that Princess Diana faked her own death, the more they believed she was murdered ("Dead and Alive").

32. Brotherton, French, and Pickering, "Measuring Belief in Conspiracy." For a similar approach, see Swire-Thompson, DeGutis, and Lazer, "Searching for the Backfire Effect."

33. Oliver and Wood, "Conspiracy Theories," 954.

34. Uscinski and Parent, *American Conspiracy Theories;* Bruder et al., "Measuring Individual Differences." Of course, other scholars reject the notion that conspiratorial thinking can be arranged along a single dimension (see, e.g., Franks et al., "Beyond 'Monologicality'?").

35. There are, in turn some scholars who seek to explore the psychological correlates of conspiratorial thinking. For example, Freeman and Bentall find that agreement with the statement "I am convinced there is a conspiracy behind many things in the world" is correlated with meeting criteria for various psychiatric disorders ("Concomitants of Conspiracy Concerns").

36. Still other scholars have drawn on other aspects of general thinking that lend certain individuals to be drawn to conspiracy theories. Garrett and Weeks propose three scales to measure individual's epistemic beliefs—beliefs about the nature of knowledge and how one comes to know—that are associated with conspiratorial thinking ("Epistemic Beliefs' Role").

37. This is not to say that there is not great value in sorting through the particulars of the kinds of dispositions that lead some individuals to conspiratorial thinking.

38. I also examined the relationship between authoritarianism and rumor holding. Authoritarianism measures the degree to which individuals subscribe to a worldview characterized by obedience to authority. The authoritarianism scale I use here is drawn from a series of items relating to child-rearing asked by the National Election Study (NES). Specifically, these items ask about attributes in children most preferred by individuals, such as respect for elders and good manners (see Feldman and Stenner, "Perceived Threat," for a description). For instance, one of the items states: "Listed below are pairs of desirable qualities. For each pair, please mark which one you think is more important for a child to have . . . independence or respect for elders." These items are especially attractive because they are explicitly nonpolitical and plausibly exogenous to beliefs concerning rumors about political events and figures. Authoritarians should be less likely to question statements that have a veneer of credulity, such as rumors that come with complex backstories. Authoritarians therefore should be more likely to accept political rumors, especially those that comport with their political beliefs. However, since the authoritarian personality is associated with right-wing politics, the authoritarianism scale is probably better at determining the degree to which individuals cling to rumors about policies and politicians on the left. The authoritarianism scale is therefore different than the other general concepts measured here—it is best thought of as a mixture of general and specific rumor-holding tendencies. Empirically, I find that authoritarianism does predict rumor acceptance from across the ideological spectrum, but it is more strongly associated with acceptance of rumors that implicate the Left—such as concerns related to Obama's birthplace. The inclusion or exclusion of the authoritarianism measure does not, however, change any of the multivariate results reported below. I therefore exclude this measure in my analysis here.

39. McClosky and Chong, "Similarities and Differences."

40. Oliver and Wood, "Conspiracy Theories."

41. Of course, it could be the case that people who tend to think about the world in dogmatic ways are more likely to either accept or reject rumors, shying away from the undecided response. Empirically, this does not appear to be the case.

42. Empirically, the items seemed to scale on a single dimension, but the relationship was not particularly strong. An exploratory factor analysis of my July 2010 data yields a single-factor solution, though the eigenvalue of the first dimension was below 1.0 and a scale formed from the three items had a reliability of only .46.

43. Removing the item relating to "important public issues" from the dogmatism scale does not change the regression results reported below.

44. As with the dogmatism items, I created a scale using items that had majority agreement from both the "far left" and "far right" subsamples examined by McClosky and Chong, "Similarities and Differences." The first two of these items were drawn from a battery of questions that they termed "estrangement from politics." The third was from a battery termed "paranoid tendencies," but fit well conceptually with the other two items. Empirically, the items scale well. An exploratory factor analysis of the July 2010 data yields a single-factor solution and a scale formed from the three items has a reliability of .65.

45. Citrin, "Comment"; Hetherington, *Why Trust Matters.*

46. Sunstein and Vermeule, "Conspiracy Theories," 209.

47. These scales are created by taking the mean over all the items a respondent answered in a particular scale. It should also be noted that both dogmatism and political disengagement are modestly positively correlated with Republican Party identification. The mean dogmatism score is 0.3 for Democrats and 0.5 for Republicans. The mean disengagement score is 0.7 for Democrats and 0.8 for Republicans.

48. Kunda, "Case for Motivated Reasoning."

49. Taber and Lodge, "Motivated Skepticism."

50. Similarly, Bullock, "Partisanship," finds that false information about political candidates can influence opposing-party candidate assessments, even after that information is revealed to be false. For instance, Republicans who hear negative stories about Democratic candidates lower their evaluation of that candidate. If that information is revealed to be false, their opinion of the candidate will rebound somewhat but will not return to its initial state.

51. Kahan, "Ideology, Motivated Reasoning."

52. Oliver and Wood, "Conspiracy Theories."

53. It is the case that most of the time, respondents are more likely to believe rumors about Democratic politicians than the same rumor about Republican politicians. But the reason might be that Democrats are seen as more expansive in matters of the role of government.

54. The difference is even more pronounced if we incorporate "not sure" responses into the analysis. These results are presented in table A5 in the appendix. The only exception to this trend is for the vapor-trails rumor (Democrat-targeted) in 2013.

55. In the discussion that follows, I will rely on the seven-point scales, but all the conclusions remain the same if I focus only on the initial branch.

56. It could be that the weak negative correlation is partially a result of a response set. Six of the seven items are asked in a format such that a "yes" response indicates rumor acceptance. Thus, the items could be partially contaminated by acquiescence bias. However, the Obama item is coded in the opposite way and appears to be related to the other rumor items in the expected manner, indicating that this problem may not be serious. To more rigorously test the possibility of response set, I ran a survey in April 2011, where I asked a small subset of rumor questions in one of two formats. Respondents were randomly assigned to question form. One-half the respondents were asked the questions in the yes/no/not sure format employed here. The other half were given similar questions, but the item response choices were statements that indicated acceptance or

rejection of the rumor. For instance, the question about John Kerry's war service read, "Which statement best describes your belief: (1) Senator John Kerry lied about his actions during the Vietnam War in order to receive medals from the US Navy, (2) Senator John Kerry accurately reported his actions during the Vietnam War, (3) Not sure." I also asked follow-up probes comparable to those used for the yes/no/not sure response options. I found that the response distributions and the inter-item correlations were very similar across the two forms, indicating that the items were not contaminated by a response set.

57. While partisanship is the most obvious and powerful political factor correlated with rumor acceptance or rejection, there are other important markers that demonstrate a stake in a given controversy. In the analyses that follow, I also examine the correlation between rumor acceptance and political ideology. Given the increased correspondence between party and ideology in recent years, ideology almost certainly measures to a large degree strong party attachment. But in any case, the results presented below are robust to the inclusion or exclusion of ideology.

58. Zaller, *Nature and Origins*.

59. Zaller, *Nature and Origins*.

60. The Democratic-based rumor scale consists of the Obama citizenship, Kerry, and two death panel rumors. The Republican rumor scale consists of the FBI-CIA and 9/11 rumor questions.

61. These items are constructed from both the initial branch and the follow-up probes, as described above.

62. I do not normalize these scales. I adjust only the minimum and maximum levels of the scale; I do not in any way alter the variance of the individual scales. For the ANES questions, I created a scale of individual items scored "1" if a respondent definitively rejected a rumor, and scored "0" otherwise. The two scales are admittedly different in their execution due to the different response categories employed in the two surveys. But while they are not directly comparable, they are similar in spirit.

63. I also conducted a set of analyses where I used an unordered multinomial logit model at the individual question level. These analyses provided some more nuance to my conclusions. For example, higher levels of political information increased the probability that respondents would be more likely to either accept or reject rumors as opposed to giving a "not sure" response. And those who scored high on my disengagement measure were most likely to accept a given rumor (relative to both rejecting the rumor and giving a "not sure" response). That said, the basic pattern of results is consistent with the analyses presented in regression tables. Because the continuous composite scales are easier to interpret, I use this format to present my results here.

64. I also measured support for the Tea Party on the survey. Not surprisingly, endorsement of the Tea Party was strongly related to the acceptance of Democratic-based rumors and the rejection of Republican-based rumors. In multiple regressions, the coefficient on support for the Tea Party was larger than either Republican partisanship or conservative ideology (borrowing explanatory power from both variables). In effect, support for the Tea Party functioned as a measure of subscription to views on the extreme right.

67. I replicated the basic tenor of these findings in a December 2017 study. The full results of this analysis are presented in figure A9 in the appendix.

68. See figures A10–12 in the appendix for details.

Chapter 4. Can We Correct Rumors?

1. In actuality, the plan included provisions to pay doctors to counsel patients about end-of-life options. For a comprehensive overview and fact-check of this rumor, see Holan, "PolitiFact's Lie of the Year." For a more recent discussion of the rumor's legacy, see Gonyea, "From the Start."

2. See Angie Drobnic Holan, "Sarah Palin Falsely Claims Barack Obama Runs a 'Death Panel'" PolitFact, August 10, 2009, https://www.politifact.com/factchecks/2009/aug/10/sarah-palin /sarah-palin-barack-obama-death-panel/.

3. Pew Research Center, "Health Care Reform."

4. For a recent study on enduring beliefs in this rumor, see Barnett and Marsden, "Death Panel Myth.".

5. Van der Linden, Panagopoulos, and Roozenbeek, "You Are Fake News." On the distrust of experts, see also Douglas et al., "Understanding Conspiracy Theories."

6. As noted below, subsequent studies have found only limited evidence that repeating misinformation within corrections causes substantial backlash against these corrections (see Swire-Thompson, DeGutis, and Lazer, "Searching for the Backfire Effect," for a review). However, as discussed in chapter 2, rumors derive their power from large-scale social transmission and repetition. It is thus important to recognize the potential risks of such repetition in enhancing a rumor's intuitive accuracy and inhibiting the long-term sticking power of corrections.

7. This is consistent with the findings from chapter 3 that individual dispositions, particularly conspiratorial orientations, are an important factor in explaining why people believe rumors.

8. Kushner Gadarian et al., "Partisanship"; Allcott et al., "Polarization and Public Health."

9. For trends on trust in experts, Pew Research Center data is available at Funk et al., "Trust and Mistrust." On attitudes toward scientists in the wake of the COVID-19 outbreak, see Funk, Kennedy, and Johnson, "Trust in Medical Scientists."

10. This finding comes from a September 2009 NPR/KFF/Harvard telephone survey that assessed the level of confidence that the public had in various groups to "recommend the right thing for the country when it comes to health care." See Berinsky, "Rumors and Health Care Reform," 259.

11. Petty and Cacioppo, "Elaboration Likelihood Model." For a political science application of this concept, see Lupia and McCubbins, *Democratic Dilemma*.

12. Pornpitakpan, "Persuasiveness of Source Credibility."

13. Guillory and Geraci, "Correcting Erroneous Inferences."

14. Jeffrey Young, "Grassley 'Resents' Obama over Healthcare," *The Hill*, September 17, 2009, https://thehill.com/homenews/senate/50526-grassley-resents-obama-over-healthcare/. Tedford, "In New Hampshire."

15. Calvert, "Value of Biased Information."

16. For a similar argument applied to national security decision-making, see Saunders, "Leaders, Advisers."

17. Calvert, "Value of Biased Information," 546.

18. See, for example, Schelling, *Arms and Influence*. Beyond the costly signaling literature, the idea of "unlikely sources" also is closely related to work in psychology on "disconfirming" or "incongruous" messaging (e.g., Eagly, Wood, and Chaiken, "Causal Inferences"; Koeske and Crano, "The Effect of Congruous"; Walster, Aronson, and Abrahams, "On Increasing the Persuasiveness").

19. Baum and Groeling, "Shot by the Messenger."

20. Johnson and Seifert, "Sources of the Continued Influence"; Wilkes and Leatherbarrow, "Editing Episodic Memory."

21. For a review, see Flynn, Nyhan, and Reifler, "The Nature and Origins."

22. Nyhan and Reifler, "When Corrections Fail"; Nyhan, "Why the 'Death Panel' Myth."

23. DiFonzo and Bordia, "Rumor, Gossip."

24. Lewandowsky et al., "Debunking Handbook."

25. Guess and Coppock, "Does Counter-Attitudinal Information"; Schmid and Betsch, "Effective Strategies"; Wood and Porter, "Elusive Backfire Effect."

26. Nyhan and Reifler, "Roles of Information Deficits"; Nyhan, "Why the Backfire Effect."

27. Oppenheimer, "Secret Life," 237.

28. Alter and Oppenheimer, "Uniting the Tribes."

29. Schwarz, "Metacognitive Experiences." For a review, see Alter and Oppenheimer, "Uniting the Tribes."

30. Begg, Anas, and Farinacci, "Dissociation of Processes"; Gilber, Tafarodi, and Malone, "You Can't Not Believe"; Unkelbach, "Reversing the Truth Effect." But see Hasson, Simmons, and Todorov, "Believe It or Not."

31. Dechêne et al., "Truth about the Truth"; Wang et al., "On Known Unknowns."

32. Jacoby and Dallas, "On the Relationship."

33. Fazio et al., "Knowledge Does Not Protect"; Fazio, Rand, and Pennycook, "Repetition Increases Perceived Truth"; but see Brashier, Eliseev, and Marsh, "Initial Accuracy Focus"; Pennycook, Cannon, and Rand, "Prior Exposure"; Murray et al., "'I've Said It Before'"; Keersmaecker et al., "Investigating the Robustness."

34. Schwarz et al., "Metacognitive Experiences."

35. Cameron et al., "Patient Knowledge and Recall"; Swire-Thompson, DeGutis, and Lazer, "Searching for the Backfire Effect"; Ecker, Hogan, and Lewandowsky, "Reminders and Repetition"; see Walter and Tukachinsky, "Meta-Analytic Examination" for meta-analytic evidence.

36. Carnahan and Garrett, "Processing Style"; Ecker, Hogan, and Lewandowsky, "Reminders and Repetition." In fact, in a comprehensive review of the literature on backfire effects, Swire-Thompson, DeGutis, and Lazer conclude that it is "extremely unlikely that . . . fact-checks will lead to increased belief in the misinformation" and note that "avoiding the repetition of the original misconception within the correction appears to be unnecessary and could even hinder corrective efforts" ("Searching for the Backfire Effect," 292).

37. Nyhan, "Why the Backfire Effect."

38. Kuklinski et al., "Misinformation."

39. Pluviano, Watt, and Della Sala, "Misinformation Lingers"; Pluviano et al., "Parents' Beliefs"; Ecker, Hogan, and Lewandowsky, "Reminders and Repetition"; Swire-Thompson, DeGutis, and Lazer, "Searching for the Backfire Effect"; Ecker, Hogan, and Lewandowsky, "Reminders and Repetition." But see Carnahan and Garrett, "Processing Style."

40. For details, see Berinsky, "Birthers Are Back."

41. From June 30 to July 2, 2012, YouGov surveyed 1,000 Americans and again asked respondents whether they thought that "Barack Obama was born in the United States of America."

42. Nyhan and Reifler, "When Corrections Fail."

43. Nyhan and Reifler note that receiving corrections from news sources that conservatives view as liberal could produce backfire effects ("When Corrections Fail," 315). As a result, they focused on ostensibly neutral formats and sources. For example, the choice to present mock news articles was designed to increase realism and objectivity: "people typically receive corrective information within 'objective' news reports" (304). The source of the news article was likewise selected because of its perceived neutrality: "we chose the Associated Press as the source for Study 1 due to its seemingly neutral reputation" (315). The corrections in all of their experiments similarly came from nonpartisan sources: the Central Intelligence Agency (324–25), the Congressional Budget Office on tax cuts (326), and unspecified "experts" on stem cells (327).

44. This replication also differs from the conditions in the original study by omitting conditions that varied respondents' mortality salience. For example, the original study asks some respondents to "Jot down, as specifically as you can, what you think will happen to you as you physically die and once you are physically dead" (Nyhan and Reifler, "When Corrections Fail," 312). Beyond these changes to the correction conditions, there were also differences in the sample. Nyhan and Reifler's sample consisted of 130 undergraduate students, whereas the replication included 304 participants recruited via Amazon Mechanical Turk between May 19 and June 2, 2010.

45. Nyhan and Reifler, "When Corrections Fail"; Goodman, "Death Panels."

46. Rutenberg and Calmes, "False 'Death Panel' Rumor."

47. Data from the Pew Research Center are available at Pew Research Center, "Health Care Reform."

48. These proportions are consistent with other contemporaneous polling on health care rumors. See Brendan Nyhan. "Why the 'Death Panel' Myth."

49. Pasek, Sood, and Krosnick, "Misinformed."

50. Robert Pear, "Reversal on End-of-Life Planning."

51. Sarah Kliff, "What Americans Think of Abortion," *Vox*, April 8, 2015, https://www.vox.com/2018/2/2/16965240/abortion-decision-statistics-opinions.

52. Goodnough et al., "Obamacare Turns 10."

53. Lewandowsky et al., "Misinformation and Its Correction."

54. The survey was administered online to a large national sample of 1,701 American adults between May 17 and May 19, 2010. The second wave of the survey was administered to 699 of the initial respondents from May 25 to May 29, 2010. The study was conducted by Survey Sampling International (SSI) of Shelton, CT. I did not employ quotas but asked SSI to construct a target population that matched the census population (18 and over) on education, gender, age, geography, and income. The resulting sample is not a probability sample but is a diverse national sample. For a description of the sample characteristics, see appendix B in Berinsky, "Rumors and Health Care Reform."

55. The treatment contained a typo, identifying Blumenauer's home state as Georgia. Follow-up studies indicate that this typo did not change the basic pattern of the results of the experiment.

56. I ran a study of 1,354 respondents on Mechanical Turk from November 17 to 25, 2014, to see if people perceived the text of the Isakson and Blumenauer quotes as functionally the same—that is, if people viewed them as equally strong denouncements of the rumor. I presented the full version of the "rumor + correction" condition but experimentally varied the final quote. Specifically, I used a 3×2 design with one dimension as the relevant quotes denouncing the rumor ("Blatant Lie" vs. "Nuts") and the other dimension as the speaker of the quote (the Republican Isakson vs. the Democrat Blumenauer vs. a third nonpartisan speaker Ben Johnson, who was identified as "the chairman of the Bipartisan Advisory Committee on Healthcare Reform"). I then asked respondents to rate how strongly they thought that [Politician X] accepts or rejects the idea of "death panels" being in the health care bill. I found that there were no statistically or substantively significant differences in the perceived strength of the two corrections, regardless of the source of the quote.

57. Respondents were also asked: (1) "Do you think the changes to the health care system that have been enacted by Congress and the Obama administration create 'death panels' which have the authority to determine whether or not a gravely ill or injured person should receive health care based on their 'level of productivity in society?'" and (2) "Overall, given what you know about them, would you say you support or oppose the changes to the health care system that have been enacted by Congress and the Obama administration?"

58. In addition, I asked two questions that measured, in a general sense, how closely the respondents were attending to the instructions on the survey. Specifically, I designed items that serve as what Oppenheimer, Meyvis, and Davidenko term an instructional manipulation check (IMC) ("Instructional Manipulation Checks"). IMCs (or "screeners") indirectly capture whether respondents are satisficing (Krosnick, "Response Strategies")—simply hurrying through the questionnaire as fast as possible—or paying close attention to the survey's contents (full text of these questions is in the appendix). Approximately two-thirds of respondents passed each one of the two screener questions and 55 percent of the sample passed both questions. In the analyses that follow, I present the results for the full sample but focus on the "attentive sample"—those

respondents who passed both screener questions. I focus on this subsample because the news story treatments contain subtle differences in presentation that are likely to have the strongest effect on those respondents who paid the closest attention to the survey. Berinsky, Margolis, and Sances show that the passage of screener questions leads to an increased power of textual treatments ("Separating the Shirkers"). This increased power arises because people who pass screeners read that text more closely. That said, because Berinsky, Margolis, and Sances also show that people who pass screener questions are different from those who fail them, it is certainly possible that there is a heterogeneous treatment effect between the attentive and inattentive subgroups. That is, even if the inattentive subgroup read the material more closely, the effect of the treatment might not be the same for the two groups. The estimates presented here for the attentive sample should therefore be best thought of as the average treatment effect for the attentive.

59. For a more detailed overview of the results of ACA Study 1, see Berinsky, "Rumors and Health Care Reform."

60. In this study, I used a three-category dependent variable: rumor rejection, acceptance, or uncertainty. In other studies, I followed up this initial question with a probe of belief strength to create a seven-point scale of rumor acceptance. The results in those studies are essentially the same with the seven- and three-point scales.

61. Though the relatively small size of the subgroup samples precludes the detection of statistically significant differences, there are strong patterns in the substantive size and direction of the effects (and sometimes these differences reach conventional levels of significance).

62. The full sample results are presented in the appendix of Berinsky, "Rumors and Health Care Reform."

63. This nine-point difference barely misses significance at the .10 level in the attentive sample.

64. Perhaps surprisingly, this backlash effect does not occur among Republicans—probably because support for the reform plan is so low across all conditions. It should also be noted that while rumor acceptance levels could mediate the effect of rumor exposure on policy choice, I do not have the data necessary to test such a hypothesis.

65. As the chi-square test of overall significance demonstrates, the differences among the experimental conditions were no longer significant. Not surprisingly, given this result, the statistically significant differences found in the pairwise comparison of conditions from the first wave disappear. To test for declining effects more formally, I estimated difference-in-differences ordinary least squares (OLS) regressions for the pairwise comparisons (the results were essentially the same using multinomial logits). Interaction terms are, of course, difficult to infer much from, as they are often very imprecisely estimated. In this regression, all p-values are greater than 0.1, but five are only slightly greater than 0.1. Nevertheless, the tests are still somewhat suggestive of a declining treatment effect.

66. See the appendix to Berinsky, "Rumors and Health Care Reform" for these results.

67. This study was fielded as part of the October/November 2010 Cooperative Congressional Election Study (CCES), a panel study administered by YouGov. In July 2010, I ran an additional study with YouGov to directly test my expectations regarding the effectiveness of different corrective strategies. The results of this experiment are consistent with the studies in this paper and are presented in the appendix of Berinsky, "Rumors and Health Care Reform."

68. The stories in these treatments were modeled on the stories used in the May 2010 experiment (and are presented in the appendix).

69. This treatment could also be thought of as the "correct information" treatment.

70. I re-ran a limited version of this study with a control group from May to July 2011. The effects of the treatment were similar to those found here, while the difference between the control and treatment groups was in line with those found in earlier experiments.

71. Admittedly, this second exposure to the rumor might have also triggered other cognitive mechanisms besides fluency that could increase the treatment effect. However, the results presented here are consistent with the mechanism of fluency.

72. Subjects who completed only the first wave of the survey are excluded from the analysis: 837 of the initial 1,000 subjects also took part in the follow up study.

73. Neither of the correction conditions is statistically distinct from the rumor only condition in a pairwise comparison test.

74. Druckman and Nelson, "Framing and Deliberation."

75. However, the differences are statistically significant at the .10 level only in the "rumor only" condition. The difference in the differences across the two conditions between the irrelevant recall and the long recall conditions is nonsignificant.

76. The substantive effect of the rehearsal treatment carries over from beliefs about rumor to health care reform opinion, though these differences are not statistically significant (see Berinsky, "Rumors and Health Care Reform," for details).

77. Bargh et al., "Additive Nature."

78. The survey was conducted from August 27 through September 13, 2009. A nationally representative sample of 1,278 adults was interviewed by landline and cell phone.

79. In total, I identified 52 news stories. Of these stories, 30 percent paired the rumor with a correction from a Democratic source, 43 percent paired the rumor with a correction from a journalist, and 4 percent paired the rumor with a nonpartisan correction. The content analysis protocol and a detailed description of the coding procedure are presented in the appendix to Berinsky, "Rumors and Health Care Reform."

80. Hochschild and Einstein, *Do Facts Matter?* 142.

81. Holman and Lay, "They See Dead People"; Benegal and Scruggs, "Correcting Misinformation"; Wintersieck, Fridkin, and Kenney, "The Message Matters."

82. See, for example, Alba, "Now Circulating."

83. Bolten, "'Sobel' Rumors"; Bhavnani, Findley, and Kuklinski, "Rumor Dynamics"; Finnström, "Gendered War"; Huang, "War of (Mis)Information"; Jo, "Diffusion of Rumors"; Ma, "Spread of SARS"; Pipes, *Hidden Hand*; Zonis, "Conspiracy Thinking"; Taub and Fisher, "Where Countries Are Tinderboxes."

84. However, this might not be enough. Ecker et al. explore such a strategy and find that even multiple retractions were insufficient to completely eliminate the continued influence of misinformation ("Correcting False Information").

Chapter 5. Rumors and Misinformation in the Time of Trump

1. Wooston, "Donald Trump: 'I Won.'"

2. Barbaro, "Donald Trump Clung."

3. Cohen and Forgey, "Trump Alleges Biden Controlled." For instance, at a Michigan rally in mid-October, Trump asked supporters, "Did you see they found 50,000 ballots in, like, a river?" This was just one of nearly 70 false or misleading claims he made over the course of three days (Dale, "Fact-checking Trump's Dishonest weekend").

4. Sherman, "Donald Trump's Pants."

5. Weissert, "Turning the Page?"

6. Salvanto et al., "CBS News Poll."

7. Lardner and Smith, "Records."

8. New York Times, "Twitter Locks Trump's Account."

9. Smith, Ballard, and Sanders, "Most Voters Say."

10. McGranahan, "Anthropology of Lying."

11. A comprehensive list of PolitiFact fact-checks of Trump statements is available at PolitiFact, "Donald Trump." For an explanation of the rating's methodology, see Holan, "Principles of the Truth-O-Meter"; Cillizza, "A Fact Checker Looked."

12. Finnegan, "Scope of Trump's Falsehoods." For a fact-checking comparison of the two candidates, see Sharockman, "Truth Check."

13. The complete archive of the *New York Times'* fact-checking effort is available at Leonhardt, Philbrick, and Thompson, "Trump's Lies vs. Obama's." For a comparison with PolitiFact's fact-checks of Obama's statements, see PolitiFact, "Barack Obama."

14. Glenn Kessler, Meg Kelly, Salvador Rizzo, Leslie Shapiro, and Leo Dominguez, "A Term of Untruths," *Washington Post*, January 23, 2021, https://www.washingtonpost.com/politics/interactive/2021/timeline-trump-claims-as-president/. The complete archive of the *Washington Post's* fact-checking effort is available at Kessler, "Fact Checker."

15. Other politicians have similarly repeated false claims but not at the same scale. See, for example, Dale, "Fact Check: Bernie Sanders."

16. Kessler, Rizzo, and Kelly, "President Trump" (2018).

17. Kessler, "Fact Checker."

18. Lind, "Donald Trump Lies."

19. Pfiffner, "Lies of Donald Trump." This trend continued even during the coronavirus pandemic and the ensuing national crisis. Peters, Plott, and Haberman, "260,000 Words."

20. Schaffner and Luks, "Misinformation or Expressive Responding?"; Patrice Taddonio, "How a Fight over Crowd Size."

21. Lauren Carroll, "Fact-Checking Trump's Claim."

22. Along these lines, there is descriptive evidence that individuals exposed to conservative media—most notably, the Fox News Channel—tend to have more misinformed beliefs about a number of topics, including the COVID-19 pandemic (e.g., Bursztyn et al., "Misinformation"; Jamieson and Albarracín, "Relation between Media Consumption and Misinformation"; Simonov, "Persuasive Effect"), among other issues (Jurkowitz and Mitchell, "Cable TV"). However, it is important to note that several of these works simply examine the correlation between media exposure and misperceptions, which may be confounded by selection bias in the types of media individuals choose to consume (de Benedictis-Kessner, Baum, and Berinsky, "Polarization").

23. For recent polling on declining trust in government, see data from the Pew Research Center available at "Americans' Views of Government." For research on democratic norms in particular, see Kates, Ladd, and Tucker, "Should You Worry."

24. On the model that Trump set for other leaders to spread misinformation, see, for example, Caby Galvin, "Globalization of 'Fake News'"; Washington Post, "Global Reach."

25. Stolberg and Weiland, "Study Finds."

26. Swire et al., "Processing Political Misinformation."

27. For example, for a claim about vaccines causing autism, participants assigned to the attributed condition saw the statement, "Donald Trump said that vaccines cause autism," whereas participants in the unattributed condition simply saw the claim, "Vaccines cause autism." Trump made this claim repeatedly, including on Twitter. See Hornsey et al., "Donald Trump and Vaccination."

28. Returning to the autism example above, the correction included the following text: "This is false. There is strong consensus in the scientific community that vaccines are not linked to autism. For example, one study by the Danish Epidemiology Science Centre tracked all children born in Denmark from 1991 to 1998 and concluded that there was no increase in the rate of autism for vaccinated as opposed to non-vaccinated children."

29. We measured support for Trump in Studies 1 and 2 by asking participants how likely they would be to vote for Trump in the 2016 election. Republicans who rated 5 or more (out of 10) on this measure were classified as Trump supporters, and Republicans who scored below 5

were classified as Trump nonsupporters. An aggregation of polls showing how levels of support for Trump versus the other candidates changed over time is available at FiveThirtyEight, "2016 National Primary Polls." For Study 3, we instead classified support using feelings thermometers. Participants were considered to be supporters of a given politician (Trump or Sanders) if they rated the candidate higher than 50 on a 0–100 feelings thermometer item and nonsupporters if they provided a rating lower than 50. If participants selected 50 exactly, they were treated as neutral and excluded from all analyses.

30. A comprehensive list of PolitiFact fact-checks of Sanders's statements is available at Polit-Fact, "Bernie Sanders." For fact-checks from the *New York Times*, see Qiu, "Fact-Checking Bernie Sanders."

31. Swire-Thompson et al., "They Might Be a Liar."

32. Because we used real-world statements that Trump and Sanders had actually made, the exact statements used (and their topics) varied. For example, one of the false statements in the Trump condition was "Donald Trump said that 'inner-city crime has reached record levels.'" Conversely, one of the false statements attributed to Sanders was: "Bernie Sanders said that the '2016 US Presidential election had the lowest voter turnout in over 20 years.'"

33. Specifically, participants in the "equal" condition saw four true and four false statements, whereas participants in the "disproportionate" condition again saw four false statements but only one true statement.

34. Pornpitakpan, "Persuasiveness of Source."

35. Housholder and LaMarre, "Facebook Politics."

36. Ecker and Antonio, "Can You Believe It?"; Guillory and Geraci, "Correcting Erroneous Inferences"; McGinnies and Ward, "Better Liked than Right."

37. Such "surprising" or "unlikely" source corrections are not very common, but they do occur. See, for example, Wall Street Journal Editorial Board, "A Presidential Smear."

38. As an alternative measure, we also calculated "accuracy scores" by subtracting participants' belief in misinformation from their belief in facts. On this measure, the higher the score, the more likely participants were to accurately discern truth from fiction. Immediately after reading the fact-checking messages, individuals were better able to distinguish true versus false statements, regardless of whether the statements they were shown were attributed to Trump. Over the course of a week, however, participants from all groups seemed to partially forget the fact-checking messages. This tendency was especially strong among participants who were assigned to view information attributed to Trump. For a full description of these findings, see Swire et al., "Processing Political Misinformation."

39. Allcott and Gentzkow, "Social Media and Fake News"; Garrett and Bond, "Conservatives' Susceptibility"; Guess, Nagler, and Tucker, "Less than You Think"; Guess, Nyhan, and Reifler, "Exposure to Untrustworthy Websites"; Marwick and Lewis, "Media Manipulation"; Faris et al., "Partisanship,"; Huszár et al., "Algorithmic Amplification"; Guess et al., "Cracking Open the News Feed."

40. Jost and Banaji, "Role of Stereotyping"; Jost et al., "Political Conservatism."

41. Jost et al., "Political Conservatism." Importantly, Jost and colleagues explicitly state that their view does not discount the effect of individuals' context on their adoption of conservative beliefs. However, they argue that such situational features primarily serve to exacerbate (or attenuate) dispositional differences, rather than wholly determine individuals' political attitudes.

42. Many of these traits are likewise associated with authoritarianism (Adorno et al., *Authoritarian Personality*), which also tends to be positively correlated with political conservatism (see Nilsson and Jost, "Authoritarian-Conservatism Nexus," for a review).

43. Jost, "Ideological Asymmetries"; Jost et al., "Political Conservatism"; Jost, Sterling, and Stern, "Getting Closure"; Barberá et al., "Tweeting from Left to Right"; Nam, Jost, and Van Bavel, "'Not for All the Tea.'"

44. Van der Linden et al., "Paranoid Style."

45. Such relationships may not be limited to the United States. For instance, Ecker and Ang investigated in Australia whether political attitudes conditioned how people update their beliefs after being presented with factual corrections ("Political Attitudes"). They found that when misinformation contradicted individuals' prior attitudes, fact-checks affected the beliefs of participants on both sides of the political spectrum. However, when the misinformation affirmed individuals' prior beliefs, retractions were only effective for left-wing—but not right-wing—participants (though see Ecker, Sze, and Andreotta, "Corrections of Political Misinformation" for contrary findings in the US context).

46. Kahan, "Ideology"; Kahan et al., "Motivated Numeracy." In addition, a small literature criticizes the purported relationship between personality traits and political conservativism because it omits the importance of genes in its analysis (Verhulst, Eaves, and Hatemi, "Correlation Not Causation"). These arguments rely on a previous body of research showing that individuals' genetics influence political attitudes and behavior (e.g., Martin et al., "Transmission of Social Attitudes"; Dawes and Fowler, "Partisanship, Voting"; Fowler and Dawes, "In Defense of Genopolitics"; Hatemi et al., "Genome-Wide Analysis"; Verhulst, Hatemi, and Martin, "Nature of the Relationship"). Smith and colleagues, for example, argue that genetic variation shapes conservative versus liberal orientation to a greater extent than do environmental factors ("How Do We Know").

47. Washburn and Skitka, "Science Denial."

48. Claassen and Ensley, "Motivated Reasoning."

49. For these analyses, I combined the equal and disproportionate ratio conditions because there were not differences in responses to corrections based on the ratio of misinformation presented.

50. Given some Sanders's supporters' resistance to criticism, this finding is encouraging. Devine, Griffin, and Bronstein, "The 'Swarm.'"

51. Koch, "Again and Again."

52. Guess and Coppock, "Does Counter-Attitudinal Information"; Swire-Thompson, DeGutis, and Lazer, "Searching for the Backfire Effect"; and Wood and Porter, "Elusive Backfire Effect."

53. Though not discussed at length here, we found nearly identical patterns in Study 2 (summarized in figure 10 of Swire et al., "Processing Political Misinformation," 15). Participants were no more or less likely to vote for Trump after viewing the fact-checking messages; in fact, individuals' self-reported voting intentions were largely independent of belief change.

54. Funk, "Impact of Scandal."

55. Basinger, "Scandals and Congressional Elections."

56. Hahl, Kim, and Sivan, "Authentic Appeal."

57. Redlawsk, Civettini, and Emmerson, "Affective Tipping Point."

58. Nyhan and Reifler, "Effect of Fact-Checking."

59. Though see Carnahan, Bergan, and Lee, "Do Corrective Effects Last?"

60. Anderson and Hanslmayr, "Neural Mechanisms."

61. Illustrative fact-checks of statements from Shorten and Turnbull are available at ABC News, "Bill Shorten," and ABC News, "Malcolm Turnbell," respectively.

62. See, for example, Andrew Bolt, "Election a Choice."

63. Note that we measured political support for each politician as a summary of three measures: self-reported voting intentions, feelings thermometer ratings, and perceptions of the politician's general veracity.

64. For a full description of our results, see Aird et al., "Does Truth Matter."

65. Trust has continued to decline in the United States to around 20% in 2020, with more recent polling data from Pew Research Center, "Americans' Views of Government." Conversely,

Australians' trust in government rose to over 60% in 2020. Malcom Farr, "Australians' trust in government and media soars as coronavirus crisis escalates," *Guardian*, April 6, 2020, https://www.theguardian.com/australia-news/2020/apr/07/australians-trust-in-government-and-media-soars-as-coronavirus-crisis-escalates.

66. Reilly and Torresi, "Voting Rights." For a broader discussion of polarization in comparative politics beyond the US and Australian contexts, see: Klein, "What Polarization Data"; Boxell, Gentzkow, and Shapiro, "Cross-Country Trends."

67. See, for example, Iyengar et al., "The Origins and Consequences."

68. This type of electoral system is relatively uncommon globally, with only 22 countries having similar compulsory voting requirements. Santhanam, "22 Countries."

69. Though Barrera and colleagues find a similar dynamic—the ability to move factual beliefs but not assessments of politicians—in an experiment conducted during the 2017 French national election, suggesting that perhaps it is Australians, not Americans, that are the outlier ("Facts, Alternative Facts").

Chapter 6. The Role of Political Elites

1. "Elite" here means "partisan political actors—leading Democrat and Republican politicians" (Berinsky, *In Time of War*, 275 n. 17). Because media and political actors shape the information environment in different ways, distinguishing between them helps identify which elites in particular have an outsized influence on partisan beliefs about rumors. This stands in contrast to Zaller, who lumps political and media actors together into a single category of elites (*Nature and Origins*). That said, as discussed throughout this book, media actors surely play a role in the spread of political rumors as well.

2. Berinsky, *In Time of War*.

3. On the importance of cue taking and heuristics in how poorly informed citizens form opinions on political issues, see Lupia, "Shortcuts versus Encyclopedias"; Popkin, *Reasoning Voter*; Sniderman, Brody, and Tetlock, *Reasoning and Choice*; Berinsky, *In Time of War*.

4. For a discussion of these implications in the context of public support for war, see Berinsky 2009, 214–15.

5. Recall that political information was assessed using a standard battery of political knowledge questions measuring factual knowledge about political leaders and institutions.

6. Here, as in the analyses that follow, I present the raw data of this relationship—the actual rate of rumor rejection at different levels of political information—rather than predicted probabilities from a multivariate model.

7. Mirroring this thinking, some prominent leaders have pointed to civics education as a solution to the problem of political misinformation. For instance, in his 2019 annual report, John Roberts, the Chief Justice of the Supreme Court, connected a rise in online mis- and disinformation to a diminished focus on civic education in the United States, saying, "We have come to take democracy for granted, and civic education has fallen by the wayside. In our age, when social media can instantly spread rumor and false information on a grand scale, the public's need to understand our government, and the protections it provides, is ever more vital" (see Supreme Court, "2019 Year-End Report"). See also Campbell et al., *American Voter*; Delli Carpini and Keeter, *What Americans Know*; and Gilens, "Political Ignorance."

8. The phrasing of this question, of course, sets aside the fact that exposing people to more political information would not change the underlying characteristics of the respondent that survey-based measures of political information almost certainly proxy, e.g., education and consciousness.

9. I first presented these results in a working paper in April 2012.

10. See table 3.1 in chapter 3 for a full description of these data collection efforts.

11. Miller, Saunders, and Farhart, "Conspiracy Endorsement."

12. Cassino and Jenkins, "Conspiracy Theories Prosper."

13. Nyhan, "Why the 'Death Panel.'"

14. Nyhan, Reifler, and Ubel, "Hazards of Correcting."

15. Nyhan, "Political Knowledge."

16. Jost, "Ideological Asymmetries"; Lewandowsky, Oberauer, and Gignac, "NASA Faked the Moon Landing."

17. Miller, Saunders, and Farhart, "Conspiracy Endorsement."

18. Levendusky, *Partisan Sort*; Mason, "Ideologues without Issues."

19. Kahan, "Ideology, Motivated Reasoning"; Ditto et al., "Partisan Bias"; and Kahan et al., "Motivated Numeracy."

20. Frimer, Skitka, and Motyl, "Liberals and Conservatives."

21. Guay and Johnston, "Ideological Asymmetries"; Jost et al., "Are Needs to Manage."

22. V. O Key, *Responsible Electorate*.

23. Berinsky, *Silent Voices*, 27–29.

24. Rosenblum and Muirhead, *A Lot of People Are Saying*.

25. Bode, Vraga, and Tully, "Do the Right Thing"; Martel, Mosleh, and Rand, "You're Definitely Wrong."

26. Butterfuss, Aubele, and Kendeou, "Hedged Language"; Gustafson and Rice, "The Effects of Uncertainty"; and Gustafson and Rice, "A Review of the Effects of Uncertainty."

27. Johnson and Slovic, "Presenting Uncertainty."

28. Gustafson and Rice, "A Review of the Effects of Uncertainty."

29. E.g., Martel, Mosleh, and Rand, "You're Definitely Wrong."

30. Bucciol and Zarri, "Lying in Politics"; Card, Lin, and Smith, "Politifact"; Ostermeier, "Selection Bias?"

31. For a comparative analysis of misinformation in more recent elections, see Sharockman, "Post-Truth Election"; Uscinski and Butler, "Epistemology"; Uscinski, "Epistemology of Fact Checking."

32. Although there is limited evidence for *ideological* bias in fact-checking, there is evidence that Republicans largely *perceive* fact-checkers as biased toward the left (e.g., Walker and Gottfried, "Republicans Far More Likely"; Shin and Thorson, "Partisan Selective Sharing"). See also Lim, "Checking How Fact-Checkers Check"; Marietta, Barker, and Bowser, "Fact-Checking"; Ostermeier, "Selection Bias?"

33. Golbeck, Grimes, and Rogers, "Twitter Use by the US Congress"; Hemphill, Otterbacher, and Shapiro, "What's Congress Doing on Twitter?"

34. Pew Research Center, "News on Twitter"; Pew Research Center, "Politics on Twitter."

35. Pew Research Center, "Journalists Sense Turmoil."

36. Data was shared via personal correspondence with researchers at the Lazer Lab at Northeastern University, directed by David Lazer. The handles and tweets were originally collected for Green et al. ("Elusive Consensus") and then continued to be collected until November 2020. The links shared by each member of Congress were labeled based on NewsGuard's rating system as well as the manual coding system described in Grinberg et al., "Political Science." The data I received was aggregated at the handle-day level and comprises counts of the number of links shared that fall into each rating category.

37. Grinberg et al., "Political Science," 374.

38. For a discussion of NewsGuard's methodology, see NewsGuard, "Rating Process and Criteria."

39. While it is always possible that some of these tweets are reshared to refute, research by Mohsen Mosleh and colleagues shows that only 3.9% of a sample of 2,000 users who shared

links to fake news on Twitter did so to refute or mock the linked article ("Shared Partisanship"). The overwhelming majority of Twitter users seem to share links to fake news in earnest. If we believe that Democrats are more likely to refute links than Republicans, then this would mean that the differences I am capturing, in fact, are smaller representations of the difference in resharing untrustworthy sites.

40. These full results are presented in figure A15 in the appendix. These measures are "black," "red," "orange," "yellow," and "pink slime." Websites were considered "black" if they "published almost exclusively fabricated stories," whereas "red" and "orange" sources were coded based on articles flagged by Snopes.com and reflect the extent to which the misinformation is a result of a "flawed editorial process." (For more information about Snopes's methodology, see "What Is Snopes' Fact-Checking Process?" Snopes, May 30, 2019, https://www.snopes.com/faq/fact-checking-process/.) Outlets labeled as "yellow" were tabloids or other low-quality journalism. More information on these classifications system can be found in the supplementary materials for Grinberg et al., "Political Science." Outlets were labeled as "pink" if they came from sources associated with "pink slime journalism," which is automatically generated and politically motivated online content (Bengani, "As Election Looms").

41. Members of Congress who identify as Independents were excluded from this analysis. However, this coding decision did not substantively change the results. Additionally, the patterns are similar, albeit slightly less stark, if we use raw counts and do not divide by total tweet activity, since Democrats are more active on Twitter overall.

42. These findings are presented in figure A16 in the appendix. A list of the super spreaders sorted by total amount of misinformation shared in presented in table A10.

43. Examples of domains rated as publishing misinformation include Daily Kos (on the left) and Breitbart (on the right). More examples can be found in the report found at Benton, "NewsGuard Considers Fox News."

44. Taking these three rumors together, 28.8% of statements were issued by Republicans, 16.8% were issued by Democrats, and 54.3% were issued by nonpartisan sources. However, this varies across individual rumors. For instance, the majority of statements on the birther rumor came from Republicans (58.5%). For the other two rumors, while the majority of corrections actually came from nonpartisan sources, Democrats were more likely to have a response than were Republicans. In fact, in the data set, there are no statements from Republicans addressing the rumor that Obama is a Muslim. This does not mean that these statements do not exist at all, but the fact that they did not come up in my searches suggests that they were less prevalent.

45. An example of a direct quote is "On Monday, while on Steve Malzberg's radio show on New York's WOR Radio, I was asked about the President Obama's birth certificate issue. In my answer, I simply misspoke when I alluded to President Obama growing up in Kenya and meant to say Indonesia." An example of a correction text that paraphrases a statement is "Huckabee did say in a radio interview that Obama grew up in Kenya and then spoke at length about the implications of that suggesting that his views of the British were shaped by a father whom he only met once and a grandfather he never met. But we should note that Huckabee quickly corrected the record and has notably rejected claims about Obama's birth place."

46. Specifically, I defined "definitive corrections" as follows: "A 'definitive' correction is very clear, and does not contain other statements that may weaken the statement/correction. The corrector appears to be sincere in their attempt to 'set the record straight.' Often, it is clear that the public figure is urging other people to dismiss the rumor as well. The public figure will also often talk as if it is a fact that the rumor is false." In contrast, a soft correction was described as one that "contains other language that undermines the initial correction. If any part of the speaker's words fosters ambiguity as to whether or not the rumor is true, it should be classified as 'soft.' If the speaker mentions the rumor, but deflects or dodges the question as 'a non-issue' without an

unambiguous correction, it is 'soft.' If the speaker insinuates that, in his/her opinion the rumor is false, but that others are entitled to their own opinion, it is 'soft.'" Coders could also indicate that the statement that addressed the rumor included no correction at all.

47. Inter-coder reliability never exceeded 60%.

48. Specifically, we recruited 257 individuals via Amazon Mechanical Turk, and each individual rated twelve different quotes, six of which were the same for everyone while the other six were selected from the corpus of 188 corrections. Each respondent would see two statements about each rumor, so the survey covered six rumors in total. For example, the corrections included statements about Obama's religion and place of birth as well as rumors that the Republicans fraudulently won the 2004 election in Ohio. Respondents were randomly assigned to rate statements using either the scale measure reported here or a binary classification of simply "soft" or "definitive," although the findings were consistent for both measures. Respondents also had the option to classify a response as "not applicable" if they believed the statement endorsed rather than corrected the rumor.

49. There were also some instances in which multiple people were involved in a correction, for instance, when the correction was in the form of a transcript in which a journalist was interviewing a political figure. These corrections were coded with the partisanship of the interviewee. It should be noted that the results are not simply the result of a pattern where Republicans offer fewer corrections than do Democrats. It is difficult to make absolute comparisons between the parties given the differences in the number of rumors examined on the Democratic and Republican side. But that said, there were more Republican corrections identified in the search process and included in this analysis.

50. Nevertheless, as mentioned in chapter 5, I did observe slight partisan asymmetries in rumor beliefs prior to correction, even though both Democratic and Republican respondents were equally receptive to later corrections. Specifically, Trump supporters consistently rated misinformation spread by Trump as more believable than Sanders supporters rated misinformation spread by Sanders. However, nonsupporters of Trump consistently rated his misinformation as *less* believable than nonsupporters of Sanders. In other words, respondents with more right-leaning tendencies tended to exhibit stronger biases in their initial perceptions of the veracity of politicians' claims.

51. Thorson, "Belief Echoes."

52. Data from this study were collected through SSI from October 8 through October 18, 2014 (N = 2,233).

53. The soft correction read as follows: "'It doesn't seem like there's any evidence they used foreign funds for political activity, but it's always hard to say in these situations . . . everyone is entitled to their own opinion.' said William Forrester, [another [Party1/Party2] Congressman from Indiana]/[a spokesperson for the nonprofit group OpenCampaigns], recently." The strong correction, on the other hand, read as follows: "'These accusations are 100% false. They have no logic, no basis and no merit. They are definitely false. And they need to stop now,' said William Forrester, [another [Party1/Party2] Congressman from Indiana]/[a spokesperson for the nonprofit group OpenCampaigns], recently."

54. See tables A21–23 in the appendix for a summary of the results.

56. This result also stands in contrast to the general finding, discussed in chapter 4, that "unlikely" sources—partisans speaking against their own apparent interests—are the most effective in pushing respondents to reject rumors. In addition, it should be noted that the partisanship of the rumor's target had the largest effect on whether respondents rejected the rumor and supported the candidate, which is consistent with the more general finding that the partisan nature of rumors strongly influences individuals' likelihood of accepting these rumors.

57. This experiment was conducted from April 11 to April 28, 2018, on a sample of 5,958 participants recruited through SSI.

58. For a history of the program, see Eschner, "What We Know." It should be noted that all subjects in my experiment were debriefed at the end of the survey with the following statement: "During this survey you may have seen an article about a reintroduced CIA mind-control program. In all cases, the articles you read were constructed by us, and the people and events described are completely fictional. We constructed these stories in order to find out how people might react when different groups are associated with different types of rumors and to test the effectiveness of subsequent rumor corrections."

59. The full soft correction was "Well, it all seems a little odd to me. It's such a crazy story. Let's hope they're not right!" whereas the definitive correction stated: "There is absolutely no truth to this claim. These so-called 'activists' are clearly just some conspiracy theorists who got bored one afternoon. Their claims are baseless and absurd, and no one should take them seriously."

60. Refer to table A24 in the appendix for the regression data used to generate the predicted effect plots for the mind control experiment (figs. 6.8 and 6.9).

Chapter 7. Conclusion

1. Madison, "Epilogue."

2. Phillip Bump, "This Might Be the Most Embarrassing Document Created by White House Staffer," *Washington Post*, December 18, 2020, https://www.washingtonpost.com/politics/2020/12/18/this-might-be-most-embarrassing-document-created-by-white-house-staffer/; Chris Marquette, "Former Trump White House Aide Peter Navarro Charged with Contempt of Congress," *Roll Call*, June 3, 2022, https://rollcall.com/2022/06/03/former-trump-white-house-adviser-peter-navarro-indicted-for-contempt-of-congress/.

3. Kay Ivey, "Stole," YouTube, April 11, 2022, https://www.youtube.com/watch?v=xztJw19j-CY.

4. Michael C. Bender, Rebecca Lieberman, Eden Weingart, Alyce McFadden, and Nick Corasaniti, "How Trump's Endorsements Elevate Election Lies and Inflate His Political Power," *New York Times*, August 21, 2022, https://www.nytimes.com/interactive/2022/08/22/us/trump-endorsements.html.

5. Clara Hendrickson, "List of Alleged Dead Voters in Wayne County Does Not Provide Evidence of Voter Fraud," *Detroit Free Press*, November 6, 2020, https://www.freep.com/story/news/local/michigan/detroit/2020/11/06/no-evidence-thousands-dead-people-cast-ballots-wayne-county/6195468002/.

6. Amy Gardner, Emma Brown, and Josh Dawsey, "Inside the Nonstop Pressure Campaign by Trump Allies to Get Election Officials to Revisit the 2020 Vote," *Washington Post*, December 22, 2021, https://www.washingtonpost.com/politics/trump-election-officials-pressure-campaign/2021/12/22/8a0b0788-5d26-11ec-ae5b-5002292337c7_story.html.

7. Hendrickson, "List of Alleged Dead Voters."

8. "Voter Fraud and the January 6th Capitol Attack | YouGov Poll: June 7–10, 2022," YouGov America, June 13, 2022, https://today.yougov.com/topics/politics/articles-reports/2022/06/13/voter-fraud-and-january-6th-capitol-attack-yougov.

9. In this book, I focus on the former in the context of the latter because of my intellectual orientation and expertise. But I recognize that mass political behavior is only one piece of the puzzle. That said, the process of individual cognition creates a weak foundation for addressing the ills of rumors and misinformation. For instance, in *The Misinformation Age*, O'Connor and Weatherall convincingly argue that the dynamics of social interaction can help spread misinformation even if individuals in that system behave in a thoughtful and rational manner. The data presented in this book show that individuals do not necessarily behave in such a way. Thus, social relations might further compound the troubling tendencies uncovered here.

10. Brakkton Booker, "Facebook Removes 'Stop The Steal' Content; Twitter Suspends QAnon Accounts," NPR, January 12, 2021, https://www.npr.org/sections/insurrection-at-the-capitol/2021/01/12/956003580/facebook-removes-stop-the-steal-content-twitter-suspends-qanon-accounts.

11. Bode and Vraga, "In Related News."

12. Allen et al., "Scaling Up Fact-Checking"; Epstein et al., "Developing an Accuracy-Prompt Toolkit."

13. Roozenbeek and Van der Linden, "Fake News Game."

14. See, for example, Brian Resnick, "A new brain study sheds light on why it can be so hard to change someone's political beliefs," *Vox*, January 23, 2017, https://www.vox.com/science-and-health/2016/12/28/14088992/brain-study-change-minds; Kalev Leetaru, "The Backfire Effect and Why Facebook's 'Fake News' Warning Gets It All Wrong," *Forbes*, May 23, 2017, https://www.forbes.com/sites/kalevleetaru/2017/03/23/the-backfire-effect-and-why-facebooks-fake-news-warning-gets-it-all-wrong/?sh=6a5f083924d7l; and Nyhan, "Why the Backfire Effect."

15. On inoculation, see Roozenbeek, et al., "Disentangling Item"; on lateral reading, see Wineburg et al., "Lateral Reading"; on media literacy tips, see Guess et al., "A Digital Media Literacy Intervention."

16. Pennycook et al., "Fighting COVID-19 Misinformation"; Epstein et al., "Developing an Accuracy-Prompt Toolkit."

17. Zaller, "What Nature and Origins Leaves Out," 618.

18. Sunstein, *Conspiracy Theories*, 209.

Abalakina-Paap, Marina, Walter G. Stephan, Traci Craig, and W. Larry Gregory. 1999. "Beliefs in Conspiracies." *Political Psychology* 20 (3): 637–47. https://doi.org/10.1111/0162-895X.00160.

ABC News (Australian Broadcasting Corporation). n.d. "Fact Check: Bill Shorten." Accessed March 4, 2021. https://www.abc.net.au/news/factcheck/bill-shorten/.

———. n.d. "Fact Check: Malcolm Turnbull." Accessed March 4, 2021. https://www.abc.net.au/news/factcheck/malcolm-turnbull/.

Adorno, Theodor, Else Frenkel-Brunswik, Daniel Levinson, and Nevitt Sandford. 1950. *The Authoritarian Personality*. New York: Harper and Brothers.

Aird, Michael J., Ullrich K. H. Ecker, Briony Swire, Adam J. Berinsky, and Stephan Lewandowsky. 2018. "Does Truth Matter to Voters? The Effects of Correcting Political Misinformation in an Australian Sample." *Royal Society Open Science* 5 (12): 1–14. https://doi.org/10.6084/m9.figshare.c.4320944.v1.

Alba, Davey. 2020. "Now Circulating on Social Media: 4 Election Falsehoods." *New York Times*, October 14. https://www.nytimes.com/2020/10/14/technology/four-election-related-falsehoods.html.

Allcott, Hunt, Levi Boxell, Jacob Conway, Matthew Gentzkow, Michael Thaler, and David Yang. 2020. "Polarization and Public Health: Partisan Differences in Social Distancing during the Coronavirus Pandemic." *Journal of Public Economics* 191: 104254.

Allcott, Hunt, and Matthew Gentzkow. 2017. "Social Media and Fake News in the 2016 Election." *Journal of Economic Perspectives* 31 (2): 211–36. https://doi.org/10.1257/jep.31.2.211.

Allen, Jennifer, Antonio A. Arechar, Gordon Pennycook, and David G. Rand. 2021. "Scaling Up Fact-Checking Using the Wisdom of Crowds." *Science Advances* 7 (36): eabf4393.

Allport, Floyd H., and Milton Lepkin. 1945. "Wartime Rumors of Waste and Special Privilege: Why Some People Believe Them." *Journal of Abnormal and Social Psychology* 40 (1): 3.

Allport, Gordon W., and Leo Postman. 1947. The Psychology of Rumor. New York: Henry Holt.

Alter, Adam L., and Daniel M. Oppenheimer. 2009. "Uniting the Tribes of Fluency to Form a Metacognitive Nation." *Personality and Social Psychology Review* 13 (3): 219–35. https://doi.org/10.1177/1088868309341564.

Amazeen, Michelle A. 2013. "Making a Difference: A Critical Assessment of Fact-Checking in 2012." *New America Foundation, 1–40*.

Anderson, Michael C., and Simon Hanslmayr. 2014. "Neural Mechanisms of Motivated Forgetting." *Trends in Cognitive Sciences* 18 (6): 279–92. https://doi.org/10.1016/j.tics.2014.03.002.

Ansolabehere, Stephen, Jonathan Rodden, and James M. Snyder. 2008. "The Strength of Issues: Using Multiple Measures to Gauge Preference Stability, Ideological Constraint, and Issue Voting." *American Political Science Review* 102 (2): 215–32. http://www.jstor.org/stable/27644512.

Anspach, Nicolas M., and Taylor N. Carlson. 2020. "What to Believe? Social Media Commentary and Belief in Misinformation." *Political Behavior* 42 (3): 697–718. https://doi.org/10.1007/s11109-018-9515-z.

Arguedas, Amy Ross, Craig T. Robertson, Richard Fletcher, and Rasmus Kleis Nielsen. 2022. "Echo Chambers, Filter Bubbles, and Polarisation: A Literature Review." Reuters Institute, January 19. https://reutersinstitute.politics.ox.ac.uk/echo-chambers-filter-bubbles-and -polarisation-literature-review.

Bakshy, Eytan, Solomon Messing, and Lada A. Adamic. 2015. "Exposure to Ideologically Diverse News and Opinion on Facebook." *Science* 348 (6239): 1130–32.

Barbaro, Michael. 2016. "Donald Trump Clung to 'Birther' Lie for Years, and Still Isn't Apologetic." *New York Times*, September 17. https://www.nytimes.com/2016/09/17/us/politics/donald -trump-obama-birther.html.

Barberá, Pablo, John T. Jost, Jonathan Nagler, Joshua A. Tucker, and Richard Bonneau. 2015. "Tweeting from Left to Right: Is Online Political Communication More than an Echo Chamber?" *Psychological Science* 26 (10): 1531–42.

Bargh, J. A., R. N. Bond, W. J. Lombardi, and M. E. Tota. 1986. "The Additive Nature of Chronic and Temporary Sources of Construct Accessibility." *Journal of Personality and Social Psychology* 50: 869–78.

Barnett, Michael D., and Arthur D. Marsden. 2019. "The Death Panel Myth among Older Adults: Political Ideology, Advance Directives, and Perceived Discrimination on the Basis of Age." *Death Studies* 45 (10): 827–37. https://doi.org/10.1080/07481187.2019.1699200.

Baron, Richard J., and Adam Berinsky. 2019. "Mistrust in Science—A Threat to the Patient—Physician Relationship." *New England Journal of Medicine* 381 (2): 182–85. https://www.nejm .org/doi/10.1056/NEJMms1813043.

Barrera, Oscar, Sergei Guriev, Emeric Henry, and Ekaterina Zhuravskaya. 2020. "Facts, Alternative Facts, and Fact Checking in Times of Post-Truth Politics." *Journal of Public Economics* 182: 1–19.

Basinger, Scott J. 2013. "Scandals and Congressional Elections in the Post-Watergate Era." *Political Research Quarterly* 66 (2): 385–98.

Baum, Matthew A., and Tim Groeling. 2009. "Shot by the Messenger: Partisan Cues and Public Opinion regarding National Security and War." *Political Behavior* 31 (2): 157–86.

Begg, Ian Maynard, Ann Anas, and Suzanne Farinacci. 1992. "Dissociation of Processes in Belief: Source Recollection, Statement Familiarity, and the Illusion of Truth." *Journal of Experimental Psychology: General* 121 (4): 446–58. https://doi.org/10.1037/0096-3445.121.4.446.

Benegal, Salil D., and Lyle A. Scruggs. 2018. "Correcting Misinformation about Climate Change: The Impact of Partisanship in an Experimental Setting." *Climatic Change* 148 (1–2): 61–80. https://doi.org/10.1007/s10584-018-2192-4.

Bengani, Priyanjana. 2020. "As Election Looms, A Network of Mysterious 'Pink Slime' Local News Outlets Nearly Triples in Size." *Columbia Journalism Review,* August 5. https://www .cjr.org/analysis/as-election-looms-a-network-of-mysterious-pink-slime-local-news-outlets -nearly-triples-in-size.php.

Benton, Joshua. 2018. "NewsGuard Considers Fox News a Healthy Part of Your News Diet." *Nieman Lab*, August 24. https://www.niemanlab.org/2018/08/newsguard-considers-fox-news -a-healthy-part-of-your-news-diet/.

Berinsky, Adam J. 2007. "Assuming the Costs of War: Events, Elites, and American Public Support for Military Conflict." *Journal of Politics* 69 (4): 975–97. https://doi.org/10.1111/j.1468 -2508.2007.00602.x.

———. 2012. "The Birthers Are Back." *YouGov*, February 3. https://today.yougov.com/topics /politics/articles-reports/2012/02/03/birthers-are-back.

———. 2009. *In Time of War: Understanding American Public Opinion from World War II to Iraq.* Chicago: University of Chicago Press.

———. 2017. "Rumors and Health Care Reform: Experiments in Political Misinformation." *British Journal of Political Science* 47 (2): 241–62. https://doi.org/10.1017/S0007123415000186.

———. 2004. *Silent Voices: Public Opinion and Political Participation in America.* Princeton, NJ: Princeton University Press.

———. 2018. "Telling the Truth about Believing the Lies? Evidence for the Limited Prevalence of Expressive Survey Responding." *Journal of Politics.* University of Chicago Press. https://doi .org/10.1086/694258.

Berinsky, Adam J., Michele F. Margolis, and Michael W. Sances. 2014. "Separating the Shirkers from the Workers? Making Sure Respondents Pay Attention on Self-Administered Surveys." *American Journal of Political Science* 58 (3): 739–53. https://doi.org/10.1111/ajps.12081.

Betsch, Cornelia. 2011. "Innovations in Communication: The Internet and the Psychology of Vaccination Decisions." *Eurosurveillance* 16 (17): 1–6.

Bhavnani, Ravi, Michael G. Findley, and James H. Kuklinski. 2009. "Rumor Dynamics in Ethnic Violence." *Journal of Politics* 71 (3): 876–92. https://doi.org/10.1017/S002238160909077X.

Blanchflower, David. 2016. "Experts Get It Wrong Again by Failing to Predict Trump Victory." *Guardian,* November 9. https://www.theguardian.com/business/2016/nov/09/experts -trump-victory-economic-political-forecasters-recession.

Bode, Leticia, and Emily K. Vraga. 2015. "In Related News, That Was Wrong: The Correction of Misinformation through Related Stories Functionality in Social Media." *Journal of Communication* 65 (4): 619–38.

Bode, Leticia, Emily K. Vraga, and Melissa Tully. 2020. "Do the Right Thing: Tone May Not Affect Correction of Misinformation on Social Media." *Harvard Kennedy School Misinformation Review* 1 (4): 1–12.

Bolt, Andrew. 2016. "Election a Choice between Terrible Twins—Bill Shorten and Malcolm Turnbull." *West Australian,* April 23. https://thewest.com.au/news/qld/election-a-choice-between -terrible-twins---bill-shorten-and-malcolm-turnbull-ng-b22c22fe5570ae0e5ef369dd640ddaae.

Bolten, Catherine E. 2014. "'Sobel' Rumors and Tribal Truths: Narrative and Politics in Sierra Leone, 1994." *Comparative Studies in Society and History* 56 (1): 187–214.

Boutyline, Andrei, and Robb Willer. 2017. "The Social Structure of Political Echo Chambers: Variation in Ideological Homophily in Online Networks." *Political Psychology* 38 (3): 551–69.

Boxell, Levi, Matthew Gentzkow, and Jesse M. Shapiro. 2020. "Cross-Country Trends in Affective Polarization." *Review of Economics and Statistics,* 1–60. https://doi.org/10.1162/rest_a_01160.

Brainard, Julii, and Paul R. Hunter. 2019. "Misinformation Making a Disease Outbreak Worse: Outcomes Compared for Influenza, Monkeypox, and Norovirus." *Simulation: Transactions of the Society for Modeling and Simulation International* 96 (4): 365–74. https://doi.org/10 .1177/0037549719885021.

Brainard, Julii, Paul R. Hunter, and Ian R. Hall. 2020. "An Agent-Based Model about the Effects of Fake News on a Norovirus Outbreak." *Revue d'epidemiologie et de sante publique* 68 (2): 99–107.

Brashier, Nadia M., Emmaline Drew Eliseev, and Elizabeth J. Marsh. 2020. "An Initial Accuracy Focus Prevents Illusory Truth." *Cognition* 194 (January): 104054. https://doi.org/10.1016/j .cognition.2019.104054.

Brashier, Nadia M., Gordon Pennycook, Adam J. Berinsky, and David G. Rand. "Timing Matters when Correcting Fake News." *Proceedings of the National Academy of Sciences* 118 (5): e2020043118.

Braun, Joshua A., and Jessica L. Eklund. 2019. "Fake News, Real Money: Ad Tech Platforms, Profit-Driven Hoaxes, and the Business of Journalism." *Digital Journalism* 7 (1): 1–21. https:// doi.org/10.1080/21670811.2018.1556314.

Brotherton, Robert, Christopher C. French, and Alan D. Pickering. 2013. "Measuring Belief in Conspiracy Theories: The Generic Conspiracist Beliefs Scale." *Frontiers in Psychology* 4 (May): 279. https://doi.org/10.3389/fpsyg.2013.00279.

Bruder, Martin, Peter Haffke, Nick Neave, Nina Nouripanah, and Roland Imhoff. 2013. "Measuring Individual Differences in Generic Beliefs in Conspiracy Theories across Cultures: Conspiracy Mentality Questionnaire." *Frontiers in Psychology* 4 (April): 225. https://doi.org/10.3389/fpsyg.2013.00225.

Bucciol, A., and Zarri, L. 2013. "Lying in Politics: Evidence from the US." University of Verona, Department of Economics. Working Paper Series.

Bullock, John G. 2006. "Partisanship and the Enduring Effects of False Political Information." Unpublished manuscript.

Bullock, John G., Alan S. Gerber, Seth J. Hill, and Gregory A. Huber. 2015. "Partisan Bias in Factual Beliefs about Politics." *Quarterly Journal of Political Science* 10 (4): 519–78. https://doi.org/10.1561/100.00014074.

Bursztyn, Leonardo, Aakaash Rao, Christopher P. Roth, and David H. Yanagizawa-Drott. 2020. "Misinformation During a Pandemic." *National Bureau of Economic Research*. Working paper.

Butterfuss, Reese, Joseph Aubele, and Panyaiota Kendeou. 2020. "Hedged Language and Partisan Media Influence Belief in Science Claims." *Science Communication* 42 (2): 147–71.

Bysow, Ludwig A. 1928. "Gerüchte." *Kölner Vierteljahreshefte Für Soziologie* 7: 301–8.

Calvert, Randall L. 1985. "The Value of Biased Information: A Rational Choice Model of Political Advice." *Journal of Politics* 47 (2): 530–55. https://doi.org/10.2307/2130895.

Cameron, Kenzie A., Michael E. Roloff, Elisha M. Friesema, Tiffany Brown, Borko D. Jovanovic, Sara Hauber, and David W. Baker. 2013. "Patient Knowledge and Recall of Health Information following Exposure to "Facts and Myths" Message Format Variations." *Patient Education and Counseling* 92 (3): 381–87.

Campbell, Angus, Phillip E. Converse, Warren E. Miller, and Donald E. Stokes. 1980. *The American Voter*. Chicago: University of Chicago Press.

Card, Dallas, Lucy H. Lin, and Noah A. Smith. 2018. "Politifact Language Audit." Unpublished manuscript.

Carnahan, Dustin, Daneil E. Bergan, and Sangwon Lee. 2021. "Do Corrective Effects Last? Results from a Longitudinal Experiment on Beliefs toward Immigration in the US." *Political Behavior* 43 (3): 1227–1246.

Carnahan, Dustin, and R. Kelly Garrett. 2020. "Processing Style and Responsiveness to Corrective Information." *International Journal of Public Opinion Research* 32 (3): 530–46. https://doi.org/10.1093/ijpor/edz037.

Carroll, Lauren. 2015. "Fact-checking Trump's Claim that Thousands in New Jersey Cheered when World Trade Center Tumbled." PolitiFact. https://www.politifact.com/factchecks/2015/nov/22/donald-trump/fact-checking-trumps-claim-thousands-new-jersey-ch/.

Cassino, Dan, and Krista Jenkins. 2013. "Conspiracy Theories Prosper: 25% of Americans Are 'Truthers.'" *Fairleigh Dickinson University's Public and Mind Poll*.

Cheathem, Mark R. 2019. "Conspiracy Theories Abounded in 19th-Century American Politics." *Smithsonian Magazine*, April 11. https://www.smithsonianmag.com/history/conspiracy-theories-abounded-19th-century-american-politics-180971940/.

Choi, Daejin, Selin Chun, Hyunchul Oh, Jinyoung Han, and Ted "Taekyoung" Kwon. 2020. "Rumor Propagation Is Amplified by Echo Chambers in Social Media." *Scientific Reports* 10 (1): 1–10. https://doi.org/10.1038/s41598-019-57272-3.

Cillizza, Chris. 2016. "A Fact Checker Looked into 158 Things Donald Trump Said; 78 Percent Were False." *Washington Post*, June 1. https://www.washingtonpost.com/news/the-fix/wp/2016/07/01/donald-trump-has-been-wrong-way-more-often-than-all-the-other-2016-candidates-combined/.

Cinelli, Matteo, Gianmarco De Francisci Morales, Alessandro Galeazzi, Walter Quattrociocchi, and Michele Starnini. 2021. "The Echo Chamber Effect on Social Media." *Proceedings of the National Academy of Science* 118 (9): 1–8. https://doi.org/10.1073/pnas.2023301118.

Citrin, Jack. 1974. "Comment: The Political Relevance of Trust in Government." *American Political Science Review* 68 (3): 973–88. http://www.jstor.org/stable/1959141.

Claassen, Ryan L., and Michael J. Ensley. 2016. "Motivated Reasoning and Yard-Sign-Stealing Partisans: Mine Is a Likable Rogue, Yours Is a Degenerate Criminal." *Political Behavior* 38 (2): 317–35. https://doi.org/10.1007/s11109-015-9313-9.

Clarke, Steve. 2002. "Conspiracy Theories and Conspiracy Theorizing." *Philosophy of the Social Sciences* 32 (2): 131–50. https://doi.org/10.1177/004931032002001.

Cohen, David, and Quint Forgey. 2020. "Trump Alleges Biden Controlled by People in 'Dark Shadows.'" *Politico*, August 31. https://www.politico.com/news/2020/08/31/trump-biden-conspiracy-theory-406729.

Converse, Philip E. 1987. "Changing Conceptions of Public Opinion in the Political Process." *Public Opinion Quarterly* 51 (4): 12–24. https://doi.org/10.1093/poq/51.4_PART_2.S12.

———. 1964. "The Nature of Belief Systems in Mass Publics." In *Ideology and Discontent*, edited by David Apter. New York: Free Press.

Crocco, Anthony G., Miguel Villasis-Keever, and Alejandro R. Jadad. 2002. "Analysis of Cases of Harm Associated with Use of Health Information on the Internet." *JAMA* 287 (21): 2869–71.

Dale, Daniel. 2016. "Confessions of a Trump Fact-Checker: I Spent 33 Days Fact-Checking 253 Donald Trump Falsehoods. Here's What I've Learned." *Politico*, October 19. https://www.politico.com/magazine/story/2016/10/one-month-253-trump-untruths-214369/.

———. 2019. "Fact Check: Bernie Sanders Has Made the Same False Claim about Health Spending for 10 Years." CNN, August 9. https://www.cnn.com/2019/08/09/politics/fact-check-bernie-sanders-health-care-spending/index.html.

———. 2020. "Fact-checking Trump's Dishonest Weekend: The President Made at Least 66 False or Misleading Claims in Three Days." CNN, October 19. https://www.cnn.com/2020/10/19/politics/fact-check-trump-dishonest-weekend-florida-michigan-georgia-wisconsin/index.html.

Danforth, John, Benjamin Ginsberg, Thomas B. Griffith, David Hoppe, Michael Lutting, Michael W. McConnel, Theodore B. Olson, and Gordon H. Smith. 2022. "Lost, Not Stolen: The Conservative Case that Trump Lost and Biden Won the 2020 Presidential Election." https://lostnotstolen.org/wp-content/uploads/2022/07/Lost-Not-Stolen-The-Conservative-Case-that-Trump-Lost-and-Biden-Won-the-2020-Presidential-Election-July-2022.pdf.

Darwin, Hannah, Nick Neave, and Joni Holmes. 2011. "Belief in Conspiracy Theories: The Role of Paranormal Belief, Paranoid Ideation and Schizotypy." *Personality and Individual Differences* 50 (8): 1289–93. https://doi.org/10.1016/j.paid.2011.02.027.

Dawes, Christopher T., and James H. Fowler. 2009. "Partisanship, Voting, and the Dopamine D2 Receptor Gene." *Journal of Politics* 71 (3): 1157–71.

de Benedictis-Kessner, Justin, Matthew A. Baum, and Adam J. Berinsky. 2019. "Polarization and Media Usage: Disentangling Causality." In *The Oxford Handbook of Electoral Persuasion*, edited by Elizabeth Suhay, Bernard Grofman, and Alexander H. Trechsel. New York: Oxford University Press.

Dechêne, Alice, Christoph Stahl, Jochim Hansen, and Michaela Wänke. 2010. "The Truth about the Truth: A Meta-Analytic Review of the Truth Effect." *Personality and Social Psychology Review* 14 (2): 238–57. https://doi.org/10.1177/1088868309352251.

Delli Carpini, M., and Scott Keeter. 1996. *What Americans Know about Politics and Why It Matters.* New Haven, CT: Yale University Press.

Devine, Curt, Drew Griffin, and Scott Bronstein. 2020. "The 'Swarm': How Some Sanders Loyalists Attack Online Dissent." *CNN Politics*, February 9. https://www.cnn.com/2020/02/07/politics/bernie-sanders-social-media-attacks-invs/index.html.

DiFonzo, Nicholas, and Prashant Bordia. 2007. "Rumor, Gossip and Urban Legends." *Diogenes* 54 (1): 19–35. https://doi.org/10.1177/0392192107073433.

Ditto, Peter H., Cory J. Clark, Brittany S. Liu, Sean P. Wojcik, Eric E. Chen, Rebecca H. Grady, Jared B. Celniker, and Joanne F. Zinger. 2019. "Partisan Bias and its Discontents." *Perspectives on Psychological Science* 14 (2): 304–16.

Doherty, Carroll, Jocelyn Kiley, Andrew Daniller, Bradley Jones, Hannah Hartig, Amina Dunn, Hannah Gilberstadt, Ted Van Green, and Vianney Gomez. 2020. "Americans' Views of Government: Low Trust, but Some Positive Performance Ratings." Pew Research Center, September 14. https://www.pewresearch.org/politics/2020/09/14/americans-views-of-government-low-trust-but-some-positive-performance-ratings/.

Donovan, Pamela. 2007. "How Idle Is Idle Talk? One Hundred Years of Rumor Research." *Diogenes* 54 (1): 59–82.

Douglas, Karen M., Robbie M. Sutton, and Aleksandra Cichocka. 2017. "The Psychology of Conspiracy Theories." *Current Directions in Psychological Science* 26 (6): 538–42. https://doi.org/10.1177/0963721417718261.

Douglas, Karen M., Joseph E. Uscinski, Robbie M. Sutton, Aleksandra Cichocka, Turkay Nefes, Chee Siang Ang, and Farzin Deravi. 2019. "Understanding Conspiracy Theories." *Political Psychology* 40 (S1): 3–35. https://doi.org/10.1111/pops.12568.

Dowd, Gregory Evans. 2015. *Groundless: Rumors, Legends, and Hoaxes on the Early American Frontier*. Baltimore: Johns Hopkins University Press.

Dropp, Kyle, and Brendan Nyhan. 2016. "It Lives: Birtherism Is Diminished but Far from Dead." *New York Times*, September 23. https://www.nytimes.com/2016/09/24/upshot/it-lives-birtherism-is-diminished-but-far-from-dead.html.

Druckman, James N., Matthew S. Levendusky, and Audrey McLain. 2018. "No Need to Watch: How the Effects of Partisan Media Can Spread via Interpersonal Discussions." *American Journal of Political Science* 62 (1): 99–112. https://doi.org/10.1111/ajps.12325.

Druckman, James N., and Kjersten R. Nelson. 2003. "Framing and Deliberation: How Citizens' Conversations Limit Elite Influence." *American Journal of Political Science* 47 (4): 729–45. https://doi.org/10.1111/1540-5907.00051.

Drutman, Lee. 2020. "Fact-Checking Misinformation Can Work: But It Might Not Be Enough." FiveThirtyEight, June 3. https://fivethirtyeight.com/features/why-twitters-fact-check-of-trump-might-not-be-enough-to-combat-misinformation/.

Eady, Gregory, Jonathan Nagler, Andy Guess, Jan Zilinsky, and Joshua A. Tucker. 2019. "How Many People Live in Political Bubbles on Social Media? Evidence from Linked Survey and Twitter Data." *Sage Open* 9 (1): 1–21. https://doi.org/10.1177/2158244019832705.

Eagly, Alice H., Wendy Wood, and Shelly Chaiken. 1978. "Causal Inferences about Communicators and Their Effect on Opinion Change." *Journal of Personality and Social Psychology* 36 (4): 424–35. https://doi.org/10.1037/0022-3514.36.4.424.

Ecker, Ullrich K. H., and Li Chang Ang. 2019. "Political Attitudes and the Processing of Misinformation Corrections." *Political Psychology* 40 (2): 241–60. https://doi.org/10.1111/pops.12494.

Ecker, Ullrich K. H., and Luke M. Antonio. 2021. "Can You Believe It? An Investigation into the Impact of Retraction Source Credibility on the Continued Influence Effect." *Memory & Cognition* 49 (4): 631–44. https://doi.org/10.3758/s13421-020-01129-y.

Ecker, Ullrich K. H., Joshua L. Hogan, and Stephan Lewandowsky. 2017. "Reminders and Repetition of Misinformation: Helping or Hindering Its Retraction?" *Journal of Applied Research in Memory and Cognition* 6 (2): 185–92. https://doi.org/10.1016/j.jarmac.2017.01.014.

Ecker, Ullrich K. H., Stephan Lewandowsky, Briony Swire, and Darren Chang. 2011. "Correcting False Information in Memory: Manipulating the Strength of Misinformation Encoding and Its Reaction." *Psychonomic Bulletin and Review* 18 (3): 570–78.

Ecker, Ullrich K. H., Brandon K. N. Sze, and Matthew Andreotta. 2021. "Corrections of Political Misinformation: No Evidence for an Effect of Partisan Worldview in a US Convenience

Sample." *Philosophical Transactions of the Royal Society* 376 (1822): 1–8. https://doi.org/10.1098/rstb.2020.0145.

Ellis, Bill, and Garry A. Fine. 2010. *The Global Grapevine: Why Rumors of Terrorism, Immigration, and Trade Matter.* New York: Oxford University Press.

Epstein, Ziv, Adam J. Berinsky, Rocky Cole, Andrew Gully, Gordon Pennycook, and David G. Rand. 2021. "Developing an Accuracy-Prompt Toolkit to Reduce COVID-19 Misinformation Online." *Harvard Kennedy School Misinformation Review* 2 (3): 1–13. https://misinforeview.hks.harvard.edu/article/developing-an-accuracy-prompt-toolkit-to-reduce-covid-19-misinformation-online/.

Eschner, Kat. 2017. "What We Know about the CIA's Mid-century Mind-Control Project." *Smithsonian Magazine.* https://www.smithsonianmag.com/smart-news/what-we-know-about-cias-midcentury-mind-control-project-180962836/.

Faris, Robert M., Hal Roberts, Bruce Etling, Nikki Bourassa, Ethan Zuckerman, and Yochai Benkler. 2017. "Partisanship, Propaganda, and Disinformation: Online Media and the 2016 U.S. Presidential Election." *Berkman Klein Center for Internet & Society Research Paper.*

Faye, Cathy. 2007. "Governing the Grapevine: The Study of Rumor during World War II." *History of Psychology* 10 (1): 1.

Fazio, Lisa K., Nadia M. Brashier, B. Keith Payne, and Elizabeth J. Marsh. 2015. "Knowledge Does Not Protect against Illusory Truth." *Journal of Experimental Psychology: General* 144 (5): 993.

Fazio, Lisa K., David G. Rand, and Gordon Pennycook. 2019. "Repetition Increases Perceived Truth Equally for Plausible and Implausible Statements." *Psychonomic Bulletin and Review* 26 (5): 1705–10. https://doi.org/10.3758/s13423-019-01651-4.

Feldman, Stanley, and Karen Stenner. 1997. "Perceived Threat and Authoritarianism." *Political Psychology* 18 (4): 741–70. https://doi.org/10.1111/0162-895X.00077.

Finnegan, Michael. 2016. "Scope of Trump's Falsehoods Unprecedented for a Modern Presidential Candidate." *Los Angeles Times*, September 25. https://www.latimes.com/politics/la-na-pol-trump-false-statements-20160925-snap-story.html.

Finnström, Sverker. 2009. "Gendered War and Rumors of Saddam Hussein in Uganda." *Anthropology and Humanism* 34 (1): 61–70.

FiveThirtyEight. 2016. "National Republican Primary Polls." https://projects.fivethirtyeight.com/election-2016/national-primary-polls/republican/.

Flaxman, Seth, Sharad Goel, and Justin M Rao. 2016. "Filter Bubbles, Echo Chambers, and Online News Consumption." *Public Opinion Quarterly* 80 (S1): 298–320.

Fletcher, Richard, Craig T. Robertson, and Rasmus Kleis Nielsen. 2021. "How Many People Live in Politically Partisan Online News Echo Chambers in Different Countries?" *Journal of Quantitative Description: Digital Media* 1: 1–56.

Flynn, D. J., Brendan Nyhan, and Jason Reifler. 2017. "The Nature and Origins of Misperceptions: Understanding False and Unsupported Beliefs about Politics." *Political Psychology* 38 (February): 127–50. https://doi.org/10.1111/pops.12394.

Forrest, Brett. 2021. "What Is QAnon? What We Know about the Conspiracy-Theory Group." *Wall Street Journal*, February 4. https://www.wsj.com/articles/what-is-qanon-what-we-know-about-the-conspiracy-theory-11597694801.

Fowler, James H., and Christopher T. Dawes. 2013. "In Defense of Genopolitics." *American Political Science Review* 107 (2): 362–74. https://doi.org/10.1017/S0003055413000063.

Franks, Bradley, Adrian Bangerter, Martin W. Bauer, Matthew Hall, and Mark C. Noort. 2017. "Beyond 'Monologicality'? Exploring Conspiracist Worldviews." *Frontiers in Psychology* 8: 1–16. https://doi.org/10.3389/fpsyg.2017.00861.

Frederick, Shane. 2005. "Cognitive Reflection and Decision Making." *Journal of Economic Perspectives* 19 (4): 25–42. https://doi.org/10.1257/089533005775196732.

Freeman, Daniel, and Richard P. Bentall. 2017. "The Concomitants of Conspiracy Concerns." Social Psychiatry and Psychiatric Epidemiology 52 (5): 595–604.

Frimer, Jermey A., Linda J. Skitka, and Matt Motyl. 2017. "Liberals and Conservatives Are Similarly Motivated to Avoid Exposure to One Another's Opinions." Journal of Experimental Social Psychology 72: 1–12.

Fu, Angela. 2021. "Embedded within a Mass Delusion: The Challenge of Reporting on QAnon." Poynter, February 10. https://www.poynter.org/reporting-editing/2021/embedded-within -a-mass-delusion-the-challenge-of-reporting-on-qanon/.

Funk, Carolyn L. 1996. "The Impact of Scandal on Candidate Evaluations: An Experimental Test of the Role of Candidate Traits." Political Behavior 18 (1): 1–24. https://doi.org/10.1007 /BF01498658.

Funk, Cary, Meg Hefferon, Brian Kennedy, and Courtney Johnson. 2019. "Trust and Mistrust in Americans' Views of Scientific Experts." Pew Research Center, August 2. https://www .pewresearch.org/science/2019/08/02/trust-and-mistrust-in-americans-views-of-scientific -experts/.

Funk, Cary, Brian Kennedy, and Courtney Johnson. 2020. "Trust in Medical Scientists Has Grown in U.S., but Mainly among Democrats." Pew Research Center. March 21. https:// www.pewresearch.org/science/2020/05/21/trust-in-medical-scientists-has-grown-in-u-s -but-mainly-among-democrats/.

Galvin, Caby. 2017. "The Globalization of 'Fake News.'" US News, December 30. https://www .usnews.com/news/best-countries/articles/2017-12-30/how-fake-news-charges-spread -around-the-globe.

Garrett, R. Kelly, and Robert M. Bond. 2021. "Conservatives' Susceptibility to Political Misperceptions." Science Advances 7 (23): 1–9. https://doi.org/10.1126/sciadv.abf1234.

Garrett, R. Kelly, and Brian E. Weeks. 2017. "Epistemic Beliefs' Role in Promoting Misperceptions and Conspiracist Ideation." PLOS One 12 (9): 1–17. https://doi.org/10.1371/journal.pone .0184733.

Gentzkow, Matthew, and Jesse M Shapiro. 2011. "Ideological Segregation Online and Offline." Quarterly Journal of Economics 126 (4): 1799–1839.

Gerber, Alan S., and Gregory A. Huber. 2010. "Partisanship, Political Control, and Economic Assessments." American Journal of Political Science 54 (1): 153–73. https://doi.org/10.1111/j .1540-5907.2009.00424.x.

Gerber, Alan S., Gregory A. Huber, David Doherty, and Conor M. Dowling. 2013. "Assessing the Stability of Psychological and Political Survey Measures." American Politics Research 41 (1): 54–75.

Gilbert, Daniel T., Romin W. Tafarodi, and Patrick S. Malone. 1993. "You Can't Not Believe Everything You Read." Journal of Personality and Social Psychology 65 (2): 221–33. https://doi.org /10.1037/0022-3514.65.2.221.

Gilens, Martin. 2001. "Political Ignorance and Collective Policy Preferences." American Political Science Review 95 (2): 379–96. https://doi.org/10.1017/S0003055401002222.

Goertzel, Ted. 1994. "Belief in Conspiracy Theories." Political Psychology 15 (4): 731–42. http:// www.jstor.org/stable/3791630.

———. 2019. "The Conspiracy Theory Pyramid Scheme,." In Conspiracy Theories and the People Who Believe Them, edited by Joseph Uscinski, 226–44. New York: Oxford University Press.

Golbeck, Jennifer, Justin M. Grimes, and Anthony Rogers. 2010. "Twitter Use by the US Congress." Journal of the American Society for Information Science and Technology 61 (8): 1612–21.

Gonyea, Don. 2017. "From the Start, Obama Struggled with Fallout from a Kind of Fake News." NPR, January 10. https://www.npr.org/2017/01/10/509164679/from-the-start-obama -struggled-with-fallout-from-a-kind-of-fake-news.

Goodman, Ellen. 2015. "Death Panels: An Obituary." *Politico Magazine*, December 30. https://www.politico.com/magazine/story/2015/12/death-panels-obit-213481/.

Goodnough, Abby, Reed Abelson, Margot Sanger-Katz, and Sarah Kliff. 2020. "Obamacare Turns 10: Here's a Look at What Works and Doesn't." *New York Times*. Accessed February 21, 2021. https://www.nytimes.com/2020/03/23/health/obamacare-aca-coverage-cost-history.html.

Graham, David A. 2010. "America the Ignorant: Silly Things We Believe about Witches, Obama, and More." *Newsweek*, August 28. https://desdemonadespair.net/2010/08/america-ignorant-silly-things-we.html.

Graham, H. Matthew. 2022. "Measuring Misperceptions?" *American Political Science Review*, 1–23. https://doi.org/10.1017/S0003055422000387.

Graham, S. Scott. 2021. "Misinformation Inoculation and Literacy Support Tweetorials on COVID-19." *Journal of Business and Technical Communication* 35 (1): 7–14. https://doi.org/10.1177/1050651920958505.

Graves, Lucas. 2016. *Deciding What's True: The Rise of Political Fact-Checking in American Journalism*. New York: Columbia University Press.

Green, Jon, Jared Edgerton, Daniel Naftel, Kelsey Shoub, and Skyler J. Cranmer. 2020. "Elusive Consensus: Polarization in Elite Communication on the COVID-19 Pandemic." *Science Advances* 6 (28): 1–5.

Greer, Jennifer D. 2003. "Evaluating the Credibility of Online Information: A Test of Source and Advertising Influence." *Mass Communication and Society* 6 (1): 11–28. https://doi.org/10.1207/s15327825mcs0601_3.

Grinberg, Nir, Kenneth Joseph, Lisa Friedland, Briony Swire-Thompson, and David Lazer. 2019. "Political Science: Fake News on Twitter during the 2016 U.S. Presidential Election." *Science* 363 (6425): 374–78. https://doi.org/10.1126/science.aau2706.

Guay, Brian., and Christopher D. Johnston. 2022. "Ideological Asymmetries and the Determinants of Politically Motivated Reasoning." *American Journal of Political Science* 66 (2): 285–301.

Guess, Andrew M. 2021. "(Almost) Everything in Moderation: New Evidence on Americans' Online Media Diets." *American Journal of Political Science* 65 (4): 1007–22. https://doi.org/10.1111/ajps.12589.

Guess, Andrew, Kevin Aslett, Joshua Tucker, Richard Bonneau, and Jonathan Nagler. 2021. "Cracking Open the News Feed: Exploring What Us Facebook Users See and Share with Large-Scale Platform Data." *Journal of Quantitative Description: Digital Media* 1: 1–80.

Guess, Andrew, and Alexander Coppock. 2020. "Does Counter-Attitudinal Information Cause Backlash? Results from Three Large Survey Experiments." *British Journal of Political Science* 50 (4): 1497–1515. https://doi.org/10.1017/S0007123418000327.

Guess, Andrew M., Michael Lerner, Benjamin Lyons, Jacob M. Montgomery, Brendan Nyhan, Jason Reifler, and Neelanjan Sircar. 2020. "A Digital Media Literacy Intervention Increases Discernment between Mainstream and False News in the United States and India." *Proceedings of the National Academy of Science* 117 (27): 15536–45.

Guess, Andrew M., and Benjamin A. Lyons. 2020. "Misinformation, Disinformation, and Online Propaganda." In *Social Media and Democracy: The State of the Field, Prospects for Reform*, edited by Nathaniel Persily and Joshua A. Tucker, 10–33. Cambridge: Cambridge University Press.

Guess, Andrew, Jonathan Nagler, and Joshua Tucker. 2019. "Less than You Think: Prevalence and Predictors of Fake News Dissemination on Facebook." *Science Advances* 5 (1): 1–8.

Guess, Andrew, Brendan Nyhan, Benjamin Lyons, and Jason Reifler. 2018. "Avoiding the Echo Chamber about Echo Chambers." *Knight Foundation* 2: 1–25.

Guess, Andrew M., Brendan Nyhan, and Jason Reifler. 2020. "Exposure to Untrustworthy Websites in the 2016 US Election." *Nature Human Behaviour* 4 (5): 472–80. https://doi.org/10.1038/s41562-020-0833-x.

Guillory, Jimmeka J., and Lisa Geraci. 2013. "Correcting Erroneous Inferences in Memory: The Role of Source Credibility." *Journal of Applied Research in Memory and Cognition* 2 (4): 201–9. https://doi.org/10.1016/j.jarmac.2013.10.001.

Gustafson, Abel, and Ronald E. Rice. 2019. "The Effects of Uncertainty Frames in Three Science Communication Topics." *Science Communication* 41 (6): 679–706.

———. 2020. "A Review of the Effects of Uncertainty in Public Science Communication." *Public Understanding of Science* 29 (6): 614–33.

Hahl, Oliver, Minjae Kim, and Ezra W. Zuckerman Sivan. 2018. "The Authentic Appeal of the Lying Demagogue: Proclaiming the Deeper Truth about Political Illegitimacy." *American Sociological Review* 83 (1): 1–33. https://doi.org/10.1177/0003122417749632.

Hasson, Uri, Joseph P. Simmons, and Alexander Todorov. 2005. "Believe It or Not: On the Possibility of Suspending Belief." *Psychological Science* 16 (7) : 566–571. https://doi.org/10.1111/j.0956-7976.2005.01576.x.

Hatemi, Peter K., Nathan A. Gillespie, Lindon J. Eaves, Brion S. Maher, Bradley T. Webb, Andrew C. Heath, Sarah E. Medland, David C. Smyth, Harry N. Beeby, Scott D. Gordon, Grant W. Montgomery, Ghu Zhu, Enda M. Byrne, and Nicholas G. Martin. 2011. "A Genome-Wide Analysis of Liberal and Conservative Political Attitudes." *Journal of Politics* 73 (1): 271–85.

Heath, Chip, Chris Bell, and Emily Sternberg. 2001. "Emotional Selection in Memes: The Case of Urban Legends." *Journal of Personality and Social Psychology* 81 (6): 1028.

Hemphill, Libby, Jahna Otterbacher, and Matthew Shapiro. 2013. "What's Congress Doing on Twitter?" In *Proceedings of the 2013 Conference on Computer Supported Cooperative Work*, 877–86. https://doi.org/10.1145/2441776.2441876.

Hetherington, Marc J. 2005. *Why Trust Matters: Declining Political Trust and the Demise of American Liberalism.* Princeton, NJ: Princeton University Press.

Hochschild, Jennifer L., and Katherine Levine Einstein. 2015. *Do Facts Matter? Information and Misinformation in American Politics.* Vol. 13. Norman: University of Oklahoma Press.

Hofstadter, Richard. 1965. *The Paranoid Style in American Politics.* New York: Vintage.

Holan, Angie Drobnic. 2009. "PolitiFact's Lie of the Year: 'Death Panels.'" PolitiFact, December 18. https://www.politifact.com/article/2009/dec/18/politifact-lie-year-death-panels/.

———. 2018. "The Principles of the Truth-O-Meter: PolitiFact's Methodology for Independent Fact-Checking." PolitiFact, February 12. https://www.politifact.com/article/2018/feb/12/principles-truth-o-meter-politifacts-methodology-i/.

Holman, Mirya R., and J. Celeste Lay. 2019. "They See Dead People (Voting): Correcting Misperceptions about Voter Fraud in the 2016 U.S. Presidential Election." *Journal of Political Marketing* 18 (1–2): 31–68. https://doi.org/10.1080/15377857.2018.1478656.

Hopkins, Daniel J., John Sides, and Jack Citrin. 2019. "The Muted Consequences of Correct Information and Immigration." *Journal of Politics* 81 (1): 315–20.

Hornsey, Matthew J., Matthew Finlayson, Gabrielle Chatwood, and Christopher Begeny. 2020. "Donald Trump and Vaccination: The Effect of Political Identity, Conspiracist Ideation and Presidential Tweets on Vaccine Hesitancy." *Journal of Experimental Social Psychology* 88: 1–35. https://www.sciencedirect.com/science/article/pii/S0022103119302628.

Housholder, Elizabeth E., and Heather L. LaMarre. 2014. "Facebook Politics: Toward a Process Model for Achieving Political Source Credibility through Social Media." *Journal of Information Technology and Politics* 11 (4): 368–82. https://doi.org/10.1080/19331681.2014.951753.

Huang, Haifeng. 2017. "A War of (Mis) Information: The Political Effects of Rumors and Rumor Rebuttals in an Authoritarian Country." *British Journal of Political Science* 47 (2): 283–311.

Huszár, Ferenc, Sofia Ira Ktena, Conor O'Brien, Luca Belli, Andrew Schlaikjer, and Moritz Hardt. 2022. "Algorithmic Amplification of Politics on Twitter." *Proceedings of the National Academy of Sciences* 119 (1): 1–6. https://doi.org/10.1073/pnas.2025334119.

Iyengar, Shanto, Yphtach Lelkes, Matthew Levendusky, Neil Malhotra, and Sean J. Westwood. 2019. "The Origins and Consequences of Affective Polarization in the United States." *Annual Review of Political Science* 22 (1): 129–46. https://doi.org/10.1146/annurev-polisci-051117 -073034.

Jacoby, Larry L., and Mark Dallas. 1981. "On the Relationship between Autobiographical Memory and Perceptual Learning." *Journal of Experimental Psychology: General* 110 (3): 306–40. https://doi.org/10.1037/0096-3445.110.3.306.

Jamieson, Kathleen H., and Dolores Albarracin. 2020. "The Relation between Media Consumption and Misinformation at the Outset of the SARS-CoV-2 Pandemic in the US." *Harvard Kennedy School Misinformation Review* 1 (2): 1–22. https://doi.org/10.37016/mr-2020-012.

Jo, Dong-Gi. 2002. "Diffusion of Rumors on the Internet." *Information Society Review* 2002: 77–95.

Johnson, B. B., and P. Slovic. 1995. "Presenting Uncertainty in Health Risk Assessment: Initial Studies of Its Effects on Risk Perception and Trust." *Risk Analysis* 15 (4): 485–94.

Johnson, Hollyn M., and Colleen M. Seifert. 1994. "Sources of the Continued Influence Effect: When Misinformation in Memory Affects Later Inferences." *Journal of Experimental Psychology: Learning, Memory, and Cognition* 20 (6): 1420–36. https://doi.org/10.1037/0278 -7393.20.6.1420.

Jost, John T. 2017. "Ideological Asymmetries and the Essence of Political Psychology." *Political Psychology* 38 (2): 167–208. https://doi.org/10.1111/pops.12407.

Jost, John T., and Mahzarin R. Banaji. 1994. "The Role of Stereotyping in System-Justification and the Production of False Consciousness." *British Journal of Social Psychology* 33 (1): 1–27. https://doi.org/10.1111/j.2044-8309.1994.tb01008.x.

Jost, John T., Jack Glaser, Frank J. Sulloway, and Arie W. Kruglanski. 2018. "Political Conservatism as Motivated Social Cognition." *Psychological Bulletin* 129 (3): 339–75.

Jost, John T., and Margarita Krochik. 2014. "Ideological Differences in Epistemic Motivation: Implications for Attitude Structure, Depth of Information Processing, Susceptibility to Persuasion, and Stereotyping." In *Advances in Motivation Science*. Vol. 1, edited by A. J. Elliot, 181–231. Amsterdam: Elsevier.

Jost, John T., Jaime L. Napier, Hulda Thorisdottir, Samuel D. Gosling, Tibor P. Palfai, and Brian Ostafin. 2007. "Are Needs to Manage Uncertainty and Threat Associated with Political Conservatism or Ideological Extremity?" *Personality and Social Psychology Bulletin* 33 (7): 989–1007.

Jost, John T., Joanna Sterling, and Chadly Stern. 2017. "Getting Closure on Conservatism, or the Politics of Epistemic and Existential Motivation." In *The Motivation-Cognition Interface*, 56–87. New York: Routledge.

Jürgens, Pascal, and Birgit Stark. 2022. "Mapping Exposure Diversity: The Divergent Effects of Algorithmic Curation on News Consumption." *Journal of Communication* 72 (3): 322–44.

Jurkowitz, Mark, and Amy Mitchell. 2020. "Cable TV and COVID-19: How Americans Perceive the Outbreak and View Media Coverage Differ by Main News Sources." Pew Research Center, April 1. https://www.pewresearch.org/journalism/2020/04/01/cable-tv-and-covid-19-how -americans-perceive-the-outbreak-and-view-media-coverage-differ-by-main-news-source/.

Kahan, Dan M. 2013. "Ideology, Motivated Reasoning, and Cognitive Reflection: An Experimental Study." *Judgment and Decision Making* 8 (4): 407–24. https://doi.org/10.2139/ssrn.2182588.

Kahan, Dan M., Ellen Peters, Erica Cantrell Dawson, and Paul Slovic. 2017. "Motivated Numeracy and Enlightened Self-Government." *Behavioural Public Policy* 1 (1): 54–86. https://doi.org /10.1017/bpp.2016.2.

Kates, Sean, Jonathan M. Ladd, and Joshua Tucker. 2018. "Should You Worry about American Democracy? Here's What Our New Poll Finds." *Washington Post*, October 24. https:// www.washingtonpost.com/news/monkey-cage/wp/2018/10/24/should-you-worry-about -american-democracy-heres-what-our-new-poll-finds/.

Kay, Jonathan. 2011. *Among the Truthers*. New York: Harper Collins.

Keeley, Brian L. 1999. "Of Conspiracy Theories." *Journal of Philosophy* 96 (3): 109–26.

Keersmaecker, Jonas De, David Dunning, Gordon Pennycook, David G. Rand, Carmen Sanchez, Christian Unkelbach, and Arne Roets. 2020. "Investigating the Robustness of the Illusory Truth Effect across Individual Differences in Cognitive Ability, Need for Cognitive Closure, and Cognitive Style." *Personality and Social Psychology Bulletin* 46 (2): 204–15. https://doi .org/10.1177/0146167219853844.

Kessler, Glenn. n.d. "Fact Checker." *Washington Post*, Accessed March 21, 2021. https://www .washingtonpost.com/news/fact-checker/.

Kessler, Glenn, Salvador Rizzo, and Meg Kelly. 2020. "False Claims and Disinformation Are the Central Feature of Trump's Presidency." *Washington Post*, June 2. https://www .washingtonpost.com/outlook/trump-fact-checker-book/2020/06/01/c6323b88-a435-11ea -b619-3f9133bbb482_story.html.

———. 2020. "President Trump Has Made More than 20,000 False or Misleading Claims." *Washington Post*, July 13. https://www.washingtonpost.com/politics/2020/07/13/president-trump -has-made-more-than-20000-false-or-misleading-claims/.

———. 2018. "President Trump Has Made 3,001 False or Misleading Claims So Far." *Washington Post*, May 1. https://www.washingtonpost.com/news/fact-checker/wp/2018/05/01/president -trump-has-made-3001-false-or-misleading-claims-so-far/.

Key, Valdimer O. 1966. *The Responsible Electorate*. Vol. 10. Cambridge, MA: Harvard University Press.

Kim, Yonghwan, Hsuan Ting Chen, and Homero Gil De Zúñiga. 2013. "Stumbling upon News on the Internet: Effects of Incidental News Exposure and Relative Entertainment Use on Political Engagement." *Computers in Human Behavior* 29 (6): 2607–14. https://doi.org/10 .1016/j.chb.2013.06.005.

Klein, Ezra. 2020. "What Polarization Data from 9 Countries Reveals about the US's Divide between Democrats and Republicans." *Vox*, January 24. https://www.vox.com/2020/1/24 /21076232/polarization-america-international-party-political.

Kliff, Sarah. 2017. "A GOP Official at a Town Hall Tried to Argue Obamacare Has Death Panels; It Did Not Go Well." *Vox*, February 12. https://www.vox.com/2017/2/12/14588086/death -panel-town-hall.

Koch, Thomas. 2017. "Again and Again (and Again): A Repetition-Frequency-Model of Persuasive Communication." *Studies in Communication and Media* 6 (3): 218–39. https://doi.org/10.5771 /2192-4007-2017-3-218.

Koeske, Gary F., and William D. Crano. 1968. "The Effect of Congruous and Incongruous Source-Statement Combinations upon the Judged Credibility of a Communication." *Journal of Experimental Social Psychology* 4 (4): 384–99. https://doi.org/10.1016/0022 -1031(68)90065-6.

Krosnick, Jon A. 1991. "Response Strategies for Coping with the Cognitive Demands of Attitude Measures in Surveys." *Applied Cognitive Psychology* 5 (3): 213–36. https://doi.org/10.1002 /acp.2350050305.

Kuklinski, James H., Paul J. Quirk, Jennifer Jerit, David Schwieder, and Robert F. Rich. 2000. "Misinformation and the Currency of Democratic Citizenship." *Journal of Politics* 62 (3): 790–816. https://doi.org/10.1111/0022-3816.00033.

Kunda, Ziva. 1990. "The Case for Motivated Reasoning." *Psychological Bulletin* 108 (3): 480–98. https://doi.org/10.1037/0033-2909.108.3.480.

Kushner Gadarian, Shana, Sara Wallace Goodman, and Thomas B Pepinsky. 2020. "Partisanship, Health Behavior, and Policy Attitudes in the Early Stages of the COVID-19 Pandemic." *PLOS One* 16 (4): 1–13. https://doi.org/10.1371/journal.pone.0249596.

Lardner, Richard, and Michelle R. Smith. 2021. "Records: Trump Allies behind Rally that Ignited Capitol Riot." *AP News*, January 17. https://apnews.com/article/election-2020-donald-trump-capitol-siege-campaigns-elections-d14c78d53b3a212658223252fec87e99.

Lasser, Jana. 2022. "Social Media Sharing of Low-Quality News Sources by Political Elites." Twitter, September 22. https://twitter.com/janalasser/status/1572845608066764802?s=21&t=EGUzePsmUJtCKewdcmGxfg.

Lazarsfeld, Paul F., Bernard Berelson, and Hazel Gaudet. 1968. *The People's Choice*. New York: Columbia University Press.

Lazer, David M., Matthew A. Baum, Yochai Benkler, Adam J. Berinsky, Kelly M. Greenhill, Filippo Menczer, Miriam J. Metzger, Brendan Nyhan, Gordon Pennycook, and Jonathan L. Zittrain. 2018. "The Science of Fake News." *Science* 359 (6380): 1094–96. https://doi.org/10.1126/science.aao2998.

Lee, Jae Kook, and Eunyi Kim. 2017. "Incidental Exposure to News: Predictors in the Social Media Setting and Effects on Information Gain Online." *Computers in Human Behavior* 75 (October): 1008–15. https://doi.org/10.1016/j.chb.2017.02.018.

Leonhardt, David, Ian Prasad Philbrick, and Stuart A. Thompson. 2017. "Trump's Lies vs. Obama's." *New York Times*, December 14. https://www.nytimes.com/interactive/2017/12/14/opinion/sunday/trump-lies-obama-who-is-worse.html.

Levendusky, Matthew. 2009. *The Partisan Sort: How Liberals Became Democrats and Conservatives Became Republicans*. Chicago: University of Chicago Press.

———. 2013. "Why Do Partisan Media Polarize Viewers?" *American Journal of Political Science* 57 (3): 611–23.

Levy, Neil. 2007. "Radically Socialized Knowledge and Conspiracy Theories." *Episteme* 4 (2): 181–92. https://doi.org/10.3366/epi.2007.4.2.181.

Lewandowsky, Stephan, John Cook, Ullrich Ecker, Dolores Albarracin, Michelle Amazeen, Panayiota Kendou, Doug Lombardi, Eryn J. Newman, Gordon Pennycook, Ethan Porter, David G. Rand, David N. Rapp, Jason Reifler, Jon Roozenbeek, Philipp Schmid, Colleen M. Seifert, Gale M. Sinatra, Briony Swire-Thompson, Sander van der Linden, Emily K. Vraga, Thomas J. Wood, Maria S. Zaragoza. 2020. *The Debunking Handbook 2020* (Climate Change Communication). https://doi.org/10.17910/b7.1182.

Lewandowsky, Stephan, Ullrich K. H. Ecker, Colleen M. Seifert, Norbert Schwarz, and John Cook. 2012. "Misinformation and Its Correction." *Psychological Science in the Public Interest* 13 (3): 106–31. https://doi.org/10.1177/1529100612451018.

Lewandowsky, Stephan, and Klaus Oberauer. 2016. "Motivated Rejection of Science." *Current Directions in Psychological Science* 25 (4): 217–22. https://doi.org/10.1177/0963721416654436.

Lewandowsky, Stephan, Klaus Oberauer, and Gilles E Gignac. 2013. "NASA Faked the Moon Landing—Therefore, (Climate) Science Is a Hoax: An Anatomy of the Motivated Rejection of Science." *Psychological Science* 24 (5): 622–33. https://doi.org/10.1177/0956797612457686.

Lewis, Rebecca, and Alice E. Marwick. 2017. "Media Manipulation and Disinformation Online." *Data & Society Research Institute*, 1–106.

Li, Jianing, and Michael W. Wagner. 2020. "The Value of Not Knowing: Partisan Cue-Taking and Belief Updating of the Uninformed, the Ambiguous, and the Misinformed." *Journal of Communication* 70 (5): 646–69. https://doi.org/10.1093/joc/jqaa022.

Library of Congress. 1995. "The World War II Rumor Project Collection." American Folklife Center, Library of Congress. March. https://www.loc.gov/folklife/guides/rumors.html.

Lim, Chole. 2018. "Checking How Fact-Checkers Check." *Research & Politics* 5 (3): 1–7. https://doi.org/10.1177/2053168018786848.

Lind, Dara. 2016. "Donald Trump Lies. All the Time." *Vox*, September 27. https://www.vox.com/policy-and-politics/2016/9/26/13016146/donald-trump-liar-media.

Lupia, Arthur. 1994. "Shortcuts versus Encyclopedias: Information and Voting Behavior in California Insurance Reform Elections." *American Political Science Review* 88 (1): 63–76.

Lupia, Arthur, and Mathew D. McCubbins. 1998. *The Democratic Dilemma: Can Citizens Learn What They Need to Know?* Cambridge: Cambridge University Press.

Luskin, Robert C., and John G. Bullock. 2011. "'Don't Know' Means 'Don't Know': DK Responses and the Public's Level of Political Knowledge." *Journal of Politics* 73 (2): 547–57. https://doi.org/10.1017/S0022381611000132.

Ma, Ringo. 2008. "Spread of SARS and War-Related Rumors through New Media in China." *Communication Quarterly* 56 (4): 376–91. https://doi.org/10.1080/01463370802448204.

Madison, James. 1910. "Epilogue: Securing the Republic." In *The Writings of James Madison*, edited by Gaillard Hunt. New York: G. P. Putnam's Sons.

Marietta, Morgan, David C. Barker, and Todd Bowser. 2015. "Fact-Checking Polarized Politics: Does the Fact-Check Industry Provide Consistent Guidance on Disputed Realities?" *Forum* 13 (4): 577–96.

Markowitz, David. 2020. "Trump Is Lying More than Ever: Just Look at the Data." *Forbes*, May 5. https://www.forbes.com/sites/davidmarkowitz/2020/05/05/trump-is-lying-more-than-ever-just-look-at-the-data/#73f483e31e17.

Martel, Cameron, Mohsen Mosleh, and David G. Rand. 2021. "You're Definitely Wrong, Maybe: Correction Style Has Minimal Effect on Corrections of Misinformation Online." *Media and Communication* 9 (1): 120–33. https://doi.org/10.17645/mac.v9i1.3519.

Martin, Nicholas G., Lindon J. Eaves, Andrew C. Health, Rosemary Jardine, Lynn M. Feingold, and Hans J. Eysenck. 1986. "Transmission of Social Attitudes." *Proceedings of the National Academy of Sciences* 83 (12): 4364–4368. https://doi.org/10.1073/pnas.83.12.4364.

Marwick, Alice, and Rebecca Lewis. 2017. "Media Manipulation and Disinformation Online." Data and Society Research Institute Report, May 15. https://datasociety.net/library/media-manipulation-and-disinfo-online/.

Mason, Lilliana. 2018. "Ideologues without Issues: The Polarizing Consequences of Ideological Identities." *Public Opinion Quarterly* 82 (S1): 866–87.

McCarthy, Ryan. 2020. "'Outright Lies': Voting Misinformation Flourishes on Facebook." *ProPublica*, July 16. https://www.propublica.org/article/outright-lies-voting-misinformation-flourishes-on-facebook.

McClosky, Herbert, and Dennis Chong. 1985. "Similarities and Differences between Left-Wing and Right-Wing Radicals." *British Journal of Political Science* 15 (3): 329–63. http://www.jstor.org/stable/193697.

McGinnies, Elliott, and Charles D. Ward. 1980. "Better Liked than Right." *Personality and Social Psychology Bulletin* 6 (3): 467–72. https://doi.org/10.1177/014616728063023.

McGranahan, Carole. 2017. "An Anthropology of Lying: Trump and the Political Sociality of Moral Outrage." *American Ethnologist* 44 (2): 243–48. https://doi.org/10.1111/amet.12475.

McKay, Spencer, and Chris Tenove. 2021. "Disinformation as a Threat to Deliberative Democracy." *Political Research Quarterly* 74 (3): 703–17. https://doi.org/10.1177/1065912920938143.

Merlan, Anna. 2019. *Republic of Lies: American Conspiracy Theorists and Their Surprising Rise to Power*. New York: Random House.

Miller, Joanne M., Kyle L. Saunders, and Christina E. Farhart. 2016. "Conspiracy Endorsement as Motivated Reasoning: The Moderating Roles of Political Knowledge and Trust." *American Journal of Political Science* 60 (4): 824–44. https://doi.org/10.1111/ajps.12234.

Mitchell, Amy, Mark Jurkowitz, J. Baxter Oliphant, and Elisa Shearer. 2020. "Americans Who Mainly Get Their News on Social Media Are Less Engaged, Less Knowledgeable." Pew Research Center, July 30. https://www.pewresearch.org/journalism/2020/07/30/americans-who-mainly-get-their-news-on-social-media-are-less-engaged-less-knowledgeable/.

Morales, Lymari. 2011. "Obama's Birth Certificate Convinces Some, but Not All, Skeptics." *Gallup*, May 13. https://news.gallup.com/poll/147530/obama-birth-certificate-convinces-not-skeptics.aspx.

Morello, Carol. 2004. "Conspiracy Theories Flourish on the Internet." *Washington Post*, October 7. https://www.washingtonpost.com/wp-dyn/articles/A13059-2004Oct6.html.

Mosleh, Mohsen, Cameron Martel, Dean Eckles, and David G. Rand. 2021. "Shared Partisanship Dramatically Increases Social Tie Formation in a Twitter Field Experiment." *Proceedings of the National Academy of Sciences* 118 (7): 1–3. https://doi.org/10.1073/pnas.2022761118.

Murray, Samuel, Matthew Stanley, Jonathon McPhetres, Gordon Pennycook, and Paul Seli. 2020. "'I've Said It Before and I Will Say It Again': Repeating Statements Made by Donald Trump Increases Perceived Truthfulness for Individuals across the Political Spectrum." *PsyArXiv*, January 15. https://doi.org/10.31234/osf.io/9evzc.

Nam, H. Hannah, John T. Jost, and Jay J. Van Bavel. 2013. "'Not for All the Tea in China!' Political Ideology and the Avoidance of Dissonance-Arousing Situations." *PLOS One* 8 (4): e59837. http://doi.org/10.1371/journal.pone.0059837.

Negroponte, Nicholas. 1995. "The Digital Revolution: Reasons for Optimism." *Futurist* 29 (6): 68.

Nelson, Jacob L., and James G. Webster. 2017. "The Myth of Partisan Selective Exposure: A Portrait of the Online Political News Audience." *Social Media + Society* 3 (3): 1–13. http://doi.org/10.1177/2056305117729314.

New York Times. 2021. "Fact Checks." Accessed March 21, 2021. https://www.nytimes.com/spotlight/fact-checks.

———. 2021. "Twitter Locks Trump's Account after He Encouraged His Supporters to 'Remember This Day.'" January 6. https://www.nytimes.com/2021/01/06/us/politics/twitter-deletes-trump-tweet.html.

NewsGuard. n.d. "Rating Process and Criteria." https://www.newsguardtech.com/ratings/rating-process-criteria/.

Nguyen, Tina. 2017. "As Trump's Problems Mount, Breitbart's Numbers Are Cratering." *Vanity Fair*, May 26. https://www.vanityfair.com/news/2017/05/breitbart-traffic-numbers-are-cratering.

Nilsson, Artur, and John T. Jost. 2020. "The Authoritarian-Conservatism Nexus." *Current Opinion in Behavioral Sciences* 34: 148–54. https://doi.org/10.1016/j.cobeha.2020.03.003.

Nyhan, Brendan. 2012. "Political Knowledge Does Not Guard against Belief in Conspiracy Theories." *You Gov: Model Politics*, November 5. http://today.yougov.com/news/2012/11/05/political-knowledgedoes-not-guard-against-belief-/.

———. 2021. "Why the Backfire Effect Does Not Explain the Durability of Political Misperceptions." *Proceedings of the National Academy of Science* 118 (15): 1–7. https://doi.org/10.1073/pnas.1912440117.

———. 2010. "Why the 'Death Panel' Myth Wouldn't Die: Misinformation in the Health Care Reform Debate." *Forum* 8 (1): 1–26.

Nyhan, Brendan, Ethan Porter, Jason Reifler, and Thomas J. Wood. 2020. "Taking Fact-Checks Literally but Not Seriously? The Effects of Journalistic Fact-Checking on Factual Beliefs and Candidate Favorability." *Political Behavior* 42 (3): 939–60.

Nyhan, Brendan, and Jason Reifler. 2015. "The Effect of Fact-Checking on Elites: A Field Experiment on U.S. State Legislators." *American Journal of Political Science* 59 (3): 628–40. https://doi.org/10.1111/ajps.12162.

———. 2019. "The Roles of Information Deficits and Identity Threat in the Prevalence of Misperceptions." *Journal of Elections, Public Opinion and Parties* 29 (2): 222–44.

———. 2010. "When Corrections Fail: The Persistence of Political Misperceptions." *Political Behavior* 32 (2): 303–30. https://doi.org/10.1007/s11109-010-9112-2.

Nyhan, Brendan, Jason Reifler, Christopher Edelman, William Passo, Ashley Banks, Emma Boston, Andrew Brown, et al. 2009. "The Effects of Semantics and Social Desirability in Correcting the Obama Muslim Myth." Unpublished manuscript.

Nyhan, B., Reifler, J. and Ubel, P.A., 2013. "The Hazards of Correcting Myths about Health Care Reform." *Medical Care* 51 (2): 127–32.

O'Connor, Cailin, and James Owen Weatherall. 2019. *The Misinformation Age: How False Beliefs Spread.* United Kingdom: Yale University Press.

Ohlheiser, Abby. 2018. "You'll Never Guess How the QAnon Conspiracy Theorists Feel about All This Media Coverage." *Washington Post,* August 3. https://www.washingtonpost.com/news /the-intersect/wp/2018/08/03/this-is-the-moment-how-a-wave-of-media-coverage-gave -qanon-conspiracy-theorists-their-best-week-ever/.

Oliver, J. Eric, and Thomas J. Wood. 2014. "Conspiracy Theories and the Paranoid Style(s) of Mass Opinion." *American Journal of Political Science* 58 (4): 952–66. https://doi.org/10.1111 /ajps.12084.

———. 2014. "Medical Conspiracy Theories and Health Behaviors in the United States." *JAMA Internal Medicine* 174 (5): 817–18. https://doi.org/10.1001/jamainternmed.2014.190.

Olmsted, Kathryn S. 2019. *Real Enemies: Conspiracy Theories and American Democracy, World War I to 9/11.* New York: Oxford University Press.

Oppenheimer, Daniel M. 2008. "The Secret Life of Fluency." *Trends in Cognitive Sciences* 12 (6): 237–41. https://doi.org/10.1016/j.tics.2008.02.014.

Oppenheimer, Daniel M., Tom Meyvis, and Nicolas Davidenko. 2009. "Instructional Manipulation Checks: Detecting Satisficing to Increase Statistical Power." *Journal of Experimental Social Psychology* 45 (4): 867–72. https://doi.org/10.1016/j.jesp.2009.03.009.

Ostermeier, Eric. 2011. "Selection Bias? PolitiFact Rates Republican Statements as False at Three Times the Rate of Democrats." *Smart Politics, February* 10. https://smartpolitics.lib.umn.edu /2011/02/10/selection-bias-politifact-rate/.

Palin, Sarah. 2009. "Statement on the Current Health Care Debate." Facebook, August 7. https:// www.facebook.com/note.php?note_id=113851103434.

Pariser, Eli. 2011. *The Filter Bubble: What the Internet Is Hiding from You.* London: Penguin UK.

Pasek, Josh, Gaurav Sood, and Jon A. Krosnick. 2015. "Misinformed about the Affordable Care Act? Leveraging Certainty to Assess the Prevalence of Misperceptions." *Journal of Communication* 65 (4): 660–73. https://doi.org/10.1111/jcom.12165.

Paulhus, Delroy L. 1991. "Measurement and Control of Response Bias." In *Measures of Personality and Social Psychological Attitudes,* edited by J. P. Robinson, P. R. Shaver, and L. S. Wrightsman, 17–59. Cambridge, MA: Academic Press.

Pear, Robert. 2011. "A Reversal on End-of-Life Planning under Medicare." *New York Times,* January 4. https://www.nytimes.com/2011/01/05/health/policy/05health.html.

Pennycook, Gordon, Tyrone D. Cannon, and David G. Rand. 2018. "Prior Exposure Increases Perceived Accuracy of Fake News." *Journal of Experimental Psychology: General* 147 (12): 1865–80. https://doi.org/10.1037/xge0000465.

Pennycook, Gordon, Jonathon McPhetres, Yunhao Zhang, Jackson G. Lu, and David G. Rand. 2020. "Fighting COVID-19 Misinformation on Social Media: Experimental Evidence for a Scalable Accuracy-Nudge Intervention." *Psychological Science* 31 (7): 770–90.

Peters, Jeremy W., Elaina Plott, and Maggie Haberman. 2020. "260,000 Words, Full of Self-Praise, from Trump on the Virus." *New York Times,* April 26. https://www.nytimes.com/interactive /2020/04/26/us/politics/trump-coronavirus-briefings-analyzed.html.

Peterson, Erik, and Shanto Iyengar. 2021. "Partisan Gaps in Political Information and Information-Seeking Behavior: Motivated Reasoning or Cheerleading?" *American Journal of Political Science* 65 (1): 133–47. https://doi.org/10.1111/ajps.12535.

Petty, Richard E., and John T. Cacioppo. 1986. "The Elaboration Likelihood Model of Persuasion." In *Communication and Persuasion*, 1–24. New York: Springer. https://doi.org/10.1007
/978-1-4612-4964-1_1.

Pew Research Center. 2020. "Americans' Views of Government: Low Trust, but Some Positive
Performance Ratings." September 14. https://www.pewresearch.org/politics/2020/09/14
/americans-views-of-government-low-trust-but-some-positive-performance-ratings/.

———. 2009. "Health Care Reform Closely Followed, Much Discussed." August 20. https://www
.pewresearch.org/politics/2009/08/20/health-care-reform-closely-followed-much-discussed/.

———. 2022. "Journalists Sense Turmoil in Their Industry Amid Continued Passion for Their
Work." June 14. https://www.pewresearch.org/journalism/2022/06/14/journalists-sense
-turmoil-in-their-industry-amid-continued-passion-for-their-work/.

———. 2021. "News on Twitter: Consumed by Most Users and Trusted by Many." November 15
. https://www.pewresearch.org/journalism/2021/11/15/news-on-twitter-consumed-by-most
-users-and-trusted-by-many/.

———. 2022. "Politics on Twitter: One-Third of Tweets from U.S. Adults Are Political." June 16
. https://www.pewresearch.org/politics/2022/06/16/politics-on-twitter-one-third-of-tweets
-from-u-s-adults-are-political/.

Pfiffner, James P. 2020. "The Lies of Donald Trump: A Taxonomy." In *Presidential Leadership and
the Trump Presidency*, 17–40. Cham: Springer International. https://doi.org/10.1007/978-3
-030-18979-2_2.

Phadke, Shruti, Mattia Samory, and Tanushree Mitra. 2021. "What Makes People Join Conspiracy
Communities? Role of Social Factors in Conspiracy Engagement." *Proceedings of the ACM on
Human-Computer Interaction* 4 (223): 1–30. https://doi.org/10.1145/3432922.

Pipes, Daniel. 1998. *The Hidden Hand: Middle East Fears of Conspiracy*. London: Palgrave
Macmillan.

Pluviano, Sara, Caroline Watt, and Sergio Della Sala. 2017. "Misinformation Lingers in Memory:
Failure of Three Pro-Vaccination Strategies," edited by Anne C. Moore. *PLOS One* 12 (7):
1–15. https://doi.org/10.1371/journal.pone.0181640.

Pluviano, Sara, Caroline Watt, Giovanni Ragazzini, and Sergio Della Sala. 2019. "Parents' Beliefs
in Misinformation about Vaccines Are Strengthened by Pro-Vaccine Campaigns." *Cognitive
Processing* 20 (3): 325–31. https://doi.org/10.1007/s10339-019-00919-w.

PolitiFact. 2020. "Barack Obama." Accessed March 21, 2021. https://www.politifact.com
/personalities/barack-obama/.

———. 2021. "Bernie Sanders." Accessed February 23, 2021. https://www.politifact.com
/personalities/bernie-sanders/.

———. 2021. "Donald Trump." Accessed Feburary 23, 2021. https://www.politifact.com
/personalities/donald-trump/.

Popkin, Samuel L. 1991. *The Reasoning Voter: Communication and Persuasion in Presidential Campaigns*. Chicago: University of Chicago Press.

Pornpitakpan, Chanthika. 2004. "The Persuasiveness of Source Credibility: A Critical Review of
Five Decades' Evidence." *Journal of Applied Social Psychology* 34 (2): 243–81. https://doi.org
/10.1111/j.1559-1816.2004.tb02547.x.

Prior, Markus. 2007. *Post-Broadcast Democracy: How Media Choice Increases Inequality in Political
Involvement and Polarizes Elections*. Cambridge: Cambridge University Press.

Qiu, Linda. 2019. "Fact-Checking Bernie Sanders on the Campaign Trail." *New York Times*, May 25.
https://www.nytimes.com/2019/05/25/us/politics/fact-checking-bernie-sanders-campaign
.html.

Redlawsk, David P., Andrew J. Civettini, and Karen M. Emmerson. 2010. "The Affective Tipping
Point: Do Motivated Reasoners Ever 'Get It'?" *Political Psychology* 31 (4): 563–93.

Reilly, Alexander, and Tiziana Torresi. 2016. "Voting Rights of Permanent Residents." *UNSW Law Journal* 39 (1): 401–20.

Roose, Kevin. 2021. "What Is QAnon, the Viral Pro-Trump Conspiracy Theory?" *New York Times*, March 4. https://www.nytimes.com/article/what-is-qanon.html.

———. 2020. "Why Conspiracy Theories Are So Addictive Right Now." *New York Times*, October 7. https://www.nytimes.com/2020/10/07/technology/Trump-conspiracy-theories.html?

Roozenbeek, Jon, Rakoen Maertens, William McClanahan, and Sander van der Linden. 2021. "Distentangling Item and Testing Effects in Inoculation Research on Online Misinformation: Solomon Revisited." *Educational and Psychological Measurement* 81 (2): 340–62.

Roozenbeek, Jon, and Sander Van der Linden. 2019. "Fake News Game Confers Psychological Resistance against Online Misinformation." *Palgrave Communications* 5 (1): 1–10.

Rosenblum, Nancy L., and Russell Muirhead. 2019. *A Lot of People Are Saying: The New Conspiracism and the Assault on Democracy*. Princeton, NJ: Princeton University Press.

Rosnow, Ralph L. 1974. "Communications as Cultural Science." *Journal of Communication* 24 (3): 26–38.

Ross, Lee, and Craig A. Anderson. 1982. "Shortcomings in the Attribution Process: On the Origins and Maintenance of Erroneous Social Assessments." In *Judgment under Uncertainty: Heuristics and Biases*, edited by Daniel Kahneman, Paul Slovic, and Amos Tversky, 129–152. Cambridge: Cambridge University Press. https://doi.org/10.1017/CBO9780511809477.010.

Rutenberg, Jim, and Jackie Calmes. 2009. "False 'Death Panel' Rumor Has Some Familiar Roots." *New York Times*, August 13. https://www.nytimes.com/2009/08/14/health/policy/14panel.html.

Salvanto, Anthony, Jennifer De Pinto, Fred Backus, Kabir Khanna, and Elena Cox. 2020. "CBS News Poll: Most Feel Election Is 'Settled' but Trump Voters Disagree." *CBS News*, December 13. https://www.cbsnews.com/news/cbs-news-poll-most-feel-election-is-settled-but-trump-voters-disagree/.

Santhanam, Laura. 2014. "22 Countries Where Voting Is Mandatory." *PBS NewsHour*, November 3. https://www.pbs.org/newshour/politics/22-countries-voting-mandatory.

Sasahara, Kazutoshi, Wen Chen, Hao Peng, Giovanni Luca Ciampaglia, Alessandro Flammini, and Filippo Menczer. 2021. "Social Influence and Unfollowing Accelerate the Emergence of Echo Chambers." *Journal of Computational Social Science* 4 (1): 381–402.

Saunders, Elizabeth N. 2018. "Leaders, Advisers, and the Political Origins of Elite Support for War." *Journal of Conflict Resolution* 62 (10): 2118–49. https://doi.org/10.1177/0022002718785670.

Schaffner, Brian F., and Samantha Luks. 2018. "Misinformation or Expressive Responding? What an Inauguration Crowd Can Tell Us about the Source of Political Misinformation in Surveys." *Public Opinion Quarterly* 82 (1): 135–47. https://doi.org/10.1093/poq/nfx042.

Scharkow, Michael, Frank Mangold, Sebastian Stier, and Johannes Breuer. 2020. "How Social Network Sites and Other Online Intermediaries Increase Exposure to News." *Proceedings of the National Academy of Sciences* 117 (6): 2761–63.

Schelling, Thomas C. 1966. *Arms and Influence*. New Haven, CT: Yale University Press.

Schmid, Philipp, and Cornelia Betsch. 2019. "Effective Strategies for Rebutting Science Denialism in Public Discussions." *Nature Human Behaviour* 3 (9): 931–39. https://doi.org/10.1038/s41562-019-0632-4.

Schul, Yaacov, and Eugene Burnstein. 1985. "When Discounting Fails: Conditions Under Which Individuals Use Discredited Information in Making a Judgment." *Journal of Personality and Social Psychology* 49 (4): 894–903. https://doi.org/10.1037/0022-3514.49.4.894.

Schwarz, Norbert. 2004. "Metacognitive Experiences in Consumer Judgment and Decision Making." *Journal of Consumer Psychology* 14 (4): 332–48. https://doi.org/10.1207/s15327663jcp1404_2.

Schwarz, Norbert, Lawrence J. Sanna, Ian Skurnik, and Carolyn Yoon. 2007. "Metacognitive Experiences and the Intricacies of Setting People Straight: Implications for Debiasing and Public Information Campaigns." *Advances in Experimental Social Psychology* 39: 127–61. https://doi.org/10.1016/S0065-2601(06)39003-X.

Settle, Jaime E. 2018. *Frenemies: How Social Media Polarizes America.* Cambridge: Cambridge University Press.

Sharockman, Aaron. 2016. "The Post-Truth Election? Comparing 2016 to Past Elections on the Truth-O-Meter." PolitiFact. August 16. https://www.politifact.com/article/2016/aug/16/post-truth-election-comparing-2016-past-elections-/.

———. 2016. "Truth Check: Clinton and Trump on the Truth-O-Meter." PolitiFact, November 1. https://www.politifact.com/article/2016/nov/01/truth-check-clinton-and-trump-truth-o-meter-1-week/.

Sherman, Amy. 2020. "Donald Trump's Pants on Fire Claim about Illegal Votes." PolitiFact. November 6. https://www.politifact.com/factchecks/2020/nov/06/donald-trump/donald-trumps-pants-fire-claim-about-illegal-votes/.

Shin, Jieun, and Kjerstin Thorson. 2017. "Partisan Selective Sharing: The Biased Diffusion of Fact-Checking Messages on Social Media." *Journal of Communication* 67: 233–55. https://doi.org/10.1111/jcom.12284.

Sides, John, and Jack Citrin. 2007. "European Opinion about Immigration: The Role of Identities, Interests and Information." *British Journal of Political Science* 37 (3): 477–504. http://www.jstor.org/stable/4497304.

Simonov, Andrey, Szymon K. Sacher, Jean-Pierre H. Dube, and Shirsho Biwas. 2020. "The Persuasive Effect of Fox News: Non-Compliance with Social Distancing during the COVID-19 Pandemic." *National Bureau of Economic Research.* Working paper.

Smith, Kevin, John R. Alford, Peter K. Hatemi, Lindon J. Eaves, Carolyn Funk, and John R. Hibbing. 2012. "How Do We Know Political Attitudes Are Inherited and Why Should We Care?" *American Journal of Political Science* 56 (1): 17–33. https://doi.org/10.1111/j.1540-5907.2011.00560.x.

Smith, Matthew, Jamie Ballard, and Linley Sanders. 2021. "Most Voters Say the Events at the US Capitol Are a Threat to Democracy." *YouGov,* January 6. https://today.yougov.com/topics/politics/articles-reports/2021/01/06/US-capitol-trump-poll.

Sniderman, Paul M., Richard A. Brody, and Phillip E. Tetlock. 1993. *Reasoning and Choice: Explorations in Political Psychology.* Cambridge: Cambridge University Press.

Stanton, Zack. 2020. "You're Living in the Golden Age of Conspiracy Theories." *Politico,* June 17. https://www.politico.com/news/magazine/2020/06/17/conspiracy-theories-pandemic-trump-2020-election-coronavirus-326530.

Stier, Sebastian, Frank Mangold, Michael Scharkow, and Johannes Breuer. 2022. "Post Post-Broadcast Democracy? News Exposure in the Age of Online Intermediaries." *American Political Science Review* 116 (2): 768–74.

Stolberg, Sheryl Gay, and Noah Weiland. 2020. "Study Finds 'Single Largest Driver' of Coronavirus Misinformation: Trump." *New York Times,* September 30. https://www.nytimes.com/2020/09/30/us/politics/trump-coronavirus-misinformation.html.

Sunstein, Cass. 2014. *Conspiracy Theories and Other Dangerous Ideas.* New York: Simon & Schuster.

———. 2001. "The Daily We: Is the Internet Really a Blessing for Democracy." *Boston Review* 26 (3): 4.

———. 2009. *On Rumors: How Falsehoods Spread, Why We Believe Them, and What Can Be Done.* Princeton, NJ: Princeton University Press.

Sunstein, Cass R, and Adrian Vermeule. 2009. "Conspiracy Theories: Causes and Cures." *Journal of Political Philosophy* 17 (2): 202–27.

Supreme Court. 2019. "2019 Year-End Report on the Federal Judiciary." https://www.supremecourt
.gov/publicinfo/year-end/2019year-endreport.pdf

Swami, Viren, Tomas Chamorro-Premuzic, and Adrian Furnham. 2010. "Unanswered Questions:
A Preliminary Investigation of Personality and Individual Difference Predictors of 9/11 Conspiracist Beliefs." *Applied Cognitive Psychology* 24 (6): 749–61. https://doi.org/10.1002/acp
.1583.

Swire, Briony, Adam J. Berinsky, Stephan Lewandowsky, and Ullrich H. K. Ecker. 2017. "Processing Political Misinformation: Comprehending the Trump Phenomenon." *Royal Society
Open Science* 4 (3): 1–21. https://doi.org/10.1098/rsos.160802.

Swire-Thompson, Briony, Joseph DeGutis, and David Lazer. 2020. "Searching for the Backfire
Effect: Measurement and Design Considerations." *Journal of Applied Research in Memory and
Cognition* 9 (3): 286–99. https://doi.org/10.1016/j.jarmac.2020.06.006.

Swire-Thompson, Briony, Ullrich K. H. Ecker, Stephan Lewandowsky, and Adam J. Berinsky.
2019. "They Might Be a Liar but They're My Liar: Source Evaluation and the Prevalence
of Misinformation." *Political Psychology* 41 (1): 21–34. https://doi.org/10.1111/pops.12586.

Taber, Charles S., and Milton Lodge. 2006. "Motivated Skepticism in the Evaluation of Political
Beliefs." *American Journal of Political Science* 50 (3): 755–69. https://doi.org/10.1111/j.1540
-5907.2006.00214.x.

Taddonio, Patrice. 2020. "How a Fight over Crowd Size Would Define Trump's Approach to the
Presidency—and the Truth." *PBS Frontline.* January 13. https://www.pbs.org/wgbh/frontline
/article/how-a-fight-over-crowd-size-would-define-trumps-approach-to-the-presidency-and
-the-truth/.

Tambuscio, Marcella, and Giancarlo Ruffo. 2019. "Fact-Checking Strategies to Limit Urban Legends Spreading in a Segregated Society." *Applied Network Science* 4 (1): 116. https://doi.org
/10.1007/s41109-019-0233-1.

Tandoc, Edson C., Jr, Zheng Wei Lim, and Richard Ling. 2018. "Defining 'Fake News': A Typology
of Scholarly Definitions." *Digital Journalism* 6 (2): 137–53.

Taub, Amanda, and Max Fisher. 2018. "Where Countries Are Tinderboxes and Facebook Is a
Match." *New York Times*, April 21. https://www.nytimes.com/2018/04/21/world/asia
/facebook-sri-lanka-riots.html.

Tedford, Deborah. 2009. "In New Hampshire, Obama Defends Health Care Plan." *NPR*, August 11.
https://www.npr.org/2009/08/11/111776077/in-new-hampshire-obama-defends-health-care
-plan.

Thompson, D. 2008. *Counterknowledge: How We Surrendered to Conspiracy Theories, Quack Medicine, Bogus Science, and Fake History.* London: Atlantic.

Thorson, Emily. 2016. "Belief Echoes: The Persistent Effects of Corrected Misinformation." *Political Communication* 33 (3): 460–80. https://doi.org/10.1080/10584609.2015.1102187.

Thorson, Katherine R., Tessa V. West, and Wendy Berry Mendes. 2018. "Measuring Physiological
Influence in Dyads: A Guide to Designing, Implementing, and Analyzing Dyadic Physiological Studies." *Psychological Methods* 23 (4): 595–616. http://dx.doi.org/10.1037/met0000166.

TMZ. 2020. "Donald Trump: I Can't Denounce QAnon . . . I Know Nothing About It!!!" October 15. https://www.tmz.com/2020/10/15/donald-trump-wont-denounce-qanon-conspiracy
-theory-white-supremacy-town-hall/.

———. 2021. "Ex-QAnon Believer Apologizes to Anderson Cooper, Thought He Ate Babies," January 31, 2021. https://www.tmz.com/2021/01/31/former-qanon-apologizes-anderson-cooper
-eat-babies-conspiracy/.

Tokita, Christopher K., Andrew M. Guess, and Corina E. Tarnita. 2021. "Polarized Information
Ecosystems Can Reorganize Social Networks via Information Cascades." *Proceedings of the
National Academy of Sciences* 118 (50): 1–9. https://doi.org/10.1073/pnas.2102147118.

Tsfati, Yariv, Hago G. Boomgaarden, Jesper Strömbäck, Rens Vliegenthart, Alyt Damstra, and Elina Lindgren. 2020. "Causes and Consequences of Mainstream Media Dissemination of Fake News: Literature Review and Synthesis." *Annals of the International Communication Association* 44 (2): 157–73.

Tucker, Joshua, Andrew Guess, Pablo Barberá, Cristian Vaccari, Alexandra Siegel, Sergey Sanovich, Denis Stukal, and Brendan Nyhan. 2018. "Social Media, Political Polarization, and Political Disinformation: A Review of the Scientific Literature." *SSRN Electronic Journal*, March. https://doi.org/10.2139/ssrn.3144139.

Tynan, Dan. 2016. "How Facebook Powers Money Machines for Obscure Political 'News' Sites." *Guardian*, August 24. https://www.theguardian.com/technology/2016/aug/24/facebook-clickbait-political-news-sites-us-election-trump.

Unkelbach, Christian. 2007. "Reversing the Truth Effect: Learning the Interpretation of Processing Fluency in Judgments of Truth." *Journal of Experimental Psychology: Learning Memory and Cognition* 33 (1): 219–30. https://doi.org/10.1037/0278-7393.33.1.219.

Uscinski, Joseph E. 2020. *Conspiracy Theories: A Primer*. United Kingdom: Roman & Littlefield.

———. 2018. *Conspiracy Theories and the People Who Believe Them*. New York: Oxford University Press.

———. 2015. "The Epistemology of Fact Checking (Is Still Naïve): Rejoinder to Amazeen." *Critical Review* 27 (2): 243–52.

Uscinski, Joseph E., and Ryden W. Butler. 2013. "The Epistemology of Fact Checking." *Critical Review* 25 (2): 162–80.

Uscinski, Joseph E., Casey Klofstad, and Matthew D. Atkinson. 2016. "What Drives Conspiratorial Beliefs? The Role of Informational Cues and Predispositions." *Political Research Quarterly* 69 (1): 57–71. https://doi.org/10.1177/1065912915621621.

Uscinski, Joseph E., and Joseph M. Parent. 2014. *American Conspiracy Theories*. Oxford: Oxford University Press.

Vaccari, Cristian, Augusto Valeriani, Pablo Barberá, Rich Bonneau, John T. Jost, Jonathan Nagler, and Joshua A. Tucker. 2015. "Political Expression and Action on Social Media: Exploring the Relationship between Lower-and Higher-Threshold Political Activities among Twitter Users in Italy." *Journal of Computer-Mediated Communication* 20 (2): 221–39.

van der Linden, Sander, Costas Panagopoulos, Flavio Azevedo, and John T. Jost. 2021. "The Paranoid Style in American Politics Revisited: An Ideological Asymmetry in Conspiratorial Thinking." *Political Psychology* 42 (1): 23–51.

van der Linden, Sander, Costas Panagopoulos, and Jon Roozenbeek. 2020. "You Are Fake News: Political Bias in Perceptions of Fake News." *Media, Culture, and Society* 42 (3): 460–70. https://doi.org/10.1177/0163443720906992.

Vargo, Stephen L., Kaisa Koskela-Huotari, Steve Baron, Bo Edvardsson, Javier Reynoso, and Maria Colurcio. 2017. "A Systems Perspective on Markets—Toward a Research Agenda." *Journal of Business Research* 79: 260–68.

Verhulst, Brad, Lindon J. Eaves, and Peter K. Hatemi. 2012. "Correlation Not Causation: The Relationship between Personality Traits and Political Ideologies." *American Journal of Political Science* 56 (1): 34–51. https://doi.org/10.1111/j.1540-5907.2011.00568.x.

Verhulst, Brad, Peter K. Hatemi, and Nicholas G. Martin. 2010. "The Nature of the Relationship between Personality Traits and Political Attitudes." *Personality and Individual Differences* 49 (4): 306–16. https://doi.org/10.1016/j.paid.2009.11.013.

Vicario, Michela Del, Alessandro Bessi, Fabiana Zollo, Fabio Petroni, Antonio Scala, Guido Caldarelli, H. Eugene Stanley, and Walter Quattrociocchi. 2016. "The Spreading of Misinformation Online." *Proceedings of the National Academy of Sciences of the United States of America* 113 (3): 554–59. https://doi.org/10.1073/pnas.1517441113.

Vinck, Patrick, Phoung N. Pham, Kenedy K. Bindu, Juliet Bedford, and Eric J. Nilles. 2019. "Institutional Trust and Misinformation in the Response to the 2018–19 Ebola Outbreak in North Kivu, DR Congo: A Population-Based Survey." *Lancet: Infectious Diseases* 19 (5): 529–36. https://doi.org/10.1016/S1473-3099(19)30063-5.

Walker, Mason, and Jeffrey Gottfried. 2019. "Republicans Far More Likely than Democrats to Say Fact-Checkers Tend to Favor One Side." Pew Research Center, June 17. https://www.pewresearch.org/fact-tank/2019/06/27/republicans-far-more-likely-than-democrats-to-say-fact-checkers-tend-to-favor-one-side/.

Wall Street Journal Editorial Board. 2020. "A Presidential Smear." *Wall Street Journal*, May 26. https://www.wsj.com/articles/a-presidential-smear-11590535397.

Walster, Elaine, Elliot Aronson, and Darcy Abrahams. 1966. "On Increasing the Persuasiveness of a Low Prestige Communicator." *Journal of Experimental Social Psychology* 2 (4): 325–42. https://doi.org/10.1016/0022-1031(66)90026-6.

Walter, Nathan, and Riva Tukachinsky. 2020. "A Meta-Analytic Examination of the Continued Influence of Misinformation in the Face of Correction: How Powerful Is It, Why Does It Happen, and How to Stop It?" *Communication Research* 47 (2): 155–77. https://doi.org/10.1177/0093650219854600.

Wang, Wei Chun, Nadia M. Brashier, Erik A. Wing, Elizabeth J. Marsh, and Roberto Cabeza. 2016. "On Known Unknowns: Fluency and the Neural Mechanisms of Illusory Truth." *Journal of Cognitive Neuroscience* 28 (5): 739–46. https://doi.org/10.1162/jocn_a_00923.

Washburn, Anthony N., and Linda J. Skitka. 2018. "Science Denial across the Political Divide: Liberals and Conservatives Are Similarly Motivated to Deny Attitude-Inconsistent Science." *Social Psychological and Personality Science* 9 (8): 972–80. https://doi.org/10.1177/1948550617731500.

Washington Post. 2021. "Fact Checker." Accessed March 18, 2021. https://www.washingtonpost.com/news/fact-checker/.

———. 2019. "The Global Reach of Trump's 'Fake News' Outrage." November 19. https://www.washingtonpost.com/opinions/global-opinions/trump-is-spreading-his-fake-news-rhetoric-around-the-world-thats-dangerous/2019/11/19/a7b0a4c6-0af5-11ea-97ac-a7ccc8dd1ebc_story.html.

Weeks, Brian E., Alberto Ardèvol-Abreu, and Homero de Zúñiga. 2017. "Online Influence? Social Media Use, Opinion Leadership, and Political Persuasion." *International Journal of Public Opinion Research* 29 (2): 214–39.

Weeks, Brian E., and R. Kelly Garrett. 2014. "Electoral Consequences of Political Rumors: Motivated Reasoning, Candidate Rumors, and Vote Choice during the 2008 US Presidential Election." *International Journal of Public Opinion Research* 26 (4): 401–22.

Weeks, Brian E., Daniel S. Lane, and Lauren B. Hahn. 2022. "Online Incidental Exposure to News Can Minimize Interest-Based Political Knowledge Gaps: Evidence from Two US Elections." *International Journal of Press/Politics* 27 (1): 243–62.

Weeks, Brian E., Daniel S. Lane, Dam Hee Kim, Slgi S. Lee, and Nojin Kwak. 2017. "Incidental Exposure, Selective Exposure, and Political Information Sharing: Integrating Online Exposure Patterns and Expression on Social Media." *Journal of Computer-Mediated Communication* 22 (6): 363–79. https://doi.org/10.1111/jcc4.12199.

Weissert, Will. 2020. "Turning the Page? Republicans Acknowledge Biden's Victory." *AP News*, December 15. https://apnews.com/article/election-2020-joe-biden-donald-trump-antony-blinken-cabinets-b6f05a0c9545f54430679d35bdddca3b.

Wilkes, A. L., and Mark Leatherbarrow. 1988. "Editing Episodic Memory Following the Identification of Error." *Quarterly Journal of Experimental Psychology Section A* 40 (2): 361–87. https://doi.org/10.1080/02724988843000168.

Wineburg, Sam, Joel Breakstone, Sarah McGrew, Mark D. Smith, and Teresa Ortega. 2022. "Lateral Reading on the Open Internet: A District-wide Field Study in High School Government Classes." *Journal of Educational Psychology* 114 (5): 893–909. https://doi.org/10.1037/edu0000740.

Wintersieck, Amanda, Kim Fridkin, and Patrick Kenney. 2018. "The Message Matters: The Influence of Fact-Checking on Evaluations of Political Messages." *Journal of Political Marketing* 20 (2): 93–120. https://doi.org/10.1080/15377857.2018.1457591.

Wittenberg, Chloe, and Adam J. Berinsky. 2020. "Misinformation and Its Correction." In *Social Media and Democracy: The State of the Field, Prospects for Reform, SSRC Anxieties of Democracy*, edited by Joshua A. Tucker and Nathaniel Persily, 163–98. Cambridge: Cambridge University Press.

Wood, Michael J., Karen M. Douglas, and Robbie M. Sutton. 2012. "Dead and Alive: Beliefs in Contradictory Conspiracy Theories." *Social Psychological and Personality Space* 3 (6): 767–73. https://doi.org/10.1177/1948550611434786.

Wood, Thomas, and Ethan Porter. 2019. "The Elusive Backfire Effect: Mass Attitudes' Steadfast Factual Adherence." *Political Behavior* 41 (1): 135–63. https://doi.org/10.1007/s11109-018-9443-y.

Wooston, Cleve R. Jr. 2016. "Donald Trump: 'I Won the Popular Vote if You Deduct the Millions of People Who Voted Illegally.'" *Washington Post*, November 27. https://www.washingtonpost.com/news/the-fix/wp/2016/11/27/donald-trump-i-won-the-popular-vote-if-you-deduct-the-millions-of-people-who-voted-illegally/.

Zaller, John R. 1992. *The Nature and Origins of Mass Opinion.* Cambridge: Cambridge University Press.

———. 2012. "What Nature and Origins Leaves Out." *Critical Review* 24 (4): 569–642.

Zehmakan, Ahad N., and Serge Galam. 2019. "Fake News and Rumors: A Trigger for Proliferation or Fading Away." *Chaos* 30 (7): 1–17. https://doi.org/10.1063/5.0006984.

Zhuravskaya, Ekaterina, Maria Petrova, and Ruben Enikolopov. 2020. "Political Effects of the Internet and Social Media." *Annual Review of Economics* 12 (1): 415–38. https://doi.org/10.1146/annurev-economics-081919-050239.

Zonis, Marvin, and Craig M. Joseph. 1994. "Conspiracy Thinking in the Middle East." *Political Psychology* 15 (3): 443–59.

INDEX

Note: Page numbers in italic type indicate figures or tables.

AARP. *See* American Association of Retired Persons

acceptance of rumors, 42–73; authoritarianism in relation to, 177n38; content factors in, 56, 60–65, *63, 64, 66,* 69; determinants of acceptance, 56–67; determinants of rejection, 67–71, *68, 70;* dispositional factors in, 56–60, *60, 61, 72,* 73, 136–37; effect of new information on, 7, 13, 61, 67, 77; motivated reasoning leading to, 61–62, 118, 125, 136–38; partisanship as factor in, 78–79, 164–65; political knowledge and information as factor in, 130–37, *131–33;* prevalence of, 7, *8,* 48, 56; reasons for, 8–9; repetition as factor in, 28, 76, 80–81, 89, 96–101, *99, 100,* 103; research on, 46–56; stability of, 54–56; types of uncertainty, 31–32, 53–54. *See also* believers; consequences of rumors; correction of rumors; disbelievers; uncertainty about rumors

accuracy nudges, 163

Affordable Care Act (2010), 11, 12, 74, 88–103, 131

Allcott, Hunt, 7

Allport, Gordon W., 23, 27, 34, 57, 171n9

AMA. *See* American Medical Association

American Association of Retired Persons (AARP), 77, 91, 102

American Medical Association (AMA), 91, 102

American National Election Study (ANES), 46, 59, 135, 175n12

American Revolution, 3

ANES. *See* American National Election Study

Angeli, Jake, 21

Australia, 16, 124–26, 187n45

authoritarianism, 177n38

backfire effects, 79–81, 85–87, 94, 104, 120

Bay of Pigs invasion, 24

belief echoes, 14

belief perseverance, 13–14

believers: authenticity of beliefs of, 42–45; instrumental or expressive function of beliefs for, 43–44; intransigence of, 14–15, 33; as misinformed, 173n41; online communities of, 34–38; role of, in rumor circulation, 30, 35; as target of information campaigns, 14–15, 33, 159, 161, 166; the uncertain in relation to, 175n11, 176n20

Biden, Joe, 1–2, 105–6, 152

birther controversy, 3, 4–5, 18, 30, 32–33, 82–83, *83, 84,* 105

Blumenauer, Earl, 91

Bode, Leticia, 161

Boebert, Lauren, 22

Bone, Robert M., 7

Bordia, Prashant, 25, 79

Breitbart, 37

Brotherton, Robert, 57

Bruder, Martin, 58

Bush, George W., 26, 54

Bysow, Ludwig A., 23

cable television, 36

Calvert, Randall, 78

CCES. *See* Cooperative Congressional Election Study

Central Intelligence Agency (CIA), 26

cheap talk, 43–44, 65, 78

Cheney, Dick, 54

Cheney, Liz, 165

Chong, Dennis, 58–59

Cichocka, Aleksandra, 57

Citrin, Jack, 13

Claassen, Ryan L., 118